GLOBAL CINEMA

Edited by Katarzyna Marciniak, Anikó Imre, and Áine O'Healy

The **Global Cinema** series publishes innovative scholarship on transnational themes, industries, economies, and aesthetic elements that increasingly connect cinemas around the world. It promotes theoretically transformative and politically challenging projects that rethink film studies from cross-cultural, comparative perspectives, bringing into focus forms of cinematic production that resist nationalist or hegemonic frameworks. Rather than aiming at comprehensive geographical coverage, it foregrounds transnational interconnections in the production, distribution, exhibition, study, and teaching of film. Dedicated to global aspects of cinema, this pioneering series combines original perspectives and new methodological paths with accessibility and coverage. Both "global" and "cinema" remain open to a range of approaches and interpretations, new and traditional. Books published in the series sustain a specific concern with the medium of cinema but do not defensively protect the boundaries of film studies, recognizing that film exists in a converging media environment. The series emphasizes a historically expanded notion of globalization rather than one of exclusive presentism; it is mindful of repositioning "the global" away from a US-centric/Eurocentric grid, and remains critical of celebratory notions of "globalizing film studies."

Katarzyna Marciniak is a professor of Transnational Studies in the English Department at Ohio University.

Anikó Imre is an associate professor of Critical Studies in the School of Cinematic Arts at the University of Southern California.

Áine O'Healy is a professor of Modern Languages and Literatures at Loyola Marymount University.

Published by Palgrave Macmillan:

Prismatic Media, Transnational Circuits: Feminism in a Globalized Present
By Krista Geneviève Lynes

Also by Krista Geneviève Lynes

From Local to Global: Making Peace Work for Women (2005), co-edited with Gina Torry

Prismatic Media, Transnational Circuits

Feminism in a Globalized Present

Krista Geneviève Lynes

palgrave
macmillan

PRISMATIC MEDIA, TRANSNATIONAL CIRCUITS
Copyright © Krista Geneviève Lynes, 2012.

First published in 2012 by
PALGRAVE MACMILLAN®
in the United States—a division of St. Martin's Press LLC,
175 Fifth Avenue, New York, NY 10010.

Where this book is distributed in the UK, Europe and the rest of the World,
this is by Palgrave Macmillan, a division of Macmillan Publishers Limited,
registered in England, company number 785998, of Houndmills,
Basingstoke, Hampshire RG21 6XS.

Palgrave Macmillan is the global academic imprint of the above
companies and has companies and representatives throughout the world.

Palgrave® and Macmillan® are registered trademarks in the United
States, the United Kingdom, Europe and other countries.

ISBN: 978–0–230–33754–1

Library of Congress Cataloging-in-Publication Data is available from the
Library of Congress.

A catalogue record of the book is available from the British Library.

Design by Integra Software Services

First edition: January 2013

10 9 8 7 6 5 4 3 2 1

For my mother,
Yvette Aloïsi

Contents

Illustrations

Acknowledgments

Roland Barthes characterizes the author as "simply that *someone* who holds together in a single field all the traces by which the written text is constituted."[1] These acknowledgments only gesture toward reconstituting the complex traces, labors and collaborations through which this project took shape over the space of nearly a decade. Teresa de Lauretis was an inspiring mentor, who gave more generously of her time and intellectual energy than I could have hoped for. It was through her texts and her mentorship that I learned to think about the complex processes of imaging and the relations between subjectivity, spectatorship and screens at the heart of the political projects in this study. James Clifford's poetic advice frequently drew me to the complex and unresolved terms of culture's most interesting predicaments. Jennifer González, Donna Haraway and Gina Dent were awesome interlocutors, and I feel privileged to have benefitted from their guidance as this project materialized.

Students and colleagues at the San Francisco Art Institute contributed immensely to the ways in which I began to think about the processes of art making. I am especially grateful to my friends and colleagues Renée Green, Javier Anguera and Allan deSouza, as well as to students in my seminars, Body Politics; Screen Histories, Screen Memories; Third Media; and Visible Evidence & the Photographic Imaginary. I am also grateful to my new colleagues at Concordia University, and especially to the students in my graduate seminar, Media & Feminist Theory, who engaged questions of feminist collectivity passionately and who demonstrated the urgency of feminist praxis by striking and taking to the streets at the end of the semester against tuition increases and neo-liberal incursions into education and public life.

The research resulting in this book was presented in lectures, seminars and workshops between 2005 and 2012. I wish to thank the individuals who chaired panels, organized events or invited me to participate: in 2005, A. Jane Johnston for the panel "Video Art: Subject, Object, Suspect, Abject," College Art Association, Atlanta; likewise in 2005, the organizers of the Visible Evidence Conference, Montreal; in 2007, Aruna D'Souza and Tom McDonough for the panel "Globalism and Its Discontents,"

College Art Association, New York; in 2010, Peter Mörtenböck and Helge Mooshammer, for the conference "space RE:solutions. Interventions and Research in Visual Culture," held at the Vienna Institute of Technology; in 2012, members of the Department of Women's and Gender Studies at Rutger's University for the workshop "The Politics of Visuality: Innovative Feminist Approaches to Race/Gender/Sexualities in Visual Culture and Social Media," and to the other participants Jafari Sinclaire Allen, Maria Cotera, Kara Keeling, Lisa Nakamura and L. Ayu Saraswati; and finally in 2012, Charles Acland, Alice Jim, Bart Simon and Haidee Wasson for the invitation to present to the Screen Culture Research Group at Concordia University.

I am particularly indebted to colleagues and friends who generously read and offered feedback on the book's introduction: Natalie Loveless generously gave her impression in the midst of organizing a transnational move; Laura Christian read the chapter with a critical acuity and generosity of spirit that surpassed my request for feedback by leaps and bounds.

My research assistants in the past year, Katerina Symes and Tamara Shepherd, assisted tirelessly in bringing the manuscript to completion. I'm grateful to Felicity Plester and Robyn Curtis at Palgrave MacMillan and to the series editors of "Global Cinema," Katarzyna Marciniak, Anikó Imre and Áine O'Healy for welcoming my project at Palgrave MacMillan.

This book was completed with the aid of fellowships from the University of California, Institute for Humanities Research, as well as the Feminist Studies and History of Consciousness Departments at the University of California, Santa Cruz.

I am grateful to the artists and galleries who granted me kind permission to reproduce photographs of their work here: Lida Abdul (Giorgio Persano Gallery), Marina Abramović (Sean Kelly Gallery), Jo Andres (Women Make Movies), Siddiq Barmak (Barmak Films), Mona Hatoum (The White Cube Gallery), Emily Jacir (Alexander & Bonin), Mandy Jacobson & Karmen Jelincić (Women Make Movies), Elahe Massumi, the Revolutionary Association of the Women of Afghanistan (World Picture Network), Milica Tomić (Charim Gallery Wien) and Akram Zaatari (Sfeir-Semler Gallery).

Finally, I am grateful to my family: to my father, Jim Lynes, and brother and sister, Phil and Emilie Lynes, for their passionate love of learning. I am utterly beholden to Jonathan Weiss, who has been a passionate interlocutor, patient and generous reader, and fount of support throughout, and who has taught me invaluable lessons about thinking *autrement qu'être*. My son, Xavier, has fueled new forms of curiosity and provided a powerful lens for refracting taken-for-granted matters. His passionate engagement with the world has moved me and taught me enormously in his three years on this earth. Finally, to my mother, Yvette Aloïsi, who, while she didn't live to see this book come to print, inspired me with her fierce intelligence, political and ethical commitment, challenging questions and powerful life drive through to the end. This book is dedicated to her.

*   *   *

An earlier version of Chapter 2 appeared in *Signs: Journal of Women in Culture and Society*. I am grateful to the publishers for permission to reprint here. I am especially grateful to Mary Hawkesworth and Karen Alexander, editors at *Signs*, for their invaluable input on the article. An earlier version of Chapter 4 also appeared in the anthology *Space (Re)Solutions: Intervention and Research in Visual Culture*. I am grateful to the editors, Peter Mörtenböck and Helge Mooshammer, for organizing the conference that brought the papers together, and for editing the vital anthology of these works in visual culture. The text is reprinted with the kind permission of Transcript Verlag.

Introduction: Prismatic Media, Transnational Circuits

The possibility of multiple monitors and of a freer play with this multiplicity, the restructuration of the space of production and performance, the new status of what is called an actor, a character, the displacement of the limit between the private and the public, a growing independence with regard to public or political monopolies on the image, a new economy of relations between the direct and the nondirect, between what is carelessly said to be "real" time and "deferred" time, all this constitutes a bundle of considerable transformations and stakes.

—*Jacques Derrida*[1]

A shattered mirror still functions as a mirror; it may destroy the dual relation of I to I but leaves the infiniteness of life's reflections intact. Here reality is not reconstituted, it is put into pieces so as to allow another world to rebuild (keep on unbuilding and rebuilding) itself with its debris.

—*Trinh Minh-ha*[2]

How might experimental media respond to the urgent demand for a complex and emancipatory unity within and between political struggles worldwide? Artworks, documentaries, amateur tapes and reportage, the disparate forms of representation that can be loosely termed "visual media," *mediate* after all: they yoke together the subjects who appear on screen, cultural producers and differently positioned audiences distributed across the paths media take through the global system. On what grounds do media appeal to unity? How might they make visible multiple (and sometimes competing) realities and political contradictions? What are the political effects of specific aesthetic strategies for feminist coalitional politics? This project is concerned with how artistic, filmic and documentary projects both figure the specificity of local political struggles and circulate transnationally, configuring and refiguring relations of looking.

The works considered here seek to challenge an interconnected set of dominant epistemological, economic, political and symbolic apparatuses, even as they make visible emergent forms of subjectivity and complex visions of social life under conditions of duress, political struggle, human rights abuse or super-exploitation. They do so across multiple genres—contemporary art installations, public art, documentary films and national cinemas. They draw inspiration from the surge of experimentation in media forms that occurred in global exhibitions and through new technologies in the late twentieth century, particularly in the medium of video. While networked interventions, public projections, large-scale installations and viral media evidence the ubiquity of video in the contemporary global media landscape, these dispersed cultural practices must be located within the history of the medium, a history that has presented important challenges to the status of the art object and authorship, as well as new access points for self-representation by communities and cultural producers who were frequently excluded from film production and broadcast media. Martha Rosler notes that the medium of video as taken up by artists and activists (predominantly in the United States) posed a challenge to the traditional sites of art production in society, to its channels of delivery and to the passivity of reception elicited by broadcast television and the mainstream film industry. She states:

> Not only a systemic but also a utopian critique was implicit in video's early use, for the effort was not to enter the system but to transform every aspect of it and—legacy of the revolutionary avant-garde project—to redefine the system out of existence by merging art with social life and making audience and producer interchangeable.[3]

The medium of video emerged in the Euro-American context specifically in relation to major social upheavals and was deeply entwined with the social movements of the period (anti-war, anti-colonial, civil rights, women's and gay liberation, class struggle). The journal *Radical Software*, published in the United States by Beryl Korot, Phyllis Gershuny, and Michael Shamberg, argued in its inaugural edition in 1970, "Unless we design and implement alternate information structures which transcend and reconfigure the existing ones, other alternate systems and life styles will be no more than products of the existing process."[4] The promise of "guerrilla television" lay in its association of alternative media channels with revolutionary praxis, linking video production with the small-scale, shifting attacks of insurgent groups against imperialist military forces.[5] Michael Shamberg's *Guerrilla Television*, from which this radical artistic practice drew its name, included images of Che Guevara, letters from the Black Panthers, and various figurations of McLuhan's "global village" throughout. The models of community video, activist video, and media collectives of the 1970s and 1980s situated media production at the intersection of social struggle and avant-garde and agitprop art practices, as for example with the short-lived group *Commediation* (a contraction of *community*, *media* and *mediation*), who collectively authored video works and engaged in social critique, drawing from the aesthetic strategies of Luigi Pirandello and Antonin Artaud.[6] This allying of the medium of video with insurgency and with a flowering culture of protest in the mid-twentieth century is both compelling and vexing—compelling because it raises important questions about the politics of representation, the truth-value of the medium, its capacity to access alternative contents or publics, and its mediation of differences and building of coalitional politics; and vexing insofar as the appeal to a "global village" frequently prematurely announced a solidarity it, in fact, needed to construct.[7] The moniker "street tape" certainly spoke to the ideal of immediacy video might underwrite. The near-simultaneity of production and reception—figured by the practice of organizing screenings on the same day when street tape was recorded, and with the very subjects interviewed—promised engagement and interaction between those behind the camera and those in front of it.[8] Nevertheless, the language of revolution masked the inaccessibility of new media for many who were all the same represented as icons of opposition. Nam June Paik's *Global Groove* (1973) exemplifies this belief in the utopic possibilities of mass communication, promising a "glimpse of a video landscape of tomorrow when you will be able to switch on any TV station on earth and TV guides will be as fat as the Manhattan telephone book," and in which cultural practices from around the world would be brought together in the seamless and distributed electronic space of broadcast television.

From a global perspective, moving-image media cut a course between community video projects (sometimes supported by transnational non-governmental organizations), emerging global conceptual art practices, and the development of national and Third Cinema.[9] The radical potential of participatory grassroots video productions in devising new modes of representation and strategies of mediation was frequently undermined by the deregulation of media landscapes, first as part of technology exports to the global South through the "three M theory" (mass media, mass culture, mass society), and second, under World Bank and International Monetary Fund austerity measures implemented in the 1970s and 1980s across much of the world, which effected a structural adjustment on social networks and public life at large, particularly through the withdrawal of state-sponsored television and community media projects, increased intervention by military and intelligence services, and the multinationalization of media companies around the world.[10] In many respects, community video productions and "narrowcasting" occurred within a social justice and development framework that isolated media production from the complex theorizations within Third Cinema on the relation between oppositional critical practice and oppositional film aesthetics. As Paul Willemen argues, filmmakers in the global south themselves were

> caught between the contradictions of technologized mass culture (its need to activate emancipatory wishes in order to redirect or defuse them by invoking an array of pleasures and organizing them in such a way that the dominant pleasures become associated with conservative or individualist gratifications) and the need to develop a different kind of mass culture while being denied the financial, technological and institutional support to do so.[11]

While video as a medium seemed to constitute a quite perfect example of "imperfect cinema," its potential role in articulating an oppositional artistic practice was frequently curtailed—at least at the outset—by the focus on national cinematic production.[12]

The vacillation between art and information was itself the subject of art movements in the era of the emergence of video—particularly in conceptual art practices that aimed to interrogate the boundaries of art and life through a dematerialization of the work of art. Video was an apt medium for shifting object-making art to idea-based practices. Conceptual art movements across the Americas, Eastern Europe and Asia employed video and mass media happenings to engage directly with social, political and economic realities.[13] In their introduction to *Global Conceptualism: Points of Origin, 1950s-1980s*, Luis Camnitzer, Jane Farver and Rachel Weiss argue that " 'idea art' was easier to slip by the censors. It could be made without expensive art materials, and was an affordable way for artists on the geographic margins to participate in international venues."[14] In these movements, new media forms emerged to critique hegemonic art institutions, the conditions of late capitalism and statist regulations. Video works provided archival documents of artistic events, ideas and actions (as with the work of Nusa and Sreco Dragan and the OHO Group in Slovenia,[15] or Adrian Piper in the United States); artists engaged mass media outlets through happenings (the Argentinian group *Arte de los medios*, for example, sought to constitute the work of art "inside mass media itself," writing and documenting a fictitious event, transmitting the documentation to the mass media to report and then denouncing the event as false);[16] and video provided an intimate means to deconstruct the very field of media representation (for instance, with Theresa Hak Kyung Cha's explorations of identity, language and history).

Thus, according to Marita Sturken, the history of video has consistently vacillated between art and technology, art and social change, individual and collective art practices, profit and nonprofit sectors, and formal and content-based analyses.[17] The drive to situate video within histories of artistic practice, and thus to "reclaim video from 'information,'" has served the interests of galleries, art markets and artists themselves.[18] In historicizing the medium so rapidly, Sturken argues that art organizations and museums constructed a "metahistory," a singular, well-contained narrative that silenced alternative interpretations of the medium and its social contexts.[19] Such a meta-history has been to a certain degree immune to revision, even while the introduction of digital video in 1997 has largely blurred the lines between video and film.[20] The historical divisions between art and information, however, still largely circumscribe technological convergence, if not in its modes of production then in its circuits of display. Works that cross generic boundaries—through activist artistic practices, the inclusion of political content, or transmission through mass culture channels, on the one side,[21] and through curatorial interventions in museum exhibits and film festivals, and around specific political issues, on the other[22]—testify more firmly to the transmedia or intermedia forces within each sphere, rather than to the disappearance of the division between art and information more broadly.

The bifurcated understanding of video's histories—between art and information—unnecessarily limits critical investigations of the videographic medium in transnational media cultures: it principally locates the representation of social reality on the side of community, documentary, and activist video, on the one side, while emphasizing the aesthetic strategies within video installation, projection and multichannel experimentation to the exclusion of social and historical content. Formal considerations in the analysis of documentary media thus circle principally around issues of transparency, realism and ethnographic authority; they are closely bound to documentary content and the moral and emancipatory imperatives of documentary and community video. Conversely, when the principal focus is on the formal strategies of video art, issues of representation are frequently reduced to genre conventions and works are deterritorialized from the specificity of their social and historical contexts.

Efforts to cross historical divisions—as with the international exhibition *Documenta XI* (2002), curated by Okwui Enwezor and organized around a series of platforms held in Vienna, Berlin, New Delhi, St. Lucia, Lagos and Kassel—mobilized artistic and documentary media not only to insist on the breaking of genre conventions and geographical exclusions in global exhibits of contemporary art, but also to address the very claims to a unified global cultural sphere (including a global art scene). According to T. J. Demos, Enwezor's inclusion of documentary photography, film and video served to "expose those zones of economic and political inequality that are normally and tragically unrepresented within the dominant mainstream and Western media."[23] While Demos cautions that the emphasis on documentary modes runs the risk of allying indexicality and realism with the spaces of alterity within the global system (an important caution in the circulation of indexical media in the global system), it is important to stress the manner in which such media might also enable what Salah M. Hassan and Olu Oguibe term an *ex-centric* artistic practice. For Hassan and Oguibe, who curated an exhibition of African art entitled *Authentic/Ex-Centric*, ex-centric artistic practices are those that point to "issues of cross-cultural and transnational aesthetics and consciousness within contemporary African art practice [. . . and] the reciprocal traffic of ideas and influences between Africa and other parts of the world."[24] In contemporary global art exhibitions, the traffic across art and documentary spheres (within curatorial practices, but also within artworks themselves) thus provides a means of engaging internally—within media practice and within the circuits of transmission—with the experiences of postcoloniality; economic, political and cultural inequality; ideals of participation and democracy; and imaginaries of global connection.

Hence, while the explosion of film, video, digital media, interactive artworks, web-based production, and database art witnessed in the past 15 years clearly locate electronic media within—and as thoroughly crossed by—mass culture and the forces of globalization, this study seeks to emphasize the manner in which contemporary visual culture resists classification, and in so doing challenges the conventions through which artworks, documentaries, emergent national cinemas, and activist videos move differentially within transnational circuits, with disparate institutional supports, audiences and engagements in mass culture, artistic spheres, activist circles and social justice movements.

Transnational Media as Imaging Machines

The case studies that follow trace the aesthetic and political strategies of video art, documentary, and narrative film in rendering sites of political struggle, and specifically in representing particular struggles around gender-based violence, sexual difference, exploitation and oppression to differently situated audiences around the globe. The central aesthetic strategy fleshed out across the case studies—which are located in the former Yugoslavia, India, Israel-Palestine and Afghanistan—involves what I will come to call prismatic visions of social life under conditions of conflict, post-conflict or political struggle. The refracted and diffracted perspectives present in the media under review here mark the shifting position of those represented on screen, cultural producers and spectators, implicated and situated through processes of mediation. The chapters also attend to the circuits through which these media travel; the contexts of their production, distribution and display; and their exchange through film festivals and exhibitions, museums and galleries, transnational social movements and nongovernmental organizations. Processes of representing specific political struggles, and their gendered dimensions, have material, social and semiotic effects; media not only represent but also configure political coalitions across global, local, and regional spatial scales within the global system. This is of critical importance given that assertions of globalization frequently erase the social and material processes through which localities or globalities come into being.[25] Prismatic media, therefore, refract both within media themselves, in their rendering of social reality, and without, in their movement through—and translation across—uneven cultural contexts traversed by intersecting lines of power and resistance.

Many of the works included in this study are multichannel installations, providing several juxtaposing screens or projections. Scenes in individual works frequently present conflicting accounts of an event or foreground the mediating apparatus of camera, television monitor or archival footage; installations regularly encompass multiple temporalities and thus situate the viewer in discontinuous locations. Loops of tape, overlays of images and the contrast between archival and fictional footage are some of the devices through which the filmic, installation-based and documentary media addressed in this study unfold the multiple perspectives and narratives that constitute sites of political struggle for internal and external audiences. By fracturing the singular perspective of a monocular camera, multichannel video provides a clear instance of what I term throughout this study "prismatic media." Prismatic media are tasked with challenging unitary visions, formally encompassing a resistance to singular narratives, and thus providing imaging processes with counter-strategies both to totalizing ideological structures and to the evidentiary prerogatives of many documentary and journalistic representations of gender-based violence.

Initially, a focus on the prismatic nature of multichannel works would seem to prop up the very opposition between experimental installations and documentary approaches to the subject discussed earlier in this chapter, appearing to restage the distinction between quick and dirty media and performative experiments with closed-circuit video in the artist's studio or gallery space. Many of the documentaries included in this study, however, just as effectively make use of prismatic strategies in their works, indicating that such complex aesthetic modalities are not simply bound to the form of multichannel video. Indeed, because video is a "parasitical medium" (depending on other media, such as the television monitor, for its existence), it is always articulated through a variety of technologies (both social and material) that complicate its indexical claims.

Video, in fact, is an exemplary medium through which to think historically about a feminist politics of visuality because, like feminism, it has always had a hybrid status across disciplinary fields, aesthetic genres, theory and practice. Similarly, feminist theory and politics have frequently been articulated alongside and through the emerging medium of video—in explorations of self-representation through closed-circuit video, engagements with mass culture through appropriation and *détournement*, documenting performances and body art practices and recording community engagements and social justice efforts.[26] Video also inherited the concerns within an emerging feminist film theory with concepts such as "the gaze," scopophilia, voyeurism and spectatorship. In this light, video has constituted an "imaging machine," a signifying practice that, in Teresa de Lauretis's definition, "articulates meaning to images, engages subjectivity in that process, and maps a social vision into subjectivity."[27]

De Lauretis describes the process of imaging with reference to the institution of cinema, in the context of an effort to theorize the semiotic processes whereby cinematic representations activate processes of spectatorial self-representation. For de Lauretis, the cinema is not simply an apparatus of representation (reproducing meanings, values and ideology in society), but also an engine of self-imaging, producing subject positions for its makers, those who appear on screen and its viewers. The semiotic process of spectatorship needs to be contextualized within non-textualized discourses, discursive formations and heterogeneous social practices, which also inform the viewer's subjective processes.[28] Examining both the subjective and social dimensions of spectatorship is of critical importance to feminism in a globalized present. As media move across cultural landscapes, divergent spatial scales and the militarized borders of the global system, they interpellate different audiences and viewing positions; they also draw from idiomatic and accented semiotic codes, and refer to social realities which may require mediating frameworks.

An extension of de Lauretis's conception of *imaging* to the transnational circuits of image practice challenges the persistent mythology of the global village that still underwrites efforts at democratization and increased access to communication around the world.[29] Lost to many (although certainly not all) global appeals to video-making is feminism's account of the constitutive nature of image culture in representing and (re)producing gendered ideologies, as well as the complicity even of socialist humanism and aesthetic modernism with forms of racism, colonialism and heterosexism. The language of video is thus often lost in its political mobilization, just as politics are lost in the focus on the specificity of videographic language. While bringing to light instances of gender-based violence, exploitation and displacement is especially urgent, the concept of *imaging* assists in parsing the specificity of the historical, social and cultural context, and their framing of conditions of reception, enunciation and address.

By mobilizing the concept of imaging to examine signifying practices across transnational spheres, I seek to highlight two indispensible elements to the notion of prismatic media advanced here: first, as will be discussed further, the unevenness of globalization across different social spheres, and the persistent borders within the world system, indicate that signifying practices work unevenly across cultural landscapes and, thus, produce subject positions which may involve scale shifts across different (and sometimes incommensurable) signifying systems in different parts of the globe. Second, as discussed earlier, imaging seeks to address the effects of ideologies of (sexual, racial, ethnic and class) difference in the construction of social subjects. Insofar as prismatic media may undertake to visualize how images are "(potentially) productive of contradictions in subjective and social processes," they may also open space for a complex and expansive notion of difference, and thus may highlight subjective processes and positions without resolving them to produce solidarity.[30] This involves a consideration of imaging both on and off screen, attention to structures of meaning, channels of fantasy and desire and the historical factors that intervene in imaging (social discourses, genre codifications, audience expectations, unconscious production).[31]

In this regard, it is interesting that one of the most widely cited considerations of the medium of video, Rosalind Krauss's "The Aesthetics of Narcissism," specifically forecloses the medium's potential to engage the social subject, in gender but also en-gendered in the experience of race, class and sexuality. Although Krauss is not a feminist scholar—and thus does not have as her aim the embeddedness of video in technologies of gender—she nevertheless resolves too quickly the vacillation of the female subject inside social and discursive determinations and, in de Lauretis's terms, "outside and excessive to them."[32] Krauss makes an opposition between the narcissistic quality of "reflection" (often characterized as "mirror-reflection") in video works such as Lynda Benglis's *Now* (1973) and the more successful (in her view) forms of "reflexivity" in works such as Joan Jonas's *Vertical Roll* (1972). She argues, "Reflection, when it is a case of mirroring, is a move toward an external symmetry; while reflexivity is a strategy to achieve a radical *a*symmetry, from within."[33] Whereas reflection "vanquishes separateness"—moving toward a fusion of subject and object and an "erasing of differences"—reflexivity in modernist art involves a "doubling back in order to locate the object (and thus the objective conditions of one's experience)."[34] The success of video art, for Krauss, lies in its capacity to express the objective conditions of the medium and its history, and thus to locate video's radical aesthetics within its self-referring character, and therefore, its autonomy. In fact, rather than a mirror-reflection, what Krauss celebrates is the mirror through which the work refers to itself, its traditions, and media, and calls this process a *dédoublement* or doubling back in order to locate the object (and thus the objective conditions of one's experience).[35] The reflexive analysis of the medium's capacity to mediate (to ensnare the subject in a closed circuit) is joined in Krauss's argument by reflexivity on the distinction between lived subjectivity and fantasy projections, in other words between the phenomenological experience of the lived body and the ideal ego.

The trouble with Krauss's analysis for feminist criticism is the absence of a consideration of the manner in which video is also a social technology, embedded in institutionalized discourses, critical practices and forms of experience. What Krauss's analysis fails to recognize in Joan Jonas's piece is the specific manner in which it theorizes how the "personal becomes political" (i.e., the ways in which "the political becomes the personal by way of its subjective effects");[36] and further, Krauss's account does not attend to the fact that what Jonas might be articulating may be grounded in the simultaneity of video's closed circuit, surely, but also the subjective and social contradictions of the category "woman."

Left out of Krauss's analysis, therefore, are the significant and generative contradictions within media that take up questions of embodiment, representation and sexual difference. De Lauretis argues that feminism's epistemological potential resides in its conceiving of the social subject and relations of subjectivity to sociality in gender, "though not by sexual difference alone, but rather across languages and cultural representations; a subject en-gendered in the experiencing of race and class, as well as sexual relations; a subject, therefore, not unified but rather multiple, and not so much divided as contradicted."[37] This is true also of feminist media, and of its representation of the processes by which subjects are en-gendered in the interaction of individuals with the outer world. The reflexivity of Joan Jonas's *Vertical Roll*—the distortion of the recorded image to produce a vertical roll, the consistent crashing and skipping of the figure of the female body and the shattering sound of a metal object banging repetitively— entails not only a rich exploration of the mediating function of video's closed circuit, but also of the process of subject constitution, especially for women, through a constant renegotiation of external pressures, social and semiotic structures and internal resistances.

The subject of Jonas's work is displaced, both inside and outside the determinations of semiotic structures and social reality, occupying what de Lauretis calls an "eccentric point of view."[38] This eccentricity (literally a displacement from the center) provides an account of subjectivity at odds with itself. More than this however, it provides an account of subject positions that do not so much fail to achieve identification (Jonas's failure to match up with the figure of the female nude, for instance), but whose excesses provide a resistance to identification, outside ideological structures of power/knowledge, as a personal and political practice.

Jonas's experiments with frequency modulation expose a foundational paradox surrounding the subject of feminism: namely, that when feminism first posed the question "Who or what is a woman?" it discovered, in de Lauretis's terms, the "non-being of woman" and the paradox of a being that is "at once captive and absent in discourse, constantly spoken of but of itself inaudible or inexpressible, displayed as spectacle and still unrepresented or unrepresentable, invisible yet constituted as the object and the guarantee of vision."[39] For De Lauretis, a historically conscious and self-conscious feminist theory cannot dispense with this paradox, with the inconsistency or internal contradiction that the question of the subject of feminism reveals.[40]

It is important to stress that the prismatic strategies articulated here are not simply formal or aesthetic. To locate them in this manner would simply repeat the foreclosures present in the analyses of reflexivity discussed earlier, make refraction curve back on itself, become reflexivity, and thus locate feminist media firmly back within the confines of modernist conceptions of art's autonomy. Processes of refraction and reconstruction, I believe, expose the very ground of feminist analyses of the politics of visuality, an analysis that, first, exposes the social technologies through which recognition and rights are conferred, differentially, across axes of gender, race, ethnicity, class and sexual identity, and second, articulates the situatedness, political-historical and personal-political of its own cultural and theoretical products.

The radical potential de Lauretis identifies in feminist theory may also be brought to bear on the processes of transnational mediation (both scholarly and artistic) I characterize as prismatic. Rather than a focus on "reflexivity," on the artwork's definition in terms of the limitations of its proper medium, prismatic forms of displacement join the strategies of refraction and diffraction to the movement between inside and outside social determinations, and thus ally prismatic media with anti-racist and postcolonial feminisms without borders.

The notion of an eccentric subject acknowledges the repressive force of systems of oppression—heterosexism, capitalism, racism and colonialism—and their mutual complicities and contradictions, even as it emphasizes that subject's capacity for resistance to such ideologies.[41]

Feminist theory's task involves displacement and self-displacement, determining "a place of discourse from which speaking and thinking are at best tentative, uncertain, unguaranteed," an eccentric point of view as a position of resistance and agency, outside or in excess of the sociocultural apparatuses of heterosexuality, capitalist globalization, racism and ethnic difference.[42] It is in this manner that prismatic media exceed the terms of reflexivity in artistic practices, providing instead refractory or diffracted viewpoints that engage questions of difference, even as they seek to represent "the complex meaning effects, habits, dispositions, associations, and perceptions resulting from the semiotic interaction of self and outer world."[43]

Documentary Reflexivity and Transnational Feminism

The limits of reflexivity as an aesthetic strategy must be kept in mind not only within artistic practices, where the self-questioning nature of works centers on their own constitutive language as art forms, but also within documentary practices, where reflexivity frequently is intended to guarantee a new form of objectivity, one not bound by transparency and neutrality, but rather by situated claims to ethnographic and documentary authority. While documentary genres certainly inherited the epistemological foundations of the structural and optical principles of the *camera obscura* (objective distance, monocular perspectives, indexicality), the "post-medium condition" has challenged the reality quotient even of indexical media. Mary Ann Doane accordingly argues that "[t]he project of extricating the real from the business of realism can be aligned with what might be called a 'politics of the index.'"[44] In the literature on indexical media—marked especially by Peter Wollen's comparison of Peircean semiotics to André Bazin's conception of realism—the semiotic function of the index is complemented by the creation in indexical media of an aesthetic world, as well as processes of spectatorial involvement.[45] Reflexivity within documentary genres is thus frequently signaled by a film's realist aesthetic strategies (its framing devices, tropes such as hand-held cameras, points of view, montage, use of non-professional actors, etc.) rather than naïve assertions of transcribing social reality.[46]

Questions of reflexivity and reflection are matters of style, located in the divide between direct-address styles of documentary (voiceover narration, framing devices and a clear narrative structure) and *cinéma vérité*.[47] Trinh Minh-ha notes that such an "aesthetic of objectivity" involves technologies such as directional microphones (to localize and restrict in selecting sounds); portable recorders (to maximally and faithfully document); lip-synchronous sounds; real-time footage and long takes, with minimal editing; wider framing; and the frequent use of a light-weight, hand-held camera.[48] Documentary studies scholars have sought to articulate a compromise between the poles of reflection and mediation in self-reflexive documentary practices that mix observational passages with interviews, and voiceovers by the filmmaker with inter-titles. While *cinéma vérité* and other forms of direct cinema have shown a preference for narrative structures that are loose and fluid, dismissing the storytelling effect of more traditional forms of documentary, Bill Nichols argues that the question of voice nonetheless has been central to all documentary practice. He defines voice as

> something narrower than style: that which conveys to us a sense of a text's social point of view, of how it is speaking to us and how it is organizing the materials it is presenting to us. In this sense, voice is not restricted to any one code or feature, such as dialogue or spoken commentary. Voice is perhaps akin to that intangible, moiré-like pattern formed by the unique interaction of all a film's codes.[49]

Nichols reproaches certain documentary filmmakers for disavowing the complexities of voice and discourse in favor of simple notions of "respectful representation."[50] Observational cinema and *cinéma vérité* rely on the trope of observation as a way of effacing the narrative structure; while no voiceovers interrupt the narrative, strategies such as a chronology of causality, shots organized into "dramatically revelatory scenes" or performances by characters who "play themselves" mark the film's voice behind the organization of observations.[51]

Nevertheless, reflexivity needs to be more than a distancing device; it needs also to challenge the constitution of authority. In Trinh's view, even where reflexivity is employed as a means of foregrounding the partiality of the documentarian's social and historical subject position, "[t]he 'social' continues to go unchallenged, history keeps on being salvaged, while the sovereignty of the socio-historicizing subject is safely maintained."[52] Reflexivity, in these cases, serves to increase rather than problematize questions of indexicality, realism and transparency. In describing the manner in which transparency reemerges as a nostalgia for plenitude, Homi Bhabha remarks,

> Despite appearances, the text of transparency inscribes a double vision: the field of the "true" emerges as a visible sign of authority only after the regulatory and displacing division of the true and the false. From this point of view, discursive "transparency" is best read in the photographic sense in which a transparency is also always a negative, processed into visibility through

the technologies of reversal, enlargement, lighting, editing, projection, not a source but a re-source of light. Such a bringing to light is a question of the provision of visibility as a capacity, a strategy, an agency.[53]

Reflexivity as a guarantor of transparency thus produces discursive closure, supporting a form of representational realism that denies the operations of authorial power Bhabha describes. In ethnographic film, according to Trinh, the trope of self-reflexivity is frequently constituted through self-exposure (a trope allied with the narrative constitution of the anthropologist's arrival in the field in ethnographic literature). Such exposure, as a formal device in documentary or experimental film and video, risks becoming merely a technique or formula if it does not engage historical questions of authority and of the constitution of social life in and through representation. Reflexive techniques in film (among these, Trinh includes visual and verbal narratives about the anthropologist, exposure of the methodology of observation and the conditions of production) thus secure rather than challenge models of scientific objectivity.[54]

Trinh's critique of renewed claims to ethnographic authority in the guise of self-reflexivity underlines how the epistemological force of realist aesthetics becomes complicitous with universal and universalizing models of political coalition. The consolidation of documentary authority on the one hand renders legible the demands of political subjects for recognition within international rights structures and transnational feminist coalitions. At the same time, the genre's aspiration to transcend particularity threatens to devolve into the universalizing tendencies of global feminism.

The consolidation of the narrative structure of many evidentiary documents—toward visibility and transparency—also involve an erasure of historical specificity.[55] As will be discussed at greater length in Chapter 1, transparency and realism become modes of signification that have their basis in Roland Barthes's understanding of myth—namely that mythical speech erases its own historicity, making itself appear "natural" and "transhistorical." He argues, "The meaning is already complete, it postulates a kind of knowledge, a past, a memory, a comparative order of facts, ideas, decisions. When it becomes form, the meaning leaves its contingency behind; it empties itself, it becomes impoverished, history evaporates, only the letter remains."[56] Thus, discourses of visibility (with their resonances of bringing to light and evidencing) frequently suppress the imaging processes that found subjectivity in complex processes of semiosis.

How then might prismatic strategies attend to questions of historical specificity, particularly for a politically engaged transnational feminism? James Clifford offers a vision of a "semiotic realism" cautiously indebted to Georg Lukács's and Erich Auerbach's theories of historical realism. Although Clifford acknowledges that the progressive direction of history posited by these authors has been clearly identified as a project of European imperialism, he is nevertheless interested in these authors' theorization of the manner in which artistic production can represent "in concrete complexity the dynamics of historical change."[57] For Clifford, it is precisely Lukács's and Auerbach's understanding that political, social and economic disruptions produce "realistic visions" of historical processes that allows us to ask in the present about the forms of representation emerging from new historical conjunctures. As such, while Lukács's and Auerbach's visions of the historical "real" marginalized the conflicting histories of concrete social subjects, distinguished on the basis of gender, class, caste and race, the complex frictions in the global system are articulated from the very sites of what Clifford calls "a politically and historically fissured realism," and thus produce complex, oppositional and eccentric forms of historical consciousness.[58]

In this way, refraction signals the displacement of the evidentiary in favor of what Clifford calls a "semiotic realism," which, rather than presenting an unmediated access to the subject of representation, instead involves "the representation of cultural, linguistic, bodily, scientific codes as they change and question each other 'in history'," and hence processes of "transcoding" rather than "in some observational sense, representing."[59] The distinction is emphasized in Hamid Naficy's observations regarding the reception of Third Cinema, noting somewhat playfully that all Third Cinema is received by international audiences as documentary film, seen to re-present social reality authentically rather than strategically. His emphasis on "accented cinema" (marked by the filmmakers' interstitial location in society and the film industry) marks the negotiation and bending of Third Cinema aesthetics across dominant and diasporic cultural traditions, and thus the complication of visions of authentic cultural transmission. In a similar vein, with regard to the Black Audio Film Collective, Clifford argues, "form and content are deployed strategically, to produce a contestation of culturally dominant representations of the historical real."[60] Clifford concludes that realist accounts "always reflect partial subjective positions."[61] It is this very partiality, historically constructed, refracted through frameworks of race, class, culture, gender and sexuality, which constitute the prismatic vision articulated here.

As media move through transnational circuits—and through rights-based discourses, institutional frameworks, genre conventions and visual cultures—they call upon existing forms of cross-cultural and global contact. While cultural producers interested in social justice across the global system must stress the transmissibility and viability of particular global trajectories, prismatic media have a role to play in making visible the friction between semiotic, social and subjective systems. It is also of critical importance that a globally-committed cultural practice not repeat the colonial and postcolonial associations between circulation and liberation.[62] Rather than forming ethical relations across cultures and in global networks, then, the images come to stand for the historically-specific and -informed work of encounter across cultural, economic, political and geographic boundaries.

Prismatic Media and Feminism Without Borders

How, then, might representational practices be more accountable to the processes by which they travel and make meaning transnationally? Account for the politics of reception and interpretation of media, as well as the histories of relations of exchange governing production, literacy, marketing and distribution? In her critique of ethnographic authority, Trinh calls for models of reflexivity that do not simply inquire into the conditions of production and representation, but also analyze the "established forms of the social that define one's limits."[63] Such a model of mediation would also take up the very ties between subjectivity and transparency for those represented on screen, cultural producers and spectators. She argues that

> reflexivity is not "a mere question of *rect*ifying and *just*ifying. (*Subject*ivizing.) What is set in motion in its praxis are the self-generating links between different forms of reflexivity. Thus, a subject who points to him/her/itself as a subject-in-process, a work that displays its own formal properties or its own constitution as work, is bound to upset one's sense of identity."[64]

Rather than reflection or reflexivity, Trinh calls for a mode of representation that she terms the "reflexive interval." The interval is constituted at the border between the textual and non-textual, "where a positioning within constantly incurs the risk of de-positioning, and where the work, never freed from historical and socio-political contexts nor entirely subjected to them, can only be itself by constantly risking being no-thing."[65] The interval provides a properly cinematic metaphor for the space between frames and cuts, as well as the resistance of narrative closure; moreover, it captures the join of subjectivity, sociality and semiosis at stake in the notion of "eccentric subjects" discussed earlier.

While Trinh's concept of the "reflexive interval" provides a compelling cinematic metaphor for critically and socially-engaged representational practices, the case studies that follow flesh out the manner in which the particularity of videographic media lends itself to specifically prismatic representational practices, joining the temporal and narratival focus of Trinh's "reflexive interval," with the decentering spatial practices of refraction and diffraction in contemporary time-based media.

In its temporal dimension, experimental video has mobilized not only a fierce and persistent repetition (looping being a function of both installations where works repeat end-to-end, and within video works themselves), but also the extended temporality of "real time," a temporality that Fredric Jameson terms an "aesthetics of boredom." Jameson notes how the question of boredom in early video art is raised in both aesthetic and phenomenological terms, providing "a precious symptom of our own existential, ideological, and cultural limits, an index of what has to be refused in the way of other people's cultural practices and their threat to our own rationalizations about the nature and value of art."[66] Rather than examine the temporality of video in axiological terms, Jameson focuses instead on the manner in which video's temporality itself binds apparatus and subject in a new kind of materialism: "It is as though [. . .] the emergence of the machine itself [. . .] deconcealed in some unexpected way the produced materiality of human life and human time," a time subject to measurement, and thus to the machine, a "time of the machine itself."[67] For Jameson, this temporality produces a new form of referent at the intersections of videographic and historical time, a demand for apprehending "a constant stream, or 'total flow,' of multiple materials, each of which can be seen as something like a shorthand signal for a distinct type of narrative or a specific narrative process."[68] This produces, in Jameson's view, a "kaleidoscopic" and synchronic image of distinct streams of elements whose historicism (whose relation to historical time, and thus also to historical fissures and frictions) may only be revealed in the specific videographic organizations of space and time. Jameson's understanding of video's temporality thus—rather than stressing the electronic effacement of the referent in post-industrial image culture—links the (non-)narrative structure within video with the fissures opened up by the uneven processes of globalization themselves.

Rather than the seamless electronic space visualized in Paik's *Global Groove*, then, Jameson foregrounds the manner in which video might foreground the asymmetries within and between spatial scales under the conditions of globalization. Video's organization of space and time accordingly reveals the tensions between proximity and distance under the force of global capitalism, and the friction between different temporalities and historical arcs in globalism's rhetoric of progress. In this respect, prismatic strategies are especially pertinent for both a feminist account of the politics of visuality (of what is represented and its relation to existing iconographies), and a postcolonial critical examination of the conflicts, differences and borders that form and inform antiracist and coalitional feminism—what Mohanty calls the urgent feminist praxis of a "feminism without borders." A "feminism without borders" signals a transnational and postcolonial commitment in feminism, attentive to the historical, cultural and methodological borders in the global system, while seeking sites of coalition in struggles for social justice. Such a praxis engages the production and reception of feminist theories and media in transnational cultures of exchange, and refracts representational tropes in the service of bringing into representation alternative histories, identities and possibilities for alliances. Rather than stressing the universality of gendered oppression (or indeed of gendered struggles), a "feminism without borders" would historicize and locate political agency in specific cultural locations.[69] In uncovering alternative, non-identical histories, a "feminism without borders" may counter the spatial and temporal coordinates of hegemonic histories (dominant among them, the hegemonic force of global capitalism). Strategies of refraction and diffraction serve to illuminate the sites of historicized struggles within the world system, to attend to the differential accessibility and assimilability of multiple locations under the conditions of globalization.

Prismatic media do not define a specifically feminist aesthetic, but rather suggest aesthetic strategies that both engage questions of difference, mediating across aesthetic, subjective and semiotic domains through a specifically situated politics of location, allied with feminist forms of critical consciousness. Donna Haraway takes up the notion of diffraction also as an optical metaphor for efforts to make a difference in the world:

> Diffraction patterns record the history of interaction, interference, reinforcement, difference. Diffraction is about heterogeneous history, not about originals. Unlike reflections, diffractions do not displace the same elsewhere, in more or less distorted form. Rather, diffraction can be a metaphor for another kind of critical consciousness at the end of this rather painful Christian millennium, one committed to making a difference and not to repeating the Sacred Image of the Same. Diffraction is a narrative, graphic, psychological, spiritual, and political technology for making consequential meanings.[70]

For Haraway, reflexivity may provide an impoverished ground for critical practices because, in her terms, "like reflection, [it] only displaces the same elsewhere, setting up worries about copy and original and the search for the authentic and really real."[71] The metaphor of diffraction as a commitment to critical consciousness sheds light on the efforts by cultural producers to create interference patterns in discourses of verisimilitude in representational practices, to highlight the mediating force of cultural products as they move through channels of transmission and sites of display and exhibition.[72] It also importantly allies such aesthetic strategies to the political praxes of oppositional consciousness—to what Chela Sandoval describes as a differential position that maneuvers, transfigures, weaves "between and among" oppositional ideologies, and emerges out of intensities, junctures and crises—and thus constitutes a critical strategy for feminist coalition in the contemporary global system.[73] In creating such interference patterns, prismatic media offer models for representational politics within feminist media studies and cultural production which, rather than specifying (even self-reflexively) one's position, instead displace that position through complex mediating processes between differential positions.

In their canonical examination of the culture industry, Adorno and Horkheimer argue "The style of the culture industry, which no longer has to test itself against any refractory material, is also the negation of style."[74] Refraction, we are reminded, involves the diversion or deflection of a ray of light from its previous course in passing from one medium into another or traversing a medium of varying density. It also, incidentally, has an archaic etymological root in rhetoric, as the use of the same word to mean opposing things, as well as in breaking open or breaking up. In contradistinction to reflexivity's emphasis on invoking the internal structure of a media form, refraction locates images and processes of signification within the context of ideological formations, formations whose values and effects are, as de Lauretis puts it, "social and subjective, aesthetic and affective, and permeate the entire social fabric, and hence all social subjects."[75]

In proposing refraction as a political and aesthetic strategy, I do not mean to suggest a dismissal of reflexivity in contemporary time-based media, and indeed in many of the works discussed in this study. Reflexivity has constituted a vital strategy for the artwork's ability to mirror itself, to write itself into its image, to reveal its conditions of production. Marcel Duchamp's renowned *Bicycle Wheel* (1913) pushed the questions of the status of the "real" object as a work of art, thus questioning the social definitions of art, the cult of the autographic gesture, and the uniqueness of the art object. Within cinema, the later works of Jean-Luc Godard such as *Le Petit Soldat* (1963), along with much *nouvelle vague* cinema, mobilized aesthetic strategies that marked his films as the exemplary instance of cinematic modernism in the service of a critique of French colonial ideologies.[76] Accordingly, reflexivity is itself not a unified or monolithic practice but a contested field of positions (both critical and creative). I mean rather to suggest that the circular paths of return embedded in reflexivity frequently involve a reconciliation of difference and externality in the service of a center or inner necessity in the work of art. Refraction, however, is a metaphor for processes of deflection, which signify the semiotic and aesthetic disruption of figuration in social practice. Rather than *self*-representation, refraction represents a subjective negotiation between inner and outer, between self and world, that forms one part of what Spivak terms "ethical semiosis" (the irreducible work of translation, encountered through patient and provisional preparation).[77]

The discursive and epistemological character of feminist theory (and, I would argue, feminist media) resides in its being "at once inside its own social and discursive determinations and outside and excessive to them."[78] Such an "eccentric point of view" may also be extended to cultural producers who must negotiate the poles of authenticity (the demand that one represent one's culture) and, in Hassan and Oguibe's terms, ex-centricity (the transnational, diasporic, and postcolonial experiences of many cultural producers in a globalized present). The very vacillations between internal and external views of cultural authenticity—and the issues of cross-cultural and transnational aesthetics within local artistic practice—serve as prismatic interventions in the narration of contemporary culture, mobilizing ex-centricity as a strategic position from which to problematize notions of originality and authenticity. What this produces in visual culture is a "feeling of internal distance, a contradiction, a space of silence, which is there alongside the imaginary pull of cultural and ideological representations without denying or obliterating them."[79]

Thus, refractory strategies point not only to the vacillation between visibility and invisibility—between framing and its exclusions—but also towards the historical and social determinants which inform the work, determinants that include also the spectator or visitors to the spaces media inscribe.[80] While a politics of location may serve to acknowledge the multiplicity and mediation at the heart of prismatic strategies, they may also serve to revalue what Mohanty names the figure of the "truth-teller" in visions of global sisterhood or "planetary feminism." Mohanty argues that the construction of a specifically female "standpoint" risks producing the figure either of "woman as victim" or "woman as truth-teller." In both cases, the testifying subject is granted a "privileged access to the real," and thus "promotes a political model of transcendence rather than engagement."[81] Similarly, Kaplan argues that a politics of location can turn into an instrument of hegemony, shoring up "Western interest in other cultures."[82]

Prismatic strategies must therefore be firmly located within a complex politics of location. In contrast to her critique of Western interests in other cultures, Kaplan defines a politically necessary politics of location as a "complex interpretive practice that acknowledges the historical role of mediation, betrayal, and alliance between women in diverse locations."[83] As such, it both serves to critique and deconstruct hegemonic or totalizing figurations of gender or of solidarity, and to identify the ground for affiliation and alliance. Such a politics cannot simply engage a poetic figuring of place or a romanticization of the space of the other, but rather must foreground "detailed historicized maps of the circuits of power."[84] For certainly, while the displacement of one's point of understanding and conceptual articulation is a fruitful arena for resisting the hegemonic sites of the articulation of race/gender/sexuality, it is also the site where social subjects are articulated and en-gendered across languages and cultural representations. Thus, rather than simply a record of authentic and unified experience, prismatic media might shed light on "the meanings attached to gender, race, class and age at various historical moments," and thus *theorize* rather than re-present experience.[85]

Transnational circuits do not necessarily create foundational or permanent ties between framing or signifying systems. Aesthetic and ethical strategies for representing the contradictions of social positions within the global system cannot be solved or resolved, but must consistently be re-established. Prismatic media, therefore, require renewed and constant effort by activists, feminists, scholars, survivors and victims' families, as well as civil society more generally, to open the possibility of an engagement across difference. Studies of media in a globalized present must pay attention to the traffic in accessibility, the routes that media take and their particular audiences.[86] Prismatic visions emphasize the translation of experience through representational regimes, attending especially to failures, spillovers, gaps and leakages in shifts between languages, semiotic codes and epistemological structures. James Clifford notes that translation processes are processes of imperfect equivalences: "To use comparative concepts in a situated way means to become aware, always belatedly, of limits, sedimented meanings, tendencies to gloss over differences."[87]

Feminism in a Globalized Present

Prismatic media are especially urgent in the light of the expansion of forces of globalization in the late twentieth and early twenty-first centuries— the erosion of local and national economic and political resources as well as democratic processes, the persistence and aggravation of exploitative social relations and structures, and the continued force of the naturalized ideas, beliefs and values of competition, valuation and accumulation. Prismatic media serve to highlight how globalization is uneven and inconsistent. While Spivak underlines that globalization itself has "vanishing outlines," which I take to mean a capacity to spread, to figure itself as expansive and limitless, the differential force of globalization establishes not universal interconnection but rather frictions and unevenness.[88] Friction is the name that anthropologist Anna Tsing gives to the "ever-present reminder that universal claims do not actually make everything everywhere the same."[89] The task of prismatic media involves negotiating the different spatial scales of the globalized present, to track the incommensurability between national, global, universalized, and planetary maps and collectivities. A further objective of this study is to define a feminist critical methodology able to unpack the relation between the incommensurability internal to the cultural object and the external frictions as objects travel through transnational circuits in the global system.

For Tsing, friction provides a useful metaphor in opposition to discourses in the 1990s of global motion:

> In this imagined global era, motion would proceed entirely without friction. By getting rid of national barriers and autocratic or protective state policies, everyone would have the freedom to travel everywhere. Indeed, motion itself would be experienced as self-actualization, and self-actualization without restraint would oil the machinery of the economy, science, and society.[90]

A critical practice of media analysis that aspires to the forging of a "feminism without borders" must pay close attention to the relations of exchange for media in transnational circuits. These include the structures of dominant and regional art gallery systems, reflections on globalization within museum exhibitions, film festivals, and specialized distribution companies such as *Women Make Movies,* transnational NGOs, artists' and activists' co-ops, transnational film production companies, and award-granting bodies, frequently located in Euro-American capitals.

Friction may occur within the incommensurable scales of national and pre-national belonging, or the exclusionary inclusions of bonded labor in transnational capital, even as the art works discussed in the following chapters themselves travel along the rarified paths of the art market and trades in symbolic capital. These art works and documentaries are critically important for understanding the repressive force of national and global ideologies (what Spivak calls "nation-state-specific globality") in their deployment of sexual difference and their reproduction of heteronormative conventions.[91] Conversely, cultural products that chafe the visual cultures through which they pass may present unified and holistic visions of social space.

Attention to the friction between spatial scales, as well as within them, is especially urgent given the continued force of mythological conceptions of gender at the national and transnational levels. Prismatic visions are charged with prying open sites of ideological foreclosure, particularly in relation to the forms of absolutism responsible for much gender-based violence. In order to take on hegemonic global frameworks and cross national and regional borders, feminist theory and prismatic media must work to complicate notions of home, belonging, nation and community.[92] Principally in this study, nationhood and nationalism become key sites within the global system for the figuration of feminine political subjects, even as they are the spaces most violently renegotiated in territorial contestations, armed conflict, and invisible forms of sexual exploitation.

The perils of nationalist discourse are thus not only evident for those excluded from territorial boundaries, but also, as many feminist critiques of nationalism suggest, within the hegemonic articulations of national identity. In their introduction to the anthology *Between Woman and Nation*, Norma Alarcón, Caren Kaplan, and Minoo Moallem argue that nationalist discourse sharpens "the defining lines of citizenship for women, racialized ethnicities, and sexualities in the construction of a socially stratified society."[93] The studies that follow seek to examine the internal and external frictions presented by a selection of visual media artifacts in contexts of crisis, armed conflict, genocide, and super-exploitation to examine the manner in which prismatic visions might articulate a feminism without borders.

The multiple and refracted images, the repetition of segments of tape or looping of a video, and the interactions between live performance and image, or between layers of objects or images, all seek to render the complexity of racial, ethnic, class or gender difference within representations, to make specific the historical configurations that differentiate women from one another and that are always already differences within women. These works then enact the kind of epistemological potential in feminist theory. They address a female spectator, acknowledging the complicity of individual women with the ideology of gender and, at the same time, maintain a persistent ambiguity of gender, multiplied through the many channels in the video works.

The central questions for an understanding of time-based media as both sociality and subjectivity are: "By what processes do images on the screen produce imaging on and off screen, articulate meaning and desire, for the spectators?" and "What historical factors intervene in imaging?"[94] The effect of such questions for cultural producers, subjects who appear on screen, and spectators across the global system is to force the question "how do I look?" to think not only about the processes of imaging—and the limits of representation—but also about the processes of imagining. De Lauretis's notion of imaging also includes a concern for the historical functions that intervene in those processes, and thus may shed light on how the position of the represented and the representer may already have been fixed by their specific positions in a world order structured by the unresolved tensions of colonialism, the global division of labor, the friction between incommensurate modernities, feminist discourses of rescue that hint to the violence of civilizing missions and so on. The historical specificity of the events covered in the case studies that follow seeks to challenge the seamlessness of globalizing forces and mark the specificity of aesthetic strategies in geographically and historically particular contexts.

Such imagining is elaborated by Spivak, in *Death of a Discipline*, in the future anterior tense of "teleopoiesis," as "[affecting] the distant in a *poiesis*—an imaginative making—without guarantees."[95] Spivak's focus on the future anterior highlights an imaginative desire for emancipation as a result of one's labor in the present, an emancipation that grounds the moral imperatives of socially engaged media as imaging machines.[96] The aesthetic strategies of refraction and diffraction are joined to the subjective and social task of "learning to live with contradictory instructions."[97] For Spivak, an aesthetic education in the globalized present presents a strategy for negotiating what she calls a double bind, most particularly the "double bind of the universalizability of the singular, the double bind at the heart of democracy."[98] Such a position allies the considerations of transnational circuits, globalization and prismatic media at the heart of this book. It is precisely in relation to this double bind that prismatic media exceed strategies of reflexivity, as well as canonization within the confines of "minor literatures."[99] The transnational dimensions of these media do not contrast the repressive aspects of globalization with a nostalgic localism, but undertake a feminism without borders in an attempt to open an oppositional and emancipatory space. For Spivak, "if, instead of each identitarian group remaining in its own enclave, some of us engage in abusing the enabling violation of our colonial past to converse with each other, we may be able not only to turn globalization around, but also to supplement the necessary uniformization of globalization with linguistic diversity."[100]

Video's mediation of multiple and often-competing realities is, in this sense, active and productive. It is for this reason that the verb tenses that govern artistic practice in this study are gerunds, representing unfinished processes that constantly balance between, in Clifford's terms, rooting (claiming a kind of ontological status) and routing (circulating between subjects).[101] Clifford's attention to how mobility, travel, negotiation, and flux always inform culture's claims to boundary or blood demonstrates how culture is contested and contingent, represented in performances, museums, documentaries, stories, and photographs. With resonances of making images and of imagining, imaging practices gather up a transnational and disparate set of social groups in articulating the very real dimensions of exploitation and oppression, expressing in images subjects' most fervent desire for an alternative reality.

The case studies that follow argue for the importance of tracing a given medium's function within the larger structure of media culture, following the mediation of the tropes of visibility and invisibility as objects move through the system. Specifically, they examine how media might highlight the disjunctions between platforms in the field of visual culture through methodological tools such as refraction and diffraction, which map the interference patterns within a system and between the actors they call upon and interpellate. It is not enough to "make visible" as a rights-granting mechanism, since the terms of visibility are already predefined by a socio-cultural system and semiotic apparatus that only bring certain subjects into visibility, and only on specific terms. Cultural producers must, instead, examine in media the manner in which framing devices limit the subject on screen herself, often in ways that elide not only differences between cultural systems but also differences within them. The aesthetic strategies traced here examine how media offer models of witnessing less bound by rules of evidence and more attentive to affect, fantasy, identification and location.

This book's interest in the social relations of production, distribution, and display of time-based media is closely enmeshed with analyses of the formal strategies employed by cultural producers to reflect on shifting points of view in media cultures. This is particularly relevant in the contemporary moment, not only because of the increased access to the tools of cultural production but also because—in an era where the indexicality or "truth-quotient" of media is no longer taken for granted—the truth of certain media lies rather in their rhetorical strength and in such tools as genre or trope. Studies of media under the conditions of globalization, then, are tasked with parsing media, tracing their movement through communities, their representational practices, and their mediation of social relations. Prismatic media open up the contradictions within representations of race, gender, and sexuality, shaping not only eccentric subjects but also complex coalitions under the conditions of a globalized present.

* * *

The first chapter, "Refracted Visions: 'Ethnic Cleansing' and the De-mythologization of Gender," examines how prismatic imaging practices might counter propagandistic representations of women in the service of ethnic nationalism, charting particularly the material effect of this rhetorical violence in the "ethnic cleansing" campaigns in the former Yugoslavia. The chapter begins with an analysis of the representational strategies mobilized by the Milošević regime during the wars. Using Roland Barthes's understanding of myth, the chapter traces the movement from women to woman (a second-order signification), and further from woman to nation (a third-order signification) in propaganda during the war. I argue that imaging practices make three key interventions in the representational practices of Serbian nationalism: first, artists such as Marina Abramović and Milica Tomić critically interrogate the mythical structure employed by the Milošević regime to make women stand in for the nation in wartime propaganda, exposing how the violence of rhetoric depends on the projection of ethnic tensions and historical wrongs onto women. Second, the art works under consideration in this study highlight the close connections between the ideological structures of the nation and the social structures of the family—particularly, in the case of videos by Abramović and Elahe Massumi, through the figure of the father—and observe how this structural similarity is responsible for gender-based violence and nationalism. Third, the documentaries considered in the chapter, Mandy Jacobson and Karmen Jelincić's *Calling the Ghosts* (1996) and Jo Andres's *Black Kites* (1995), critically interrogate the evidentiary imperative in documentary video, especially the impossibility of providing visible evidence for the torture and abuse suffered during the war. In all cases, multichannel video is placed in the service of defying the repressive representations offered by the Milošević government (and by wartime discourse more broadly). By providing prismatic visions of the experience of war, these artists and documentarians also fracture the space of the viewer so that the category "woman" cannot become a reductive placeholder for the work of transnational solidarity.

The second chapter, "Visual Currencies: Documenting India's Red Light Districts," draws out the ties between imaging processes and multichannel video, particularly as these representational practices situate subjects within the circuits of transnational capitalism. I compare Ross Kauffman and Zana Briski's popular documentary *Born into Brothels* (2004) with Elahe Massumi's multichannel video installations, *The Hijras* (2000) and *A Kiss Is not a Kiss* (2000). All three projects turn to India and thus frame the problem of sexual exploitation in a space of postcoloniality. The chapter explores how each work defines a specific site and scale where the problem of sexual exploitation is located, interrogating the "ethnographic turn" in art and documentary practice with respect to the social relations produced around the work (between the artist or documentarists and her subjects, and between the videos and their audiences). The chapter further articulates how the representation of women's bodies (as sex workers) locates

them in particular economies of value (the women's bodies certainly circulate in economies of loans, indenture, and exchange, but the images to
some extent do so as well).

The third chapter, "Discontinuous States: Palestinian and Israeli Border
Imaginaries," focuses on art produced in the multiple internal and external borders of Israel and Palestine, and explores the paradoxes of exile
and statehood embodied in these works. I examine how videos by Mona
Hatoum, Michal Rovner, Emily Jacir, and Akram Zaatari participate in a
critique of the border—a space of violent determinations of movement and
stasis—while at the same time make visible the artists' firm commitment
to various forms of statehood or national mobilization. The chapter argues
that the artists' representational strategies seek to challenge cartographic
abstractions by focusing on the social relations that uphold and reproduce militarized borders, as well as on the border's active role in forming
national subjects, disciplined bodies, and cultural cohesion. The chapter
focuses especially on how video plays a unique role in making visible both
the experiential and the embodied space of the traveling subject (the camera close to the artist's body as she walks through borderlands) and the
articulation of other forms of collective belonging that make claims for
statehood even as they are suspicious of it.

The final chapter, "Diffracted Mediations: The Framing of Gender in
the 'War on Terror,'" extends the considerations of previous chapters to
questions of gender, cultural production, and social relations in a world
considerably redefined by the "war on terror." It treats several works made
by Afghanis living in Afghanistan and abroad, as well as by North American
and European cultural producers, in the years following September 11,
2001. This chapter examines how cultural producers negotiate the reductive binaries in representations of war, and especially the double bind of
visibility/invisibility in the visual culture of armed conflict. The desire to
make visible the experience of Afghani women, then, must both resist
transforming them into simplistically drawn icons of post-intervention liberation and, by the same token, avoid repeating the repressive aspects of
their banishment from public life. In this context, the chapter asks how cultural producers might offer visions of Afghanistan that fracture the binary
of visibility/invisibility in both Western and Afghani contexts. Examples of
such works include Lida Abdul's *White House* (2005) and Cyrus Frisch's
Why Didn't Anybody Tell Me It Would Become This Bad in Afghanistan?
(2007). The second focus of this chapter involves an examination of modes
of looking bound by the very prohibitions of visibility and invisibility,
characterized primarily by mediations across the field of visual culture.
The chapter performs a close reading of the movement of footage shot by
the Revolutionary Association of the Women of Afghanistan, Saira Shah's

Beneath the Veil (2001), as well as the feature film *Osama* (2003) by Siddiq Barmak, and Sandra Schäfer and Elfe Brandenburger's documentary, *Passing the Rainbow* (2008). The chapter concludes that prismatic visions must be extended in the contemporary moment to examine the new sites of closure, channels of visibility, new forms of footage taken "on the ground," and new claims to immediacy provided by the democratization of cultural production.

1

Refracted Visions: "Ethnic Cleansing" and the De-mythologization of Gender

In 2009, the artist Milica Tomić walked through the streets of Belgrade, casually carrying an AK-47 assault rifle and a plastic shopping bag, passing through the sites where the People's Liberation Movement carried out successful resistance operations against Nazi occupation during World War II. The action/intervention was accompanied by a video work, which used the film-making technique of Russian avant-garde filmmaker Lev Kuleshov to construct a "creative geography" where various locations, places and times all appeared to occur in the same site over a continuous period. Tomić argues that the use of "creative geography" actually imprisoned her character in the editing loop of the video, "unable to find a way out, for this newly-created/old territory. This territory, even though it is made up of emancipatory politics, decisions and actions, is imprisoned and occupied by a new time, the era of permanent war."[1] Through her action and media work, Tomić sought to resist the forms of collective forgetting in Belgrade, not only regarding the recent violence in the Balkans, but also in the global context of increased militarization around the world. Dedicated to the "Belgrade 6," the performance created a doubled vision, tying the current climate of militarism and "security" to the resistance to fascism in World War II. The "Belgrade 6" were activists accused of inciting, assisting in and executing an attack on the Greek Embassy in Belgrade in 2009, in solidarity with the hunger strike of the political prisoner Thodoros Iliopoulos. Members of the Serbian Anarco-Syndicalist Initiative (ASI), they were arrested and held in custody for six months, charged with "international terrorism" (Figure 1.1).

Figure 1.1   Milica Tomić, *One day, instead of one night, a burst of machine-gun fire will flash, if light cannot come otherwise (Oskar Davico—fragment of a poem).* Action/intervention in the public space, Belgrade, 2009. Photo: Srdan Veljovic. Courtesy of the artist

This work, like most of Tomić's pieces, centers on issues of nationalism and identity, political violence and responsibility through a pointed engagement of her own embodied identity in the place of historical figures or oppositional political subjects. It points both to the critical importance of the female figure in wartime violence (many of the partisans were actually women) and, specifically, to the gendered dynamics of nationalist discourses in the political history of the former Yugoslavia.

This chapter turns specifically to the tightly wound knot of gender, nationalism and violence during the "ethnic cleansing" campaigns in the mid-1990s. Three key issues informed art and documentary projects in the postwar era, shortly before or following the Dayton Peace Accords of December 1995: first, there was an urgent need to compile information and evidence about abuses committed during the wars, to gather interviews and statements, frequently in collaboration with women's centers in Zagreb and elsewhere. Second, projects emerged that sought to understand and challenge the violent and exclusionary representations that incited ethnic violence. Finally, cultural producers assessed the postwar period, seeking to resist the normalization of postwar relations where residues of those totalizing gender and ethnic structures still remained. In the face of the violent material and epistemic practices undergirding the "ethnic cleansing" campaigns, many cultural producers were particularly invested in restoring the multiplicity of differences between and among Bosnians, Croatians and Serbians, as well as in breaking apart the totalizing structures that permitted and produced state-sanctioned violence on the basis of gender, ethnicity, religion and nationality.

Among the many works by cultural producers created after 1995, this chapter will examine five that address head-on the urgency of making visible the abuses committed during the war and the need to trace their continuing effects in the postwar period.[2] In 1995, prior to the signing of the peace accords, Jo Andres created a single-channel experimental documentary entitled *Black Kites* (1995). Drawing from the journals of Bosnian artist Alma Hajrić, who was forced into a basement shelter to survive the siege of Sarajevo, the video makes visible the psychic landscape of captivity. Mandy Jacobson and Karmen Jelincić produced *Calling the Ghosts* (1996), a documentary that followed Jadranka Cigelj and Nusreta Sivac, survivors of the Omarska Detention Camp. The following year, Marina Abramović produced a multimedia installation and performance for the 1997 Venice Biennale entitled *Balkan Baroque*, which recorded alternately a scientist discourse about "wolf rats" and the artist herself as a Balkan tavern singer. In 1998, Tomić created *I Am Milica Tomić*, a video installation where the artist, dressed in a white cotton dress and posed against a dark background, repeated in 30 languages "I Am Milica Tomić; I am [nationality]." Finally, Elahe Massumi's *Blood of My Father* (2000) is a three-channel installation project that looped documentary footage of a doctor recounting the discovery of her father's body during the war and juxtaposed this image with a rapid succession of visions of the war's aftermath. The videos present widely different contents and are exhibited in varied contexts. They all, however, point to a key representational strategy, one that disrupts the revelatory force of the news media's visions of the wars.

Mythologies

The aesthetic strategies of the aforementioned artworks and documentaries were in large part a response to the essentialized and violently purified collective identities presented in mass culture during the war. The complex mediation of gender-based violence, discourses of nationalism and ethnic identity served to challenge national (and international) media representations of gender and ethnicity in totalizing terms, and thus to critically interrogate the mythologies that supported "ethnic cleansing" during the war, as well as the categories with which peace-makers sought to address the postwar period. The image culture of wartime and the gendered force of propaganda were then of critical importance to understanding media that took up questions of gender-based violence.

A series of articles published in the pages of the Belgrade newspaper *Politika* in 1988 serve as an important example of the importance of gender to articulations of ethnic nationalism during the war, taking up the nation-state as a cluster of meanings, affect, boundaries and regulatory effects in the spheres of the law, culture, economy and national identity. Here, reports sought to draw the picture of a Serbian identity threatened by its neighbors. Among the stories is a series of reports that commented on the "national distribution of babies" and particularly on Albanian birth rates in Kosovo. On November 5, 1988, Djordje Jankovic reported that Albanians'

> numerical superiority and the high birth-rate are not a natural consequence of historical development but rather a result of their political will. It is obvious and need not be proved (there's a design to their settling and re-settling; high birth-rate is propagated; bigamy is tolerated, etc.). It is essential that we understand this as an act of violence against ordinary social development and handle it accordingly, using violent means. While the creation of a Greater Albania is the publicly proclaimed goal of the Albanian separatists, their covert goal, in the foreseeable future, is the break-up of Yugoslavia.[3]

Given the politics of "ethnic cleansing" later adopted or advocated by the Milošević regime (and the specific strategy of rape, sexual violence and forced pregnancy), this early statement, repeated frequently in the pages of *Politika*,[4] not only foreshadowed how other "ethnic" groups were construed as a threat to "Greater Serbia," but also marks the inseparability of this campaign from issues of gender and biopower.

This in itself is not exceptional. Anne McClintock argued convincingly over a decade ago that all nationalisms are gendered, indeed that "nations have amounted to the sanctioned institutionalization of gender *difference*."[5] Anne McClintock contends that Benedict Anderson's understanding of the nation as an "imagined community" should not lead to the belief that nations are fantasies (although they rely heavily on the collective fantasy of a group ideal); rather, nations should be seen as historical practices through which "social difference is both invented and performed," predicated on the institutionalization of gender difference.[6] The figure of "woman" is not simply differentiated from "man" in this regard, but is mobilized primarily as mother, as reproducer of both the body politic and the nation's citizens. Nira Yuval-Davis and Floya Anthias conclude that women are thus implicated in nationalism in five ways:

(1) as biological reproducers of the members of national collectivities
(2) as reproducers of the boundaries of national groups (through restrictions on sexual or marital relations)
(3) as active transmitters and producers of national culture
(4) as symbolic signifiers of national difference
(5) as active participants in national struggles.[7]

Gender is itself a powerful representational practice, since nationalisms are not only gendered, but also *engender* subjectivity and self-representation for their citizens. And yet, a gulf appears to separate these two concepts (the construction of nation through gender, the constructedness of gender itself) in the interpretative battles around the meaning of gender-based violence in times of conflict. Thus, while one might expect campaigns of "ethnic cleansing" to target women (as the reproducers of national culture), it might come as a surprise that the gendered and ethnic distinctions mobilized in wartime are also taken up within transnational feminist communities to reference the wrongs committed against a *national* community and to support urgent demands for accountability or justice on that basis.[8]

For example, Beverly Allen, even though she is particularly aware of the construction of gender in the conflict in the former Yugoslavia, puzzles at the paradox that forced pregnancies (which are, on the surface, procreative) might be tools in a genocidal campaign, which aims at the elimination of a population. She resolves this paradox by arguing, "Serb policy erases the victim's cultural identity and treats her as nothing more than a kind of biological box."[9] Thus, in this logic, Bosnian women contribute nothing of their ethnic identity to their infants and are mere receptacles for Serbian infants. While Allen is right to point to the paradox of a genocidal campaign based on the forced pregnancy of an ethnic "other"—and her explanation that Bosnian women are transformed into a "biological box" is consistent with the rhetoric of Serbian nationalism—she does not probe how this logic coheres in the Serbian "ethnic cleansing" campaigns (or even, less overtly, in the critical efforts by the international human rights community to draw attention to gender-based violence by linking mass rape and genocide nonreflexively).[10]

The images of war that appeared in the international and national press inadvertently confirmed the mythical status of women in the discourses of wartime violence. Vesna Kesić critiqued these images, recounting: "women dragging frightened and exhausted children; weeping women, angry women, women impregnated by rape, traumatized women. Whatever happens, women are depicted as bodies."[11] In Kesik's view, women stood as powerful proxies for national groups in the news media. Images of women functioned as metaphors for national or ethnic identities, and the rape of Croatian or Bosnian women was read as the rape of Croatia or Bosnia itself. The intersection of militarized patriarchy and ethnic nationalism produced the violent collapse of gender and ethnicity and set the stage for rape and forced pregnancy to make "sense" as a genocidal campaign.

Kesić noted that the tension between reading the mass rapes in terms of their "gendered" dimension (as a crime against women) or their "ethnic" dimension (as a crime against a specific community) strongly divided the feminist community in Zagreb, as well as in the West. Emphasis on the former might attend to the prevalence of rape as a wartime phenomenon and create a basis for cross-ethnic solidarity among women, but it could not account for the mobilization of rape and forced pregnancy as part of an "ethnic cleansing" campaign. Emphasis on the latter might take as a given the very collapse of "woman" and "nation" responsible for gender-based violence in times of armed conflict. This latter approach further made strange bedfellows of the media campaigns of nationalist governments, who sought to use the incidence of rape to make clear the wrongs committed against their civic body, and local and international feminist groups, who sought to make visible the genocidal dimension of the mass rapes.[12] In this case, Kesić noted:

> Because war rapes and other forms of violence against women were so tightly enmeshed within the categories of nation and ethnicity, they could be recognized as a war strategy, subjected to indictments as war crimes, and juridically sanctioned—in short, taken seriously—only if they occurred in large numbers (whatever "large" means), if they were "systematic" and "followed a pattern," and if they supported the claim of genocide or ethnic cleansing.[13]

Kesić concluded that the gendered dimension of mass rapes recognized not only the commission of rape by all parties, but also the worldwide prevalence of sexual violence against women. While this argument importantly stresses the interconnectedness of gender-based violence in times of armed conflict and in peace times, it also runs the risk of erasing the particular articulation of gender *and* ethnicity in the specific campaigns of Serbian (and Croatian) nationalists in the post-Yugoslavia era. In this respect, Catherine MacKinnon's argument that Serbian militia both mimicked pornographic material in their torture of women and filmed rape tortures that were then distributed as pornographic videos not only linked sexual violence in the "ethnic cleansing" campaigns to gender-based violence around the world, but also intimately tied considerations of rape and forced pregnancy to her larger efforts to legislate the injurious effects of pornography on women in North America and around the world.[14] The argument, which appeared on the pages of the American *Ms. Magazine*, thus served to consolidate the efforts by MacKinnon and Dworkin to have ordinances enacted in several U.S. cities granting women legal courses of action if they could demonstrate that they were physically harmed as a result of their attacker's having viewed pornography.[15]

How to plot one's course between the Scylla of ethnic nationalism and the Charybdis of woman-as-difference? What are the sociocultural structures that produce the sliding signification from specific women to the figure of "woman," and from "woman" to the collective "nation," the mythical structures that, according to Roland Barthes, transform facts into "tokens for something else?"[16] Croatian women, for instance, were often referred to during the conflict as "Ustasha whores," referencing the fascist militia in Croatia during World War II that detained and tortured Serbians, Jews and Roma (with the support of Hitler and Mussolini). Bosnian women were called "Turks," and thus identified with the Turkish victory in the fourteenth century at the Battle of Kosovo Polje, where Serbians came under the occupation of the Ottoman Empire. The stage of struggle for a "Greater Serbia" was thus signposted with female figures that marked the site of historical wrongs, sometimes dating back centuries. The prescription for righting those wrongs lay also in a vengeance against sites of perceived threat to Serbian nationalism, sites where gender and ethnicity were impossible to separate.

Barthes's understanding of myth as a "second-order semiological system" provides remarkable insight into the workings of the complex figuration of Bosnian or Croatian women, cast at the intersection of gender and ethnic difference. In Barthes's understanding of myth, the sign becomes itself a signifier for something else, creating a "second-order sign." The mythical sign is not composed of signifiers and signifieds, then, but of signs themselves, associated with new signifieds. Barthes names these alternately sign/signified or forms/contents.[17] In order to make a sign, which is already full of meaning, into a signifier for another content, myth must empty out the meaning of the sign, transforming it into a "parasitical" form. Barthes argues that, for myth to appropriate a sign, it must "drain out" its history and replace it with new content, which becomes the myth's motivation or drive. Indeed, Barthes states, "through the concept, it is a whole new history which is implanted in the myth."[18] Thus, in Barthes's famous example, the image on the cover of *Paris Match* of a black colonized subject in a French uniform saluting the French flag loses its contingent historicity (French colonization in North Africa), and becomes a form, implanted with the concept of the "French Empire." Similarly, when Bosnian women are called "Turkish whores" in Serbian nationalist discourse, the mythical history of the Turkish impalement of Serbian men is implanted in Bosnian women. The implantation's drive (the motive for the myth) is the possibility of vengeance, both through an emasculation of Turkish men (they are transposed onto the bodies of women) and through the violence of rape (a retribution, as I will discuss below, for the myth of Turkish impalement of Serbian men).

Many have noted that the Milošević regime relied heavily on tightly controlled media campaigns, and particularly on television programs, to draw out and articulate Serbian nationalism and to produce a powerful image of a "Greater Serbia" for Serbs living in Serbia, Bosnia-Herzegovina, Croatia and Kosovo.[19] These media campaigns relied on heavily controlled public media structures, restrictions of freedom of speech for independent media, taxes and fines imposed on independent newspapers, withdrawal of broadcasting licenses and the appointment of select editors-in-chief for newspapers and news programs or director-generals of radio and television. Journalists were demoted or publicly condemned.[20] The mobilization of the figure of woman-as-nation served not only to make the connection between gender-based violence and crimes against an *ethnie*, but also to make women the site of action for nationalist campaigns. For instance, a document written by Major Milovan Milutinović at the Serbian headquarters in Banja Luka, entitled "Laying Violent Hands on the Serbian Woman," alleged that Muslims and Croats were committing genocide against the Serbs:

> By order of the Islamic fundamentalists from Sarajevo, healthy Serbian women from 17 to 40 years of age are being separated out and subjected to special treatment. According to their sick plans going back many years, these women have to be impregnated by orthodox Islamic seeds in order to raise a generation of janissaries on the territories they surely consider to be theirs, the Islamic republic. In other words, a fourfold crime is to be committed against the Serbian woman: to remove her from her own family, to impregnate her by undesirable seeds, to make her bear a stranger and then to take even him away from her.[21]

Roy Gutman, the *Newsday* foreign correspondent who broke the story of the genocide to Western audiences (and specifically the mass rapes and forced pregnancy of women detained there), spoke with Milutinović about this tract. He was particularly struck by the use of the term "janissaries," the Turkish military elite composed of Christian youths forced to convert to Islam in the Middle Ages. For Gutman, Milutinović's document rehearsed, through the image of the violation of Serbian women's body, Turkish rule over Serbia in the fourteenth century. The purported forced impregnation of Serbian women was thus made to stand in for territorial conquest by the

Ottoman Empire at the Battle of Kosovo Polje in 1389.[22] While Gutman was aware of the projective resonances of this document, and made a mental note to look for evidence of Serb camps of the same description, he did not identify how "Serbian women" in this iteration came to stand in for Serbian people under Ottoman occupation centuries before.

This elision between the figure of women and "the nation," between the occupation of women's (reproductive) bodies and national territory, follows the logic of Barthes's understanding of mythical language. Serbian women were emptied of their historical specificity and implanted with a violent and violating ethnic nationalism. There is, however, something beneath this mythical schema that makes the figure of "Serbian women" a particularly potent sign for mythology, that the figure "woman" is *itself* already mythical. Here, it is worth returning to Teresa de Lauretis's argument in "The Violence of Rhetoric: Considerations on Representation and Gender."[23] De Lauretis stresses that gender is a representation not only of an object but, critically, also of a social relation—male/female— that preexists each individual. The gender system within each culture is "a symbolic system or system of meanings, that correlates sex to cultural contents according to social values and hierarchies."[24] Thus, "Bosnian women" or "Serbian women" emerge as figures in the conflict through a complex system that constructs relations of belonging (to a class), and delimits categories of absolute difference (male/female, Bosnian/Serbian, Muslim/Christian, etc.).

De Lauretis also stresses that gender functions like ideology (in the Althusserian sense)—it constitutes concrete individuals as (gendered) subjects. Gender is thus the product of social technologies (for example, the capitalist division of labor, or the reproduction of labor power), institutionalized discourses, epistemologies, or narrative and symbolic processes.[25] The representation of women in the articulation of nationalisms (and of Serbian nationalism in particular) is therefore deeply rooted in a sociocultural system, on the one hand, and a semiotic apparatus, on the other. The figure of the "Bosnian woman" or the "Serbian woman" is a gendered as well as an ethnic sign, constructed through representation, which interpellates individuals as (gendered and ethnic) subjects.

In dominant discourses, gender is collapsed with sexual difference, *tout court*; this difference is articulated particularly as a difference of women *from* men. The result in ideology is that the differences among women, and further the differences within women, are collapsed into the singular difference that is woman.[26] This figure then becomes the site of an essential difference, and the location of ethnic identity (Bosnian women, Croatian women, Muslim women, Serbian women). The close ties between ethnic nationalism and control of reproduction, population and lineage rely already on the mythical reduction of women (Serbian, Bosnian, Croatian, or Albanian; Muslim or Christian, living in the various republics of the former Yugoslavia) into "woman," and specifically into woman *as* (sexual) difference. The collapse of the category "woman" with the nation is thus not a second-order semiological system, but a third-order system, relying already on the mythical figure of "woman."

The image of "Serbian women" mobilized by Milutinović is convincing because it relies on ideologies of gender and sexual difference and grounds them in traditional figurations of national identity. Lynda E. Boose's incisive analysis of representations of Turkish occupation, especially as they are retooled for the wars in the 1990s, highlights the specific ideological function of gender in Serbian nationalist mythology.[27] Boose stresses that the campaigns of ethnic nationalism in the Balkans were played out as a cultural fiction of difference. Racial ethnicity was made synonymous with religious difference (principally of Serbian Christian Orthodox vs. Bosnian Muslim), and ethnic identity was delimited along national (or regional) boundaries. Against the commonalities between these groups (Serbs, Bosnians, and Croats are all Southern Slavs), Serbian heroic and nationalist narratives sought to construct a unity around what Boose terms "fantasies of ethnic purity" and a concomitant campaign to "ethnically cleanse" territories assumed to be a part of a "Greater Serbia."[28]

Central to the "fantasies of ethnic purity" was the notion of a quasi-primordial Slavic Christianity betrayed by conversions to Islam in the fourteenth century following Ottoman rule in the Balkans.[29] Serbian national mythology thus targeted Bosnian and Albanian Muslims as enemies by conflating them with "Turks." Boose notes that that figure of the "Turk" in Serbian cultural memory threatened to "conquer, victimize, feminize, and humiliate Serb national selfhood (always a masculine construct) and infantilize all Serbia's attempts to achieve independent adulthood."[30] The epic and heroic component of Serbian culture then tempered this defeat by the Turks at the Battle of Kosovo through the mythical construction of a "heroic masculinity kept alive by Serbia's implacable determination to avenge its captivity."[31]

The dual construction of a Turkish conqueror and a Serbian heroic masculinity was captured in Serbian myth by the repeated image of Turks impaling Serbs on stakes. Although the historical record does not bear this out, Boose notes that Serbian mythical, cultural and national traditions drew repeatedly from the image of Serb peasant heroes who resisted the Turkish occupation and were publicly impaled. While the image of impalement was partially invigorated through recourse to Christian myths (especially in evocations of crucifixion), Boose is sensitive to the gender dynamics of the image of impalement. With regard to a vivid description in Ivo Andrić 1945 novel *The Bridge on the Drina*, Boose argues:

> For what the male population of Visegrad as well as Andrić readers have been compelled to witness is a four-hour rape scene in which the rebel against Turkish rule is literally skewered by the Turkish phallic emblem of power and then hoisted up in the feminized image of the penetrated body, the enormous Turkish phallus fixing in place the unforgettable picture of a grotesque and horrific sodomy.[32]

For Boose, the image of impalement is understood as a practice of feminizing Serbs in conquest, through the image of Serbian impalement on Turkish stakes. In this regard, Serbian heroism could be reclaimed only through a re-masculinizing of the Serb national subject through a vengeful impalement of Turkish proxies (Bosnian and Albanian Muslims).[33] The violence of the mass rapes, detentions, murders and forced pregnancies, Boose argues, could not be accounted for only as a campaign to produce "Serbian babies," but also as a radical refiguring of masculinity and femininity along ethnic lines.[34] The focus on women (and even "raped women") on either side of the war thus occluded the complex representations of gender in Serbian nationalist policy and myth that produced sexual difference along ethnic and religious lines.

The recourse to the figure of "the Serbian woman" in Major Milutinović's document was effective, therefore, precisely because of the mythical figuration of Serbian history through a violent negotiation of sexual difference. According to Barthes, myth both impoverishes meaning and draws from it, vacillating in this case between the presence and indisputability of specific women and the impoverished figure of "woman," easily implanted with Serbian nationalist content (Serbian masculine heroism, purity and valor). Gender-based violence not only enacts a Serbian vengeance against perceived historical wrongs, but is also placed in the service of confirming essential and pure ethnic identities, figured in mythical language.

The representational practice of the Milošević regime was thus essential both to the production of a Serbian (masculine) heroism and to the articulation of women's bodies as the site of nationalist struggle. Forms of propaganda, state edicts, journal articles, museum exhibits and press images all worked to consolidate a mythical and totalizing system of signs. The rhetoric of violence in Serbian campaigns therefore must also be understood—as de Lauretis's chiasmic intervention makes clear—as a violence in rhetoric.[35] Already, the figuration of "woman" resolves the apparently paradoxical campaign of gender-based violence in the service of genocide. The belief that forced pregnancies would produce "Serbian babies" replicates the myth of women as "empty container" into which a Serbian nationalism may be violently implanted.[36] This paradox was resolved in the constant mythical vacillation between individual women and the figuration of women as representatives of national culture.

Refracted Media

I asked above in this chapter how to plot the course between an unwitting reconfirmation of ethnic nationalism and transnational feminists' articulation of the overly unified category "raped women." How to represent the war otherwise, to attempt to counter the violent material and epistemic practices of Serbian nationalism? How might cultural producers emphasize and restore the multiplicity of differences between women after the war? This was not simply a matter of replacing a totalizing structure with the proliferation of voices, but also of radically challenging and breaking apart the representational regime that permitted and produced state-sanctioned violence on the basis of gender, ethnicity, religion and nationality.

The radical epistemological potential of feminist thought is its understanding that the subject is constituted in gender (rather than simply by sexual difference), and further that this subject is en-gendered in race, class, ethnicity or sexual relations.[37] Difference is then not simply between Serbian men and Bosnian women, for example, but also among women and, most importantly, within women. What this means—specifically in relation to the mythical construction of the figure of woman outlined above—is that the subject of feminism is both inside and outside of the ideology of gender and nationalism. De Lauretis notes that feminism's radical epistemology produces a conception of the female subject distinct from "woman" and also distinct from women as real historical beings. In effect, what this produces is a "doubled vision," acknowledging complicity with the ideology of gender as well as a "refusal to resolve or dispel the ambiguity of gender."[38]

The video projects I have selected in this chapter share a common strategy that owes to this "doubled vision," and hence to the aesthetic strategies of prismatic media articulated in this study. The analysis that follows tracks three strategies in the following sections, where refraction serves to critique the totalizing representations of gender during the war: first, I examine artworks that challenge the mythical figuration of women as proxies for the nation; second, I analyze how several works foreground the close connections between the structures of nation and the structure of the family, noting how this structural similarity is responsible for the logic of gender-based violence and nationalism; and third, I investigate how some of these works critically interrogate evidentiary and documentary treatments of the war, especially as they become tied to the totalizing solidarity of national or ethnic identity. These three strategies, mobilized through multichannel video, serve to reconstitute wartime representations of gender by challenging the state's singular representational regime.

De-Mythologizing Women

Marina Abramović's *Balkan Baroque* is a somber and haunting work, combining performance with multichannel installation. Along the back wall of the installation space, three figures are projected on three screens: the first screen contains a close-up image of Abramović's father, the last screen a similar image of her mother. These two framing figures remain still throughout most of the installation. The central screen is more videographic, alternating between two segments of tape: the first consists of Abramović, dressed in a white lab coat, providing a clinical report explaining a fictional history of rats in the Balkans. In this account, rats are killed in order to produce a "wolf rat"; their natural behavior is thus "perverted" so that the rats actually destroy each other. Once Abramović has finished her report, she strips off her lab coat and glasses, and dances to Serbian and Romanian folk songs—dressed only in a black slip—until she collapses, breathless and exhausted. The screens on the left and right are motionless throughout the lecture, but when Abramović begins to dance to the nationalist folk songs, her father suddenly appears holding an upraised pistol, and her mother simultaneously covers her eyes with her hands.[39] In front of the video screens, the artist placed three large copper vessels filled with water and a large pile of cow bones. In the middle of this pile, Abramović sat for several hours each day of the Venice Biennale, wearing her white lab coat stained with blood and scrubbing the bones with disinfectant.[40] Critic Marcia Vetrocq noted specifically not only the visual effect of the work, but also the marked stench that increased throughout each day of the performance (Figure 1.2).

Balkan Baroque occupied the central exhibition in the Italian pavilion of the 1997 Venice Biennale. Its location marked the continued controversy over representation, culture and politics in the former Yugoslavia. Although it was officially selected to represent Yugoslavia at the Venice Biennale, the Minister of Culture for Montenegro, Goran Rakocević, objected that Abramović's work did not reflect "authentic art from Montenegro." The landscape painter, Vojo Stanić, was elected to take Abramović's place. As a result, Germano Celant (the curator of the Biennale) invited Abramović to participate in the Italian Pavilion,

Figure 1.2 Marina Abramović, *Balkan Baroque*, 1997. Washing 1,500 fresh cow bones. June 1997. Performance, 4 days, 6 hours. XLVII Venice Biennale. © Marina Abramović. Courtesy of Sean Kelly Gallery, New York

organized according to the theme *Future, Past, Present*. These vexed origins should, in fact, be considered part of the significance of the artwork itself. Indeed, an *Art in America* review of the Venice Biennale called this work a "refugee," noting that its location "in a covert, cellar-like space in the Italian pavilion adds substantially to the work's atmosphere of suppressed horror."[41]

In her review of the Biennale, Vetrocq claims that Abramović's work had the potential to be the "conscience of an exhibition that is all but purged of direct political expression." Instead, she argues that *Balkan Baroque* did not give the viewer any deeper insights into the wars in the former Yugoslavia, relying instead on what the viewer already knew about the events. She states, "If anything, Abramović interposes her own drama of suffering between the audience and critical knowledge," and concludes that the piece is narcissistic, a "self-indulgent drama of abjection and penance, with no prospect of redemption."[42] At first glance, the piece may provide few markers to the events of the war, articulating instead the feats of psychic and physical endurance characteristic of Abramović's performance works. But Vetrocq's critique may dismiss too readily the kind of critical intervention made by *Balkan Baroque*.

Vetrocq notes that Abramović's organization of the multichannel work—with a single figure projected on each screen—resembles the figural patterns of Eastern Christian iconography. Indeed, each element of the installation is profoundly symbolic: the reference to Eastern iconography, the trinity of the family as the site of sociality, the folkloric discourse of "wolf rats," and the Balkan tavern songs. The scientistic discourse on the wolf rats glides seamlessly between the folkloric and the propagandistic, employing the narrative devices of folk tales, but referencing also the anti-Semitic propaganda of the Third Reich. Vetrocq also notes that the red scarf Abramović twirls when she dances to Serbian folk songs in the video actually derives from the uniform of Marshal Tito's young pioneers. The symbol of a unified Yugoslavian national identity thus becomes reduced to a tawdry prop, flung about by a feminine symbol of Serbian ethnic culture. Abramović's performance in the installation space also responds to the contents unfolding on the screens, but it does so by examining the symbols as myths. The performance responds to Serbian nationalism, violence and genocide with a ritualistic mourning practice, which Abramović calls an "exodus" from the condition of killing.[43] This live performance also provides a counterpoint to the video image of Abramović, half-dressed, dancing to Serbian cultural folk songs. Instead of being moved (literally) by Serbian folk music, she produces a response that is both ritualistic and hauntingly domestic, "cleaning up" after the horror of the war.

Maureen Turim has argued that "gestures of cleaning [...] represent duration not simply as waiting or endurance, but as a never finished process of work—work that is coded as proletarian or domestic and female."[44] The live performance hints at the sociocultural conditions of gender in the postwar period (the sexual division of labor, the distinction between productive and reproductive activities, between performance art and reproductive labor), while the dancing body on the screen calls up the ideological figure of a gendered nationalism (the figure of woman as the battleground of ethnic nationalism, as discussed above). In this way, the work may also be situated within histories of feminist performance art, including Mierle Laderman Ukeles's "Maintenance Art" performances, Mary Kelly's *Post-Partum Document*, and the *Womanhouse* project.

Abramović's work is also deeply concerned with the viewer's role in the performance. Viewers are often called upon to perform with Abramović, as for example in many of her *Rhythm* performances, where the audience is invited to intervene by either engaging with Abramović's body or by stopping the performance altogether. Abramović states that she sees her work as divided between two categories, first her own body and second the public body. These categories are foregrounded in another work, *Soul Operations Room*, where Abramović removes her own body, asking spectators to engage with the objects she installs in the space. In this regard, she argues that "the public has to take on a more radical responsibility."[45] Abramović's *Balkan Baroque* entreats its viewers to take on the responsibility of witnessing, and it specifically tests the endurance limits of the audience in witnessing pain or danger.

The full experience of *Balkan Baroque* is not so easily settled by any of its elements: the scientistic testimony or the Balkan tavern songs, the still footage of her mother and father, Abramović's own neurotic performance, or the olfactory impact of the putrefying cow bones. The relay between these different elements of the installation effects a disidentification, a distancing mechanism that precludes the kind of sympathy that would join too clearly the viewer's sense of trauma to the experience of war in the former Yugoslavia. Instead, the viewer struggles with the mythical and essentialized origin stories that are at the root of violence. With no escape from this violent myth-making toward an image worthy of sympathy, the viewer must constantly negotiate her own projections, affective responses and expectations. The viewer's affective response is further framed by the very international context of the Venice Biennale, in the interstices of its failed vision of a community of nations.

Abramović does not dispel the mythical language of the Milošević regime with recourse to images of the reality of war. And yet, in my view, her work engages in a critical intervention in wartime mythical language and its gendered ideological presumptions. Abramović draws the critical force of the piece from her very reiteration of nationalist mythical language. Here, Barthes's understanding of mythical language, and of the role of the reader in relation to this semiotic order, is again relevant. For Barthes, there are three central ways of reading myths. The first is to focus on the *empty* form (in keeping with the terms outlined in the first part of this chapter, this signifier will be called "woman") and infuse it with a concept ("Serbian ethnic nationalism"). This form of reading is essential to the myth-maker (politician, academic, journalist), who must mobilize forms and make them speak particular contents. The second method is to focus on the *full* form (the sign made up itself of a signifier and signified). This second strategy undoes the signification of myth by de-mythologizing language. The fullness of the sign prior to its appropriation by mythical language is restored, and the form is revealed as an "impostor" or an "alibi." The third method focuses on the mythical signifier as an inextricable whole, inseparable into forms and contents. The mythologist then "respond[s] to the constituting mechanisms of myth, to its own dynamics."[46]

Abramović's installation works by de-mythologizing mythical language, focusing on the *full* form of the mythical signifier. It thus most closely resembles Barthes's second approach to reading myth. The relation between the projected figures appearing on the central screen and Abramović's own body in the installation space engages the relation between the sign "woman" in the discourses of Serbian nationalism and the lived reality of individual women as subjects of ideology. The central screen, as noted above, begins with an authoritative testimony about "wolf rats," spoken by a figure whose glasses and white lab coat are meant to guarantee the authority of her analysis. As Abramović begins to undress, miming the codes of the sexualized strip tease, the figure of authority is also unmasked. The removal of these superficial markers reveals not an authentic subject or lived reality, but the driving force of the mythical language itself, namely Serbian cultural nationalism. Beneath the "neutral" discourse, then, lies the figure of woman-as-nation, and Abramović's strip tease on screen highlights how "the Serbian woman" performs a gendered ethnicity. Abramović's own live performance, by contrast, highlights the labor and violence involved in such figuration; it therefore makes visible the relation between individual subjects and the mythical structures of gendered, nationalist ideology.

The multichannel nature of the installation is central to the critical force of Abramović's work and to her de-mythologizing practice in it. Even as Abramović performs her scientistic disquisition, the representation is partially displaced by the still images of her parents, looking out from their separate screens. Abramović's performance in the installation space also disrupts the mythical figure by alternating between the scientist and the dancer. The horrific vision of Abramović, dressed in a blood-stained lab coat and surrounded by bones, intervenes in the clinical image on screen, re-infusing the figure with meanings evacuated by the language of Serbian nationalism itself. Taken together, the elements of the installation thus stage fractured and multiple representations of the very singular and totalizing icons of national identity.

The multiplicity of visions is enacted not only in the three screens included in the installation, but also in the various narrative times enacted within and across each screen. Thus, for example, the narrative structure of the central screen in *Balkan Baroque* is always held in tension with the stillness of the surrounding screens. Further, while viewers of the piece may not remain at the installation site long enough to feel the effect of this strategy, when the narrative ends and Abramović collapses from her frenzied dancing, the video loops back to the beginning, replaying the scientistic discourse that introduces the piece. Because Abramović performs for several hours each day at the site, she smoothes over the break in the video as it loops back to the beginning and replays. The reproductive labor she performs also mimics the cyclical nature of the video playing continuously throughout the installation.

While the narrative repetition of the video loop is outside the narrative content of the video in Abramović's case, such repetition is essential to Milica Tomić's video installation and web-based artwork entitled *I Am*

Milica Tomić (1998–1999). In its installation in a museum setting, a large-scale projection contains a stark image of Tomić herself, dressed in a white slip, her hair pulled back in a long braid.[47] Her figure, fully illuminated in front of a black background, appeals to the mythical codes of a virginal femininity, but also signifies her status as a blank slate (partially undressed, stripped of the cultural markers of national identity), invoking also the iconography of the strip search in military or police interrogations.

Throughout the video loop, Tomić repeats her name in 30 different languages, and associates herself with the national identity associated with that language (*"Ich bin Milica Tomić, Ich bin Deutsch; Jaz sem Milica Tomić, Jaz sem Slovenka,"* etc.). As she begins her declarations, her body turns very slowly, as if on a pedestal. When she completes a full rotation, the viewer observes a bloody wound emerging in her hairline at the nape of her neck. Subsequent declarations are accompanied by bloody gashes appearing on her arms, chest and face, staining her clothing (Figure 1.3).

While the viewer is initially presented a panoramic and surveillant vision of Tomić's body, this vision is consistently interrupted. First, the video includes a series of syncopated cuts that segment her statements, vacillating between long shots and abrupt interruptions. The cuts in the video

Figure 1.3 Milica Tomić, *I Am Milica Tomić,* 1998–1999. Courtesy of the artist

are further emphasized by jolting frame shifts, so that the viewer is presented alternately with her head and shoulders, her upper body and most of her figure. Her body also speeds up and slows down, her head at times turning to face the camera as she completes a rotation. At several moments during the 9-minute, 58-second video, the audio and video tracks are discontinuous, presenting either overlapping declarations of identity or declarations voiced over her silent, turning body.

These formal strategies create a mirroring between the work of representation and the violence of national identification, joining the cuts on Tomić's body with the cuts in the video itself. The discontinuities in the videographic language attune the viewer to the discontinuities in the video's contents, even if the viewer cannot understand many of the languages Tomić speaks. For example, not all collective identities are national; at times these identities reference local independence struggles (e.g., Québecois, Catalan). The use of language is not always an indicator of national identity either, since Tomić declares that she is "American" and "English" in the English language. In this way, the performance destabilizes the natural associations between culture, individual subjects and national identity.

While Tomić's work may appear to address national formations rather than questions of gender, the work clearly articulates the gendered dimensions of national identity (and hence of violence on the grounds of nationalism) within the piece. One of the more distressing aspects of the work, for me, is Tomić's blank expression throughout the recitations. The wounds that crisscross her neck, the blood that trickles down her forehead, are endured without reaction, as Tomić continues to declare various national affiliations. Almost seven minutes into the video, however, Tomić gasps, closes her eyes and draws in her stomach, as a splatter of blood appears in the middle of her dress, located at the level of her uterus. After this point, her declarations name a series of contested ethnic, regional and pre-nationalist identities for several minutes, prior to returning to European national identities.

The infliction of pain in this moment of the video situates *I Am Milica Tomić* within the specific historical context of the tactics of forced pregnancy in the war in the former Yugoslavia, and thus joins a visualization of gender-based violence to the patriarchal foundations of articulations of ethnic identity during the war. The work notes the violence of forced pregnancy, rather than of rape, and thus illuminates the specific role of sexual violence within nationalist and ethnic ideologies. It therefore undermines both the uncritical association of women's bodies with national territory (in statements that the rape of women was a crime against a people) *and* the claim made by Catherine MacKinnon and others that rape in the context of the war was not dissimilar to the widespread incidence of sexual violence around the world (that women were raped because they were women, rather than because of their ethnic identities).

Because the work articulates a series of national, ethnic, cultural and anti-colonial collectivities, however, Tomić also highlights the cost (as well as the necessity and appeal) for women of interpellation into national and ethnic collective identities more broadly. Hence, while the work addresses the historical specificity of gender-based violence in the Balkans, it also addresses collective identity-formation across Europe (and especially within the "fortress Europe"), in hegemonic and counter-hegemonic formations, in its xenophobic and anti-colonial forms. *I Am Milica Tomić* invites this broader audience in the circuits of its exhibition in Europe (Austria, Belgium, Denmark, Russia, Serbia, among others), as well as its inclusion in the 8th Istanbul Biennale ("Poetic Justice") curated by Dan Cameron in 2003. Its inclusion in the *Global Feminisms* exhibit at the Brooklyn Museum in 2007 specifically brought the work into conversation with other artists theorizing militarization and gendered embodiment, particularly the Israeli artist Sigalit Landau's *Barbed Hula* (2000) (a video of a woman rotating a hula hoop made of barbed wire on her hips), Afghani-American artist Lida Abdul's *White House* (2003) (in which the artist endeavors to paint a ruin in Kabul with white paint) and Palestinian artist Emily Jacir's *Crossing Surda* (2002) (a video of the artist's crossing militarized checkpoints between Ramallah and Birzeit University).[48] Tomić's work was included in the "Politics" theme of the exhibit (the other themes were "Life Cycles," "Identities" and "Emotions"), placed into dialogue with the other works in order to emphasize, in curator Maura Reilly's terms, their "common differences."[49] The curators were interested specifically in how works from disparate parts of the globe might be brought into relational analysis not on the basis of previous grounds for feminist coalition building (especially the terms of sexual difference) but around women's participation in anti-colonialist as well as anti-patriarchal and anti-heterosexist movements. Reilly and Nochlin sought to stress the manner in which identities were contradictory or partial, focusing on the intersection of gender, racial, class and geo-political structures negotiated in specific contexts. Tomić's work does not dismiss out of hand the powerful desire to articulate one's subjectivity through nationalism, but articulates at what cost one's lived reality becomes interpellated as a generalizable category, and hence provides an important framework for the kinds of "common differences" elicited by the exhibition.

Whereas Abramović seeks to examine the full signifier as a strategy of de-mythologization, Tomić's work performs a slightly different critique. I noted above that Barthes's third strategy for reading myth focuses on the mythical signifier as an inextricable whole. In his famous example, the black soldier saluting the French flag cannot be returned (in this reading) to his historical context. Instead, the black soldier saluting the flag *is* the very presence of French imperialism. Such a reading examines the dynamics of myth, consuming it "according to the very ends built into its structure."[50] The whole mythical signifier is both true and unreal, in Barthes's view; it is transformed from a system of values into a system of facts.

Nothing is natural in Tomić's piece, not the body, the wounds or the declarative statements, yet the piece still speaks to a weighted (political and personal) reality. *I Am Milica Tomić* thus exposes the violence inherent in the mythological emptying out of the signifier, in the abstraction of the figure of "woman" and in the metaphorical inscription of nationality at the level of the subject. Unlike Abramović, who fractures the unitary and mythical figure of woman (the dancer in the central screen) with a multiplicity of positions and forms of embodiment, Tomić demonstrates that the same form, emptied of meaning, may become a marker for a range of ethnic identities, even as they do violence to both the figure and the specificity of subject positions. Tomić's piece therefore takes seriously how the forms of gender-based violence in times of war are already at stake in the semiological structures of mythical nationalist language.

And yet, like Abramović's piece, Tomić's video installation tackles head-on the singular structure of woman-as-nation proposed by the discourses of Serbian nationalism, and it does so through a refractive strategy that pries open the closed figures employed by the news media, certain articulations of transnational feminism and official high culture. Neither work attempts to disprove the figuration of women in war, but accounts for how myth—in Barthes's words—*vacillates,* alternatively drawing from and impoverishing the meaning of the sign it employs.

Engendering Nation and the Family

I noted above that Marina Abramović's prismatic strategy in *Balkan Baroque* involves the dispersal of a singular perspective between the three screens in the installation. It is of critical importance also that those three screens reproduce the tripartite structures of the nuclear family. Cultural mythologies rely not only on the figure of woman as the bearer of culture (hence, Abramović's frenzied dance to Serbian folk music in the central screen), but also on the family as the model for a naturalized understanding of a national community (which, as I will argue below, accounts for the potency of the images of Abramović's parents on the two framing screens). Particularly in the iconography of war, the link between women and peace is often articulated through the image of the mother. Similarly, it is argued that militarization relies on patriarchal patterns and, conversely, that patriarchy itself relies on militarization.[51]

War counts on this figuration because nations themselves rest on the logic of a sociocultural system based on the private sphere and the heterosexual family unit (nuclear or extended). Women are gendered feminine in nationalist discourse primarily through their reproductive function (reproducing bodies, reproducing culture). In times of war, this function takes on the tenor of a patriotic duty. This is made clear in the two press stories discussed above, which frame ethnic nationalist claims in terms of birth rates. The family becomes both the model for a naturalized understanding of the nation (Anne McClintock notes that the term "nation" derives from *natio*, the first-person conjugation of the verb "to be born") and the site for the reproduction of nationalism. This point is made even clearer in light of the "ethnic cleansing" logic behind Serbia's quest for a "Greater Serbia" across the Yugoslavian territory. The Serbian family is identified as the site for the reproduction of ethnic cultural identity, while Bosnian, Albanian and Croatian families are targeted as threats to Serbian ethnicity.

Given this context, Abramović's *Balkan Baroque* takes on not only the nationalist articulation of culture through the figure of woman, but also the production of nationalist belonging through the trope of the family. This is particularly poignant for Abramović, whose own father was a commander in World War II and was acclaimed as a national hero after the war.[52] The images of her parents, projected on either side of the central screen to frame Abramović's filmed performance in the installation, show them simply looking out into the installation space for most of its duration. They structurally support the dialogical relation between Abramović's performance on screen and her live cleansing ritual. When Abramović switches, however, from her scientistic disquisition to her role as a Balkan tavern singer, Abramović's father suddenly appears wielding a gun and her mother covers her eyes with both hands.

If, as I argued above, Abramović is engaging in a critical de-mythologizing of Serbian nationalist discourse, her staging of her family also participates actively in this de-mythologizing project. First, by including three different positions in the installation, Abramović exposes the complex social relations that produce a singular or unified vision of the nation and the national ethnic subject. At the same time, Abramović uncovers how the logic of Serbian nationalism—and also the logic of gender-based violence committed by Serbian forces—presupposes the production of gender difference in the family. Abramović's gun-wielding father is clearly the site not only of possible violence but also of phallic power. The mother's refusal to see indicates both her position as the object of the look (in the space of the installation) and her disavowal of the psychic and ideological structures of the family drama. Abramović's piece then makes visible the construction of nationalism on the basis of the differentiated gender relations at stake in the family itself. Serbian discourse, in this installation, is located firmly within the confines of a rigid structure that reproduces not only citizens but also families.

Elahe Massumi's *Blood of My Father* (2000), included in the international exhibit Channel Zero (curated by Katerina Gregos) at the Netherlands Media Art Institute, makes clear the close ties between nationalism and the structure of the family, although she examines the wars in the former Yugoslavia from the perspective of Bosnians and Kosovan Albanians. Unlike Abramović's, Massumi's piece thus marks a different shift in gender relations as a result of the violence of genocide in the Balkan wars. In the installation, three screens are organized along the same wall: the two outer screens are tinted sepia, intercutting Massumi's own footage with wartime documentary footage. The center screen appears to use a blue filter, and includes a testimony used in a BBC documentary of a doctor from Kosovo who discovers her father's body during the war (Figure 1.4).

The doctor's testimony is short and traumatic, but loops twice throughout the run of the video:[53]

> I saw my father lying on the floor on stretchers. I looked at his face. One eye was open, one eye was closed, and he didn't have this side of his face [*she touches the side of her face*]. And I could see his teeth [*an explosion resounds on the soundtrack*] and in that moment I thought, "It's okay, it's only a face. We can fix it. He'll have a scar. So what? He doesn't have to be beautiful." And I looked down and I uncovered him and I saw a huge hole here. He wasn't bleeding; it was just a red hole. And I tried to touch the shrapnel. You used to do it when you worked in a hospital, you touched to establish where the shrapnel is, is it deep inside or . . . I start doing it and my hands were [*her voice wavers*] full of my father's blood.

Figure 1.4   Elahe Massumi, *Blood of My Father*, 2000. Courtesy of the artist

This raw testimony glides between a clinical description of the scene and the surge of affect when she speaks of her father's blood on her hands. At the moment when her speech wavers, when she can no longer tell the story, the narrative cuts off and begins again, revisiting the moment when she discovers her father's body. In the space of the installation, the haunting narrative consistently returns to the time when the doctor discovers her father's body, holds off this discovery and then realizes that her father is dead.

The testimony guides the viewer through the cyclical nature of the other images depicting the detritus of war, refugees, wartime footage, rusting tanks or children playing with toy guns. The left-hand screen begins with a traveling landscape: the camera is positioned in a vehicle, traversing a burnt yellow countryside. An abandoned and broken fence, posts jutting out at odd angles and barbed wire loops frame the foreground zooming by. The flat countryside in the background looks static. The posts mark the video's tempo as the camera travels through this landscape. Eventually, the fields give way to some abandoned buildings, and the fence becomes more solid, filling the screen. Now unable to see over the fence, the viewer sees only the grating and barbed wire, with disused buildings behind. Finally, the camera's gaze rests upon two tanks on the ground by the fence and cuts to a close-up of half a tank with a figure to the right, heading away from the camera.

On the right-hand screen, a series of scenes unfold: laundry pinned up on a barbed wire fence, children playing ball between bombed out buildings, and a dead cat surrounded by a swarm of flies. As the left-hand screen pans across the tanks, the right-hand side tilts upward to reveal a small boy playing with a toy gun, pretending to shoot into the distance. Next, both screens cut to reveal a street, a pile of wreckage, a woman's face, and again, the right-hand screen returns to the young boy. This time, however, he is facing the camera, shooting out at it (and at the viewer). As he plays at shooting for the camera, the left-hand screen shows wartime footage of wounded people being carried off a truck and refugees fleeing with their belongings tied to their backs. The video begins its loop again after the camera pauses on the image of an old man crying on the left-hand screen and on the image of a young girl smiling for the camera on the right.

In the center screen, the doctor's narrative exposes the slow diagnosis of the body, staving off the surge of affect that her father's corpse produces in her. The tape is a talking-head interview, but the viewer notices especially the doctor's hands, moving along her own face to show the condition of her father's body. This intimate point of view collapses the distance between the viewer and the doctor, preparing the scene for the traumatic narrative. Her description of her father's body moves from one site of injury to another, from the teeth that show through her father's cheek to, finally, the hole she discovers in her father's chest when she lifts a blanket covering him.[54] In marked contrast to Abramović's gun-wielding father, the father here is not only dead, but also absent, lacking and powerless. The testimony ends with the doctor's quivering voice, describing her father's blood on her hands.

The interview culminates when the repression of the father's death erupts, meaning collapses and the story begins its obsessive repetition of the scene. It cannot express what happens after staring into that abyss, but can only repeat the revelation. On either side of this testimony, Massumi's sepia images of postwar Bosnia both mitigate this revelation and increase its senselessness. The stockpiling of weapons, the detritus of a meaningless war, the children exposed as impatient apprentices of violence and the displaced persons in the postwar era all make clear delineations between the social/cultural and the personal, and contain a threat: under the postwar social fabric lies the horror of children playing with guns, decomposing animals, fractured and displaced peoples and piles of bones.

Massumi's installation thus makes clear the reversal of the family dynamic as a result of the war and specifically the mass rape, torture and detention of Bosnian men and women. As Lynda Boose's analysis discussed above makes clear, Serbian mythology involved not only the threat of an emasculating Turk occupation, but also a Serbian vengeance through the rape of Bosnian men and women. The trauma suffered by the doctor in *Blood of My Father* might then be read not only as the trauma of death and mourning, but also as the dissolution of the family for Bosnian-Herzegovinians and the destruction of the patriarchal father as essential to the symbolic force of gender-based violence in the war. Both Abramović's and Massumi's video installations thus expose the mythological dependence of nationalism on the structures of the family, and thus how nationalism itself resolves gender contradictions along the lines of a patriarchal, nuclear and heterosexual family structure.

Gathering Evidence: Documentary Visions of Gender-Based Violence

I noted above that artists and documentarians, in challenging the totalizing representations of gender and nationalism deployed by the Milošević regime, sought to gather evidence of abuse that belied propagandistic claims. In gathering evidence, however, many human rights workers and feminist groups either focused on the gendered dimensions of the mass rape, detention, torture and killing of Bosnian and Croatian women, asserting the universal preponderance of sexual violence around the world, or sought to emphasize the genocidal quality of mass rape, forced pregnancies and deaths, collapsing crimes against women with crimes against a national or ethnic community.

Thus far, the videos under examination grapple with the mythical status of the figuration of women, and specifically of women as symbols of a national community. Abramović's, Tomić's and Massumi's videos break apart the singular representation of "woman" mobilized by the Serbian news media, and make clear the purifying practices by which the multiple differences among and between women are erased in order to produce a gendered image of, for example, a "Greater Serbia" under threat. The final two videos I examine in this section are experimental documentaries. They deal with what it means to gather evidence in the light of media campaigns by Serbian newscasters and politicians in Belgrade, providing a critical appraisal of the effects of such documentary practices for survivors of gender-based violence who testified about their experiences.

Such an examination is particularly charged—and specifically challenging—in the context of the mythical figuration of woman-as-nation. Barthes argues with respect to myth's force that the ubiquity of the signifier in myth reproduces the "physique of the alibi": one place is full; another is empty. The signifier and signified are linked together by a negative identity. Unlike the structure of the alibi, however, where reality fixes meaning, in myth there is no fix. For Barthes, myth is a value unguaranteed by truth. Myth can be a perpetual alibi, unaffected by the charges of reality. The pervasiveness of mythical images thus replaces historical specificity; their sheer number becomes self-confirming, acting as a mode of verification for the connotative meanings associated with these images. Given this, evidence gathering that does not itself take up mythical language risks leaving mythical structures intact, or worse, reconfirming the totalizing violence of particular mythical structures in taking up their categories and presumptions.[55]

The two videos discussed here deal with the evidentiary, engaging in a critical interrogation into the processes of making visible, and make clear that such visibility is itself a painful reconstituting process. The documentary *Calling the Ghosts* in particular exposes the working of myth as a signifying function with real effects on subjects who must on all counts live in relation to these imaginary relations. The testimonies that are offered in both documentaries do not reconfirm the category "woman" as a counter-hegemonic position, but instead examine how that position itself produces its own hegemonic structures.

The documentary project in this context is complicated by the fact that the process of remembering is itself a destabilizing evidentiary mode. Jennifer González, in discussing the role of past events and objects in subject constitution, makes a distinction between memory ("an intrusion of the past into the present") and remembering ("a retrogressive movement from the present into a reconstruction of the past").[56] For González, both processes may be at work in the construction of a representation of the past. Indeed, she emphasizes that representations may be objects of forgetting as much as of remembering, producing screen memories to protect the subject from unconscious traumatic contents. While these documentaries seek to record the experience of the war, and vividly foreground the lived reality of that experience, both are also sensitive to the distortions and multiple impressions produced by the nature of remembering and by the trauma of the events. Their representational practices address a fragmentation of our perception of the verifiable and the production of refracted visions of facts and objects.

González's analysis unfolds the complex and unfixed relations between subjects and objects, tracking how the trace of the object persists in the visual fabric of the present, and also how those objects coalesce around a particular identity formation (whether it be individual or collective). The relation between subjects and objects, and the status of representations in video, should thus be located as the site of both congealed social relations and psychic investments. In this regard, the objects serve as a deposit of the violations that occur, a trace of that time that is both difficult to bring to memory and consistently haunting at the same time.

Prismatic media accomplish two things in relation to this complex understanding of objects proposed by González: first, they make clear the semiotic and ontological instability of the object for those who have suffered trauma. The dispersal of the image of the object across multiple screens thus resists a single narrative thread, drawn out from the object to the present day. Second, multichannel representations make clear the broader social and psychic network in which objects intervene. Rather than fetishizing the object as the source of value or information, multichannel images reenact the social relations that constitute the object from the outset.

Jo Andres's *Black Kites* is an experimental documentary, based on the journals of the artist Alma Hajrić, who went into hiding in the theater basement where she worked during the siege of Sarajevo. Andres, who is a choreographer and filmmaker, met Hajrić in 1988 in Spain when both of their theater groups were on tour. At the start of the siege in 1992, Hajrić sent Andres her journals, comprised of written accounts as well as drawings and collages. These journals became the basis for the video, which narrates the conditions of captivity, the struggle to find food and water and the stories told of violence and death in Sarajevo during the time of the occupation.

The images that appear in this video have little of the evidentiary: they are all elements of an internal landscape, refracted or projected into the empty space of the *mise-en-scène*. The scene is dark; images appear out of this darkness. An "Exit" sign burns, an image of the shattered pane of glass from the front door of a house appears and the actor who plays Hajrić lies in bed, as the text from the journal is narrated as a voice-over. The images from Hajrić's sketchbook appear projected onto the surface of water; they are unstable and shimmer in the darkness. The artist's body is also projected onto this surface. Slowly across the screen, an arm reaches out in the darkness. Red light ripples across it as if the water has refracted the beams before they reach the skin. Across the bottom of the screen, a press image of a street protest fades into a drawing of a body in a sketchbook; it looks like the chalk outline of a corpse. The screen contains layers of translucent images, piled one on top of the other.

The narrator recalls how machine gun fire could be heard at night, like the rhythm of music. The video displays a staccato set of images of an arm and a hand, still with the ripples of light (as if through water) across the surface of the skin. It gives the effect of a strobe light, visually mimicking the description of the machine gun fire that we do not hear. In a later scene, the artist has her back to the camera and is washing herself. Her back then becomes a screen, onto which is projected the drawing of a large insect that appears as pure white light glowing on her back. The voice-over recounts, "I have such a strong feeling that the human body is very, very soft, very unprotected. I remembered my friend saying that she feels the passing of time only by the growth of her nails. I am even more skilled; I am a living clock." Images of the artist appear to glow under a depth of water as drops on the surface distort her face below (Figure 1.5).

In this regard, the images employ a similar strategy to the artist Shimon Attie's *Portraits of Exile* (1995). In part of the installation entitled *Sites Unseen*, Attie submerged nine transparency images mounted on large light boxes several feet underwater in the Børsgraven Canal, in front of the Danish parliament building. The images included portraits of Danish Jews who fled to Sweden during World War II on fishing boats and of refugees from the former Yugoslavia, Pakistan, Cyprus and Afghanistan seeking asylum in Denmark. Each image was itself a collage of two images, the portrait alongside a background that served to contextualize the figure. The refraction of the images by the water rendered a vacillation between presence and absence that informs both historical memory and the very condition of being a refugee. The water's play on the surface of the image also transformed the still photographs into moving images, providing a filmic temporality to the work.

Figure 1.5   Jo Andres, *Black Kites*, 1995. Courtesy of *Women Make Movies*

This kind of image is echoed in *Black Kites*, but in the more domestic (and less monumental) setting of the theater basement where Hajrić and others are in hiding. Over the image of the actor playing Hajrić, the voice-over narrates the problems with finding enough water to drink and clean with in captivity. Water is thus figured as both a distorting lens and a mode of survival. The refraction of the image by the water's movements stages a psychic space as much as a physical one, emphasizing the relation between the inside (in hiding) and the outside (Sarajevo under siege). The refraction of light, the layering of projected, submerged and emerging objects, paints a vivid scene of a psychological landscape.

At the same time, the video fails to adequately draw connections between this internal landscape and the weight of reality in war-torn Sarajevo. The lack of indexicality (or of a negotiation between this internal struggle and the reality of war) may mark an excessive fictionalization of the experience of war.[57] Attie's installation, by contrast, ties the fluid and unstable processes of remembering to social frictions in contemporary Copenhagen. The light boxes submerged in the canal signify the reemergence of historical events in the present, constituting an irruption and intervention in contemporary discourses of immigration and nationalism (much like Tomić's work *One day* [...] activated historical events to rupture the ideological force of the language of "security" in contemporary Belgrade).

In *Calling the Ghosts*, the aesthetic strategy of refraction holds in tension the psychic impact of the objects, their nature as traces of violent and violating social relations and the evidentiary nature of those same objects. *Calling the Ghosts* was produced in 1996 by two human rights activists, Mandy Jacobson and Karmen Jelincić.[58] The documentary records the testimonies of Jadranka Cigelj and Nusreta Sivac, who were imprisoned in the Omarska Detention Camp, where they were raped and tortured, and it follows their efforts to bring their captors to justice at the International Criminal Tribunal for the Former Yugoslavia (ICTY) in The Hague. It is driven largely by the testimonies of Cigelj and Sivac, and includes documentary footage, personal videos and photographs, along with other sources that revisit the occupation of the town of Prijedor and the aftermath of the war. It aims to make visible the practice of rape as a genocide crime and place pressure on the criminal tribunal in The Hague to fully prosecute those responsible for the politics of "ethnic cleansing."[59]

The most haunting object in this documentary is the Omarska Camp, where Cigelj and Sivac were detained and tortured. Unlike *Black Kites*, *Calling the Ghosts* mobilizes multiple visions to reconstruct the impossibly layered, mythical and traumatic resonance of the evidentiary objects contained in the film (letters, photographs, footage of the camps, etc.). In the documentary, the viewer travels up the road to the Omarska Camp three separate times: first, in a reconstruction of the abuses that took place by survivors of the camps; second, with the BBC correspondent, Ed Vulliamy, during the occupation; and third, as a memorial site, through Nusreta Sivac's reflections on the camp's relevance in the present moment. Each encounter with the site, however, is mediated by complex shifts between the documentary footage and found footage, between voice-over narration and diegetic interviews. The viewer's encounter with the site is thus both in the present and in the past, through news footage and through testimony. Further, each account of Omarska (testimony, footage, schematic map, photograph) reveals aspects of the events that are foreclosed by the other accounts.

For example, the first time the viewer approaches the camp, the documentary reconstructs the abuses that took place through the testimony of Cigelj, Sivac and Hasiba Harambasic. The camera approaches the Camp's buildings (an abandoned office complex) and Cigelj's voice-over recounts: "We didn't know where they were driving us. After some time the car stopped. The door opened and all at once the women and men were separated." The video then cuts to an interview with Cigelj, who has drawn a map on a large piece of paper. She points to the position of the guards, on the driveway during the day and in the hanger and the garage at night. She identifies one structure on the sketched map as "the white house." The viewer then sees footage of the abandoned structure in the present moment. Cigelj continues, "In the red house they killed them." The camera pans across from the white house to the red house. "They killed them in the white house too, but no one left the red house," Cigelj continues. The map Cigelj has drawn—with the positions of the guards marked by X's around the periphery of the structure—and the footage of the abandoned houses, the site of torture and killings, provide different representations of the camp. The map signals Cigelj's active processes of remembering, calling to account and presenting evidence. The video images of the cavernous buildings, however, seem desolate and abandoned, and the viewer must work to imagine the crimes that took place there.

As the testimony proceeds, the viewer is presented with footage of the camp during the war. The camp is filled with thin young men, lined up against a wall in the courtyard, and guards watching over the men with rifles. The source of this footage is not revealed until the second time the documentary approaches the Omarska Camp, through the eyes of Vulliamy, the BBC correspondent who has entered the camp to ensure that the conditions of detention conform to international standards. Vulliamy narrates this second encounter, noting the bombed-out vacant houses where people used to live. Three cars approach the back gates of the camp, in a scene now familiar, since the viewer has traveled this same road when Cigelj and Sivac narrated their approach to Omarska. A report shown here reads, "Omarska Detention Camp. Wednesday, August 5, 1992." In his voice-over, Vulliamy described how entering through the gates was like entering another world—another planet—at that time. The BBC crew were told they could talk to anyone they wished, but when they approached people, a large group of guards with submachine guns would come over and listen to what was being said. One prisoner said to Vulliamy, "I do not want to lie, but I cannot tell the truth." Despite the prisoner's claim, Vulliamy argues that it was perfectly clear what was happening. The footage is the same news footage that visualized the survivors' testimony at the beginning of the film.

The use of the same footage in both testimonies positions the viewer in two distinct historical times. Since the film has already included the testimonies that Vulliamy is seeking, the viewer knows the information that the international community is coming to collect at this point in the film. Nevertheless, when the viewer first saw the images, their source was enigmatic. The familiarity of the footage positions the viewer so that she views the reportage retrospectively, knowing that the footage does not reveal the abuses to which Cigelj and Sivac testify. Further, the footage that was meant to elucidate the women's testimony was actually recorded by news reporters who suspected cruel and inhuman treatment of detainees, but could not find evidence of it. The images then do not elucidate the women's testimony; instead, they open up a gap between the possibility of visualizing the trauma that occurred at Omarska and the retrospective recollection of the events that took place there. Because of the repetition of the footage in the documentary (and the decision not to integrate Vulliamy's testimony with that of Cigelj and Sivac), the tension between the narratives and the images remains unresolved.

The third time the viewer approaches the Omarska Camp, a man herds sheep across its paved parking lot. Sivac narrates in a voice-over, "I would especially like to go to the place of suffering, to the Omarska Camp, to bring flowers, at least. I fear the discovery of graves, the uncovering which might force me to realize that all those people who have been missing until now have been killed." The camera cuts from its pan across the detention camp, following the sheep who keep their heads close to the ground, to a gruesome site: a leafy area in the woods where several human remains lie scattered on the ground. It cuts to a close-up of a skull, awkwardly tilted in relation to the clothes that still hang from the skeleton; its eye sockets meet the look of the camera. This final scene is shocking for its juxtapositions, where the evidence of mass abuse is contrasted with the farmer herding sheep across the site of horror.

The complex dispersal of vision presented by the three perspectives on the Omarska Detention Camp is also foregrounded within the documentary itself. In one scene, the documentary records a television set in the corner of the room, on which Jadranka Cigelj is giving an interview. She rubs her eyes, holding her cigarette away from her face, between her closed fingers. The camera zooms out. Cigelj is still being interviewed on the television screen (again, this appears to be footage not included in the final video—except, of course, that it is included here). Next, the camera frames the television monitor again. On the monitor, Cigelj is pointing to another television monitor, on which appears footage from the red brick barracks of the Omarska Detention Camp. She is pointing to one of the windows with a pen. We do not hear the interview, and instead see only the three monitors (the video we are watching, the television screen containing Cigelj's commentary and the original footage she points to on a third monitor). The original image of the Omarska Camp is thus refracted through the multiple screens that represent it, signaling that the testimony also is reworked, refracted and dispersed, as the footage from the video is picked up, reinterpreted and explained (Figure 1.6).

Calling the Ghosts not only refracts events through multiple layers of footage, but also thereby enfolds multiple times within the narrative

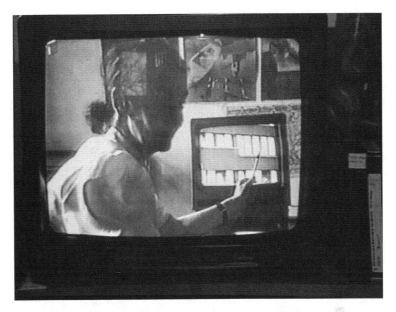

Figure 1.6 Mandy Jacobson and Karmen Jelincić, *Calling the Ghosts*, 1996. Courtesy of Women Make Movies

structure of the documentary itself. Two possible temporal schemas emerge from the play of images through the multiple frames: first, as seen above with the representations of the Omarska camp, a strategy of looping allows a segment of tape to be repeated in contrasting narrative contexts, switching between various recordings, narratives or representations. Second, the embedding of found footage encompasses divergent narrative times, straying toward different iconic regimes, genres or forms of narrative closure. This second schema most closely resembles the temporal shifts provided by multichannel video works, which may simultaneously screen footage that advances at distinct paces or loops on divergent schedules. In the "loop," the repetition of a segment of tape highlights the reiteration of the event, its cyclical quality or ubiquity as a symbolic structure. In the "stray," the visual regimes on multiple screens move in varying times and toward conflicting conclusions. The segment of tape unfolds a narrative; it moves toward something. And yet, that movement cannot anticipate the future it does not reveal. The video *Calling the Ghosts* then enfolds within its narrative time a heterogeneous collection of artifacts that move along different narrative paths. It is specifically this tendency of the found footage to disrupt a totalizing structure that differentiates the multiple narrative times within the documentary.

Take for instance Nusreta Sivac's reflection on her exile and on the loss of her hometown. She says in the interview, "I would like to go to Prijedor. I dream of it often, like it was before the war." The footage accompanying this melancholic reflection comes from a home video. On the tape, trees are reflected into the clear surface of water. On the bottom right-hand side of the screen, the camera has imprinted the date: 18:39, 9.9.1990 (prior to the war and the occupation of Prijedor). The shot is taken from an awkward angle, where it hovers over the reflection of the sky in the water, and then tilts down to reveal people on a dock, grilling over a barbecue and sitting in deck chairs. Sivac's voice-over continues, "However, to go back and live there, I think that there is no more life in Prijedor, at least for now, while it is still occupied by the Serbs." The home video thus relays a small fragment of another time, before the war, that has been absolutely lost to Sivac.

In another instance, Jacobson and Jelincić choose to represent the town of Prijedor prior to the Serbian occupation through footage that looks like it was obtained from a tourist bureau. Scenes show the waterfront, young men jet skiing, a crowded street lined with shops and an aerial view of the town's skyline. The footage not only has a horrifying *insouciance* about it, but is also directed toward a radically different narrative conclusion than the one toward which the film is building. From the viewer's perspective, the tape enacts a kind of shattering not simply because the possible futures are all left for divination, but because the time of the video itself moves toward other ends.

The dispersal of time functions as a critical political strategy. Martha Minow, a law professor who examines strategies of justice and truth-gathering after mass abuse, argues that closure must be resisted because no response can ever be adequate to the horrors faced by survivors of mass abuse: "any closure would insult those whose lives are forever ruptured. Even to speak, to grope for words to describe horrific events, is to pretend to negate their unspeakable qualities and effects."[60] To close the story is thus to deny the practices of working through that are indispensable for those devastated by the mass abuse, and for a community attempting to come to terms with the past and rebuild civil society. In this way, the strategies of refraction in narrative and sculptural video installations serve to open the narrative of mass abuse to the forms of discontinuity, non-sense and alternative narratives that work against closure.

Such strategies are especially important to the transnational scope of the film's reception. *Calling the Ghosts* garnered several awards, within both documentary and human rights frameworks (the Human Rights Watch International Film Festival Nestor Almendros Award in 1996 and the Robert F. Kennedy Journalism Award in 1998) and international film festivals (Minsk and Sarajevo International Film Festivals and the U.S. Emmy Awards in 1998). Katarzyna Marciniak argues that the film challenges audience members to "question their own complicity in watching—and consuming—spectacles of violence," a challenge that is of particular importance in the light of new forms of media that provide access to "portable and transferable" spectacles of violence.[61] For Marciniak, the filmic narrative exposes the dilemmas of representations of violence, particularly across national and transnational scales, for audiences for whom "war is boring because it is someone else's."[62] The temporal and spatial dispersions in the film not only work against the mythical erasure of history, but also take up the question of utopic visions in hegemonic and counter-hegemonic narratives, situating both the tasks of justice and memory-work in the spaces of internal reconciliation and global accountability.

Prismatic Media and the Witness

Prismatic strategies thus involve both an approach to witnessing and an aesthetic strategy. For example, consider a scene from *Calling the Ghosts* shot in a television recording studio, where Jadranka Cigelj explains that she has been cooperating with the foreign correspondent for *Newsday* Roy Gutman, who had been writing a series of articles about violence against women in the Serbian camps. Cigelj notes that Gutman had contacted the Banja Luka Press Centre to see if they would provide him with a statement commenting on Cigelj's testimony. In the scene, Cigelj is sitting in a darkened theater, watching images on two television screens. The camera zooms out to include the screens she's watching and the room, filled with floating images. One large projected screen in the middle shows an image of Zeljko Mejakic, the commander of security for the Omarska Camp and one of Cigelj's main torturers. On either side of that screen, in the front and back of the room, smaller monitors repeat the image. These five screens float in the darkness of the auditorium. The camera then zooms into the larger screen, revealing only three screens rather than five. Across the three screens, the image of Mejakic shifts to reveal a room that appears to be one of the "investigation" sites at the Omarska Camp. The camera returns to Mejakic, who is responding to a question, although we hear Cigelj's voice-over, and not his. Cigelj explains, "The Banja Luka Press Centre sent Mr. Roy Gutman a response from Zeljko Mejakic by fax, and he forwarded it to me so that I could see what the reply to my charges was" (Figure 1.7).

The camera then zooms forward again. It contains the large screen with Mejakic talking, and a smaller monitor on the left-hand side of the screen.

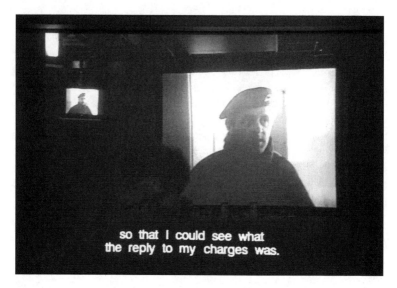

so that I could see what
the reply to my charges was.

Figure 1.7 Mandy Jacobson and Karmen Jelincić, *Calling the Ghosts*, 1996. Courtesy of Women Make Movies

Cigelj sits between the two images, and her silhouette blocks off a corner of the larger screen. She continues, reading excerpts from Mejakic's response:

> The response goes like this: "In the Investigation Centre Omarska, there was no space where Muslim women were held. However, for the purposes of investigation, from time to time, the following women were brought in . . . [The documentary cuts to an image of Cigelj, sitting at her desk, reading from the fax]. They were all from Prijedor, stayed for a couple of days, and were brought back home." That sounds like we strolled from the camp to home and back and forth. "Therefore, the women were treated properly and all of the policemen were given orders to stay as far away from them as possible. I take responsibility in claiming that there were no attempts at rape, much less that I tried to rape Jadranka Cigelj. I don't know why I would have done that: she is 45 years old and I am 26, especially since the woman in question is bad and unattractive. The way she was, I would not have leaned my bicycle against her, let alone raped her."

The scene situates Cigelj in the center of the screen, surrounded by multiple images of Mejakic. The footage appears to come from Ed Vulliamy's investigative report, at the time that Cigelj was detained at the Omarska Camp. The image's repetition across the monitors in the room disrupts the simple dialogical relation between Cigelj and Mejakic. Indeed, the truth of the detention camps lies in the multiplication of Mejakics, in the whole structure of guards, assistants and officers. Cigelj's relation to the multiple images enforces this mode of encounter: Mejakic is both an individual and a larger structure of oppression and violence.

For the viewer, the multiplication of images signals at least two things. First, that the figure of Mejakic haunts the documentary, since the fragment of tape multiplied in this scene does not reveal what it should: that Mejakic was responsible for the mass detention, torture and rape of women at the Omarska Camp, yet the staging of the scene in relation to the testimony, specifically Mejakic's testimony, allows the viewer to reflect on these multiple images. Mejakic's stringent denial of Cigelj's testimony denies the violence that Cigelj claims occurred; nevertheless, the violent and debasing language used in the statement confirms that violence in its narrative form, if not in content.

Second, by highlighting the multiple images, kinds of footage and letters—and noting the relation between these media and Cigelj—the viewer is invited to pay attention to the connections between fragmentary bits of evidence that never amount to a totalizing, clear or self-evident singular image or text. The use of multichannel images inside the singular documentary frame highlights the profound mediation of the images for the viewer. Jacobson and Jelinčić make clear in numerous scenes how the camera lens acts on its subjects. This occurs right from the beginning of the documentary, when Cigelj admits:

> In the beginning I had the reruns of my own film. There was a period of self-questioning before me. To stay silent or speak . . . If I stay silent, how moral would that be? When I remember the night when I was taken out, my own broken bones start to hurt. If I speak, how good is that for me? I would actually have to expose myself.

In the scene, Cigelj is swimming in a lake, looking back at a town in the distance. The camera is focused initially on her in the water from above, but then joins her in the water, looking at the town in the distance, the threshold of water and air dividing the frame. The video thus makes clear to the viewer the labor of testifying and the pain of making visible the policy of "ethnic cleansing" in the Balkans.

The documentary also makes clear how ambivalent people's reactions were to the camera crews in Bosnia and Herzegovina. On the one hand, the investigative reports of Gutman and Vulliamy uncovered the abuses taking place, putting pressure on the Serbian government and the international community to account for the human rights abuses taking place there. On the other hand, the camera is held to account for its impact on processes of remembering. In one scene, the documentary camera films women being interviewed by Cigelj. One woman leaning out of the window shouts, "I am telling you: If you are going to help, then shoot! If not—then don't film us!" In another scene, Sivac recalls, "Journalists and TV crews would come, always with the same question: 'Are there any women here who were raped?' I mean, as if one could divide women between those who were raped and those who weren't! As if they were in some sort of display!" Each of these scenes foregrounds the emplacement of the viewer in the world of the documentary, her relation to the fragments of evidence collected and the impact of visibility on those recorded and those watching.

These strategies are especially important for the activist aims of Cigelj and Sivac, to include rape as a war crime at the International Tribunal in The Hague.[63] After the film screened at the New York Human Rights Film Festival in 1996, the filmmakers and Cigelj and Sivac toured the United States with the support of Amnesty International and testified before the U.S. Congress regarding war crimes against women in Bosnia-Herzegovina. The film aired in the documentary series on the Showtime channel, and "60 Minutes" included a report on Cigelj and Sivac and the man accused of their rape. The documentary thus circulated within rights-based, political and juridical frameworks in which calls for justice were allied with a critique of unengaged and voyeuristic spectatorial positions.

Indeed, the very vacillation between the gendered and ethnic dimensions of nationalist discourse in many of the artworks discussed in this chapter resisted not only the totalizing force of wartime propaganda but also the resolution of violence and conflict within transnational discourses that sought to universalize the specificity of the historical events into broader themes (pornography, rape, ethnic conflict, European instability). The multiple channels of footage utilized by all these video pieces thus situate the viewer in relation to the historical events that took place. These videos replicate the position of the viewer in a larger network of data, information, images and affect, and ask her to draw out her connection, reaction, empathy and dis-identification with those images. The prismatic nature of the representations do not simply reflect the wartime events; they work to position the viewer in multiple sites of investigation, sites that are held open to the multiple stories, testimonies and lived experience of the most untenable of times. This representational strategy works to counter the kinds of totalizing and monocular perspectives that often contributed to the campaigns of violence and, paradoxically, contributed to the collapse of survivors' experiences to that single fate of having *survived* the camps. Such prismatic visions thus shatter our illumination of the events without refusing representation.

The multiple and refracted images, the repetition of segments of tape or looping of the video work itself and the interactions between live performance and image, or between layers of objects or images, seek to return difference to women, to make specific the historical configuration of gender, race, ethnicity, religion and location that differentiate women from each other and that are always already differences within women. These works then enact the kind of radical epistemological potential of feminist theory. They address a female spectator, acknowledging the complicity of individual women with the ideology of gender and, at the same time, maintain a persistent ambiguity of gender, multiplied through the many channels in the video works.

Near the end of *Calling the Ghosts*, Cigelj is interviewed again. She says, "This day is a very special one. The first year since I got out of the camp." The camera pans across a valley, identifying it as Ljubuski, Bosnia and Herzegovina. "Ten months of work in Croatia, meeting a friend, my Grozdana. Grozdana is my present, my return to normal life." She and Grozdana walk, cutting across a path lined with trees—their yellow leaves form a canopy on the ground as they walk. "You found me when I was completely broken. What motivated you to follow what I was doing, to lift me up?" Jadranka asks. Grozdana replies, "I thought you could pull yourself out. You remembered everything so precisely that I knew that you didn't remember it in order to take it with you and forget it, but in order to tell someone. Those who have something to say, those who want to fight should be supported." This scene engages in a radical refiguring of the sites for female sociality after the trauma of "ethnic cleansing" campaigns in the former Yugoslavia. This engagement offers the possibility of a form of sociality not based on the violent mythical structures of Serbian nationalism or (in response) Bosnian-Herzegovinian nationalism and independence. Alternative sites of sociality are also present in Abramović's ritual domestic labor following the violence of the war, in Andres's attention to the minutia of captivity rather than the public horrors, or in Massumi's attention to the dissolution of family relations after the war. These prismatic images point to the forms of domestic or reproductive labor, gendered feminine, that are ignored in representations of the cost of war and postwar reconstruction.[64]

Prisms of course act to refract light, reflect it or disperse it into its constituent spectral colors. Each of these actions implies a very different visual regime and mode of looking. Refraction thus serves as a critical tool for approaching the structures of myth employed by nationalist discourse. Reflection calls up the rich terrain of projection and introjection that forms the basis of cinematic viewing. The reflection of light signals the importance of the spectator, while the dispersal of light enacts a kind of shattering vision, one that breaks apart the singular shaft of light and scatters it. This most closely resembles the multichannel form that many of these video works take, breaking apart an image into a series of visions of a site, an event or a subject. Prisms also make visible a process that is invisible, the movement of light through the atmosphere, and thus also make visible the process of seeing, the conditions of visibility and the importance of a medium to the vision produced.

Prismatic strategies thus point to the specificity of the representational form, the multichannel video installation or loop or re-run in a single-channel work, but they also point to a mode of observation and to a politics of looking. Thus, prismatic media might serve to define a form of critical consciousness with regard to the proliferation of images of "woman" and "nation" in times of war, and specifically in relation to mass abuse. Such prismatic media denaturalize those images, running interference between the mythical figures of a potent nationalism or ethnic belonging and the lived realities of particular communities of individuals caught up in the material and epistemic violence of war. Prisms refract light; they offer mediated representational strategies, inside and outside the structures of ideology, or of a particular visual regime.

Postscript

As I was completing an early draft of this chapter, Slobodan Milošević died of a heart attack in his jail cell at the UN Detention Centre in The Hague on March 11, 2006. Controversy emerged whether Milošević had sought to aggravate his condition to seek temporary medical leave or whether the UN Detention Centre had provided Milošević with inadequate medical attention. Milošević's death also raised judicial controversy regarding the prolonged nature of his trial, its inadequacy in seeking redress or justice for those who were victims of violence in the Balkan Wars. Many also felt that his death preempted a juridical decision on Milošević's responsibility for war crimes, including crimes against humanity and genocide. Carla Del Ponte, the chief prosecutor for the trial at the *International Criminal Tribunal for the Former Yugoslavia* (ICTY), expressed regret that Milošević had died just as his trial was coming to an end: "His crimes affected hundreds of thousands of people [...] there were just 50 hours of hearing left."[65]

At the same time, war crime tribunals are not necessarily the only avenue for public retribution after such atrocities. Giorgio Agamben, in *Remnants of Auschwitz*, seeks to pry apart questions of ethics from the juridical notion of "responsibility." He notes that the Nuremberg trials produced the fiction that the problem of Auschwitz had been "overcome." He argues "it has taken almost half a century to understand that law did not exhaust the problem, but rather that the very problem was so enormous as to call into question law itself, dragging it to its own ruin."[66] Responsibility, in Agamben's view, is inadequate to the task of witnessing an event that one can never assume. At stake here is the question, What does it mean to "bring to light"? Jadranka Cigelj and Nusreta Sivac asserted that the trial at the ICTY was most important to them in confirming the truth of their testimonies. And yet, as Agamben's point makes clear, the ICTY is a particularly cumbersome and slow-moving mechanism, inadequate even to the ethical desires of those who have survived trauma.

Carla Del Ponte expressed hope that Milošević's death would lead the ICTY to be more active in pursing other actors who committed atrocities. The death of a figurehead and deflection of efforts to other multiple sites might be positive in the project of illumination, allowing for multiple testimonies, actions, and perspectives to be held up against one another. This must leave room, though, for forms of ethical response not tied to the juridical.

At the end of *Calling the Ghosts*, Jadranka Cigelj and Nusreta Sivac walk through The Hague. They stop by a postcard stand and pick out a card. Cigelj decides to send a postcard to her former colleagues at the court in Prijedor, where she worked prior to being taken to the Omarska Camp, those who gladly took over her job and her apartment when she was taken away. She addresses the postcard as follows: "Dear Colleagues, Zika, Drasko, Milenko, Slavko, and all the rest. We hope that you will join us shortly in this lovely city. Your colleagues, The Hague." The failure to resolve the trial of Slobodan Milošević, and the upsurge of popular nationalist support for him following his public wake in Belgrade, mean that the ICTY is on shakier ground in providing an account and producing an official response to the genocide that took place during the Balkan Wars. While the postcard, then, does not succeed in bringing those colleagues to justice (indeed, their opportunism and inaction could not be tried in The Hague), it makes visible something else, calling for an ethical response on the part of bystanders to the horrors of war, creating a circuit between an imagined space of retribution and the town to which Cigelj and Sivac cannot return. This singular image may do much also to disperse the judicial view of redress into smaller acts of visibility, attribution of blame, vengeance or forgiveness. This is all the more necessary given that, at the end of *Calling the Ghosts*, we learn that a woman witness in the ICTY case withdrew from testifying at The Hague out of fear for her safety thereafter. The resurgence of nationalism in Serbia, and the upsurge of popular support for Milošević at the time of his death, also make clear the urgent need for a persistent critique of the mythical structures of national identity.

2

Visual Currencies: Documenting India's Red Light Districts

New York-based artist Elahe Massumi traveled to India in 2000 to document the conditions of life of sex workers in New Delhi, specifically those workers most economically and socially vulnerable—children and members of the hijra community. One resulting multichannel video installation, *A Kiss Is not a Kiss* (2000), reveals the trade in children, bought and sold through bonded labor in the countryside and forced to work in abject conditions in urban brothels. The installation frames the four walls of the exhibition space.[1] On each screen, multiple frames scroll past the viewer; in one, the image of sex between a young child sex worker and a john is positioned alongside the image of her shaking her head, refusing the kiss he insists on taking. The juxtaposition of images, like the title of the piece itself, signals that things are not quite what they seem, that indeed a kiss is not a kiss.

Massumi's title indicates that the subject depicted is inadequately represented, and it points to the broader struggles that artists and documentarians face in making visible the nature of sexual exploitation, its causes and effects, demonstrating how closely these politics of representation are bound to the solutions that the videos propose to the problem of sexual exploitation. To represent prostitution is to wrestle with the production of images that may reinforce the looks by which sex workers are eroticized and exploited. Cultural producers also contend with visual regimes that (directly or indirectly) pass moral judgment on sex work. To get at the truth of life in the red-light district, artists and documentarians must attend to the ways in which life is deeply inflected by fantasy and desire, most often generated by clients and traders. In these conditions, a sex worker's own desires are almost impossible to represent without implying her complicity in scenes where she is commonly viewed as a victim.

In the previous chapter, I noted that multichannel video served to make visible the contradictory position of women, both inside and outside the ideological structures of ethnic nationalism. Prismatic media were thus mobilized to adequately image this contradictory and displaced positionality. Here, multichannel video serves to account for the ambivalent and in-between space of the gendered subaltern subject, both within and outside the political economy of transnational capitalism. Two key considerations frame my analysis of documentary practices in such contexts: first, how do the videos foreground and frame the causes of women's oppression and exploitation? Second, what scale—local, national or transnational—is adopted by each work? These questions address the chains of responsibility and relationality that produce the red-light district's activity and exploitation, as well as the position of the intended audience, calling for either charity, empathy or accountability. The videos I consider here offer different representational strategies for making visible the various forms of sexual exploitation in India's red-light districts.

Ross Kauffman and Zana Briski's documentary *Born into Brothels* (2004) records a series of photography workshops set up for the children of sex workers in a Kolkata brothel.[2] Briski originally traveled to Kolkata to live in the red-light district and photograph brothel life. Faced with the sex workers' resistance to being photographed, and with her own sympathy for the children born in the brothel, she began to teach the children photography. The documentary folds into its narrative both Briski's quest to place the children in boarding schools, away from the threats of the brothels, and the children's own representations of life in the Sonagachi red-light district.

Massumi's multichannel artworks *A Kiss Is not a Kiss* and *The Hijras* (2000) blur the lines between fiction and documentary, at times using actors or having participants reenact a rite for the camera, thereby fracturing a more singular and authoritative vision into multiple projections. *A Kiss Is not a Kiss* charts a young girl's sale into sexual slavery, the brutal conditions of a New Delhi brothel, a recreated sex act between a child prostitute and a john and images of a dying child in a hospital bed. *The Hijras* also uses multiple screens to juxtapose and draw out the multifaceted experience of the hijra community, including ceremonial blessings and dances, castration rituals and sex work.[3] Each screen moves at a different pace and exposes varying aspects of the subjects' experience. Some images are slowed down to the point where they resemble still photographs; others demonstrate the fast-paced exchange of bodies and rupees. This representational instability echoes for the viewer the multiplicity of conditions and experiences that make up sex work in India, conditions that are not reducible simply to discourses of sexual exploitation, the traffic in women or the gendered dynamic of sexual oppression.

How the subjects are situated in each video either bolsters or undermines international articulations of the causes of sex trafficking and strategies for the prevention of sexual exploitation. While it is true that a geopolitical distinction might be made between the traffic in bodies across borders and such traffic within a state's national borders, it would be a mistake to imagine sexual exploitation as a national problem. Such a collapse—where physical geography becomes the key index of the scale of the problem—has far-reaching effects on one's understanding of sex work performed within those sectors of society most vulnerable to exploitation and abuse.[4] Rapid urbanization, the creation of red-light districts, the increase in urban poverty, the concentration of large (mostly male) labor forces in urban slums and the articulation of different identities in the urban social system are all phenomena of the postcolonial megacity. And while they do take place within national borders, it makes very little sense to imagine their coherence on a national level. Yet *Born into Brothels* often portrays the red-light district as a failure of Indian modernity, erasing the force of the transnational economy (in its material and semiotic dimensions) in producing the Sonagachi district in Kolkata. It is not just that trafficking benefits from the trade routes opened up by global capitalism, but that it participates in those economies, creating distinctions between national and transnational scales of sexual exploitation that mask their deep imbrication.

The adoption foremost of a national lens in analyzing the question of sex work in India also serves to obscure the sex workers' local experiences of larger structural relations, both within transnational capitalism and without. Dimensions of life outside the global capitalist system are certainly oppressive, but they also provide alternatives to the simple reproduction of labor power in the family unit by creating ties in excess of the valuation of social relations under capitalism. The sites foreclosed by the reach of global capital thus also paradoxically shape alternative forms of sociality outside normative social relations. *Born into Brothels* imagines that the children's insertion into democratic systems and liberal citizenship will free them from a life of exploitation. The documentary is a medium for that transition, enfranchising the children through its representations.

Massumi's work, by contrast, demonstrates that the sex workers she represents are not outside the structures of capitalist democracy, but thoroughly a part of its logic of election (political) and exchange (economic). *The Hijras* and *A Kiss Is not a Kiss* situate the question of exploitation within the structures of democracy and global capitalism that shape the experience of sex workers in India and highlight the larger structural logic that produces both postcolonial Indian modernity and the conditions of bonded labor, postcolonial subjectivity and sexual exploitation in a New Delhi brothel. The subjects are not simply victims, even though they are violently excluded from the privileges of citizenship and subjectivity. The videos thus belie the more clearly drawn line between inside and outside proposed by a project like *Born into Brothels*. Instead, Massumi's installations might be seen as tools for responsibility and responsiveness rather than enfranchisement or recognition. They call to account the interconnected structures (in which the viewers also participate) that produce both the conditions of the subjects' exploitation as well as the international community's demand for redress. In this case, a national scale of analysis becomes a trap: too close and too far from the conditions of life in the red-light district, it erases both the local specificity of the sexual economy and its transnational dimensions. Prismatic media offer ways of reconstituting such erasures, however, by providing multiple scales for the representation of intersecting and overlapping subjectivities within transnational sexual economies.

Visualizing Sexual Exploitation

Massumi's videos are complex multichannel installations. As a viewer, one's eye travels the length of three or four screens, struck by the simultaneity of the action, the multiplication of frames, the disappearance of narratives and the contrasts between different visual regimes (filmic, pictorial, digital). As the notion of prismatic media described in the previous chapter makes clear, the multiplicity of screens marks the shifting positions of the artist and viewer, who are implicated in the multiple visions of the site of oppression. While here these prismatic strategies are not so much mounted against a totalizing and mythical figure (as they are in Marina Abramović's and Milica Tomić's works), they allow Massumi to negotiate the complexity of her subjects' eccentric positions, dependent on and simultaneously excluded from the circuits of transnational capitalism.

The *Hijras* is a three-panel installation. Each projected screen contains a series of layered "windows," each representing a different facet of hijras' experience in contemporary Indian society. It is also a visual catalogue, at times resembling French colonial paintings, early Hollywood cinema, Internet pop-up windows and early digital video. These different visual schemas play against each other, offering contrasts between stillness and movement, light and color, greater or lesser depth of field and restrained or free mobility for the viewer. In the first, the central dramatic action depicts a ceremony whereby a young initiate is castrated at puberty and becomes a hijra. Multiple windows also fragment the space between the viewer and the action unfolding, sometimes tightly framing the initiate's kohl-lined eyes, at other times barring the viewer from the action by columns or garlands of flowers. In the second screen, where a hijra sex worker is shown undressing for a client, the fragmentation of the screen's visual field is more tightly orchestrated. On the right-hand side there is an organization of looks that conforms to the structures of voyeurism; specifically, the relation between the male gaze, represented by the john, and the woman-as-image, although here that position is occupied by the liminal body of the hijra. On the left, there is a series of digital frames that break up the sequential filmic montage by repetitively returning to the hijra's undressing, particularly to the exposure of her ambiguously gendered body. The third projection shows hijras blessing a wedding ceremony. Unlike the second screen's verticality, this screen offers a scrolling panorama of images. In each of these projections, the multiple screens fragment the unified space and temporality of the images, engaging the viewer with the multiplicity of positions of hijra subjectivity.

The same is true for Massumi's second video project, *A Kiss Is not a Kiss*, a four-channel installation on the theme of child prostitution. Here, too, Massumi offers a series of fragmented and diffracted screens to make visible the many perspectives of sexual exploitation in a New Delhi brothel. Three of the four projections reveal the movement of a young girl, traded from a rural village to the red light district of New Delhi, exchanged by a brothel madam for sex with a john, and finally sick and perhaps dying in a hospital bed. The three sets of images are displayed all at once rather than sequentially, simultaneously showing the viewer the chains of exchange by which the young girl's body is abstracted into currency and how her body is violently rematerialized through a forced sex act and through her illness. The fourth projection displays portraits of two young girls alongside smaller frames scrolling along the bottom of the screen that reveal their life in the brothel. The portraits look initially like photographs, but as one child blinks—a slow and deliberate flutter—the viewer realizes that the video is slowed down dramatically, so that it hovers somewhere between photography and film. In contrast with the other screens, this projection serves to witness the events occurring in the other frames.

With a similar thematic preoccupation, Kauffman and Briski's *Born into Brothels* appears closer to a traditional documentary at first glance. In giving photography equipment and lessons to the children born in Kolkata's brothels, Kauffman and Briski's documentary method can be situated within a tradition of self-representation.[5] The children's photographs disrupt the singularity of the framing narrative and arrest the tempo of the film's progress, pausing for moments on a child's view of the street or the interior of an apartment. They also break up the documentary's gaze and diffract the central view of the Sonagachi neighborhood in Kolkata among the videographers, translators and children in the photography class. The documentary thus begins by staging a relay of looks: Briski initially foregrounds the transfer of the look from her camera to the children and then largely gives up her photographic eye, allowing the video camera to narrate the children's experiences and record the photographs taken.

The documentary itself focuses on two elements. First, Kauffman and Briski interview the children, who recount their life stories and contextualize the photographs they finally take in the class. Second, the documentary focuses on Briski's efforts to find placement for the children in boarding schools so that they might escape a life of poverty and avoid "joining the line," an omnipresent pressure in the red-light district. As opposed to the movement of the children's photographs into increasingly transnational and established circuits of circulation, Briski descends into the intricacies of the postcolonial Indian administration, confronting an unreliable and eccentric postcolonial bureaucracy. The documentary dwells on Briski's multiple trips to the Ration Card office, where the petty bureaucrat repeatedly informs her she must return in a week's time, and thus reiterates the tension between regressive forces (the brothel, a site of gross human rights abuses against women, and the antiquated local and national bureaucracy) and progressive ones (the international photography exhibit and the modern metropole).

Siting Sex Work and Transnational Visions

The networks between New York and Kolkata or New Delhi are well-traveled routes, filled with the traffic of trade agreements, migration, political negotiations, technology transfers, postcolonial relations, the global art marketplace, news agencies, human rights organizations and translocal nongovernmental organizations (NGOs). *Born into Brothels* and Massumi's multichannel installations cross these worlds, traveling through certain channels and challenging others, and this negotiation shapes the figuring practices of each artist. What site is figured by the videos, and how do they make present the red-light districts of Kolkata and New Delhi?

As part of their production processes, both Massumi and Kauffman and Briski engaged with their respective communities of subjects. Massumi made contacts on the ground—those willing to network and help in producing the tapes (local NGO workers, camera people and interpreters), but also those willing to be filmed (on the one hand, the hijra community or child prostitutes; on the other hand, actors who took on the ignominious role of child trader, brothel madam, young prostitute or john). Her large-scale, multichannel installation pieces circulated in museums in Madrid, Stockholm, Sao Paolo, Antwerp, Bogotá, New York and Barcelona. *Born into Brothels* is deeply imbricated in humanitarian institutions and practices, signified by their collaborations with Sotheby's, Amnesty International and other organizations. Both artists' claim to representing the reality of sexual exploitation may be viewed in light of the "ethnographic turn" Hal Foster diagnoses in contemporary art practice.[6] Suspicious of the trend to locate art practice and installations *elsewhere,* Foster examines the relation between the artist and the subaltern subject in relation to early-twentieth-century revolutionary art practice that sought to "side with the proletariat." With the "ethnographic turn," however, the subject of association became defined in terms of cultural identity, race or ethnicity, rather than in terms of economic relation or class. Despite this shift, Foster argues, assumptions from the social realist paradigm persist in the "artist as ethnographer" model: the site of political transformation is also the site of artistic transformation; the site is always *elsewhere,* "in the field of the other"; and the postcolonial artist has automatic access to this alterity, whereas the Western artist has only limited access to it. This produces, according to Foster, a "realist assumption," where "the other, here postcolonial, there proletarian, is somehow in reality, in truth, not in ideology, because he or she is socially oppressed, politically transformative, and/or materially productive."[7] The effects of such a move are twofold: first, the realist assumption involves a *projection* onto that other-outside, such that the other becomes a foil of the self, the site from which narratives of history, civilization or development may be displaced. Second, the realist assumption figures a pure *outside,* one that exists problematically in relation to the pervasiveness of transnational capital and its permeation even of those spaces that resist its logic.

Kauffman and Briski make explicit their relation to the transnational worlds in which they participate, tracing those routes in and through the documentary itself. Indeed, the video might seem to document Briski's efforts to produce visible evidence of brothel life and open out on the conditions of production of her own work. Further, Briski is well aware of the limits of her own vision of the brothel. An opening scene of the video is spatially and temporally halted by the slowly paced sequence of Briski's photographs of the brothel. In one black-and-white image, a woman's face is barely visible in the stark shadows of her room; in another, a woman sits on a bed, framed through a narrow doorway bathed in darkness. The collection of images is replete with barriers and doorways, intimately proximate bodies or distant and distanced ones. Briski is rarely in the same space as the sex workers, and her vision of them is furtive and frustrated. Indeed, a review of the filmmakers' process in *American Cinematographer* notes that Kauffman and Briski obtained footage of the red light district by "holding their cameras low and shooting blind as they ushered the children home from field trips" or by constructing a hidden camera out of a button camera rigged to a Sony DCR-PC5, which pointed out of a hole in a backpack.[8]

The film thus narrates from the outset Briski's own difficulties shooting in a district where everyone's actions are illegal and outsiders are met with suspicion. At the same time, however, Briski's focus on the children alters her figuration of the site. If she had focused on the women sex workers in the Sonagachi neighborhood, the documentary would have laid out a more complex site of sexual labor and exploitation inside the circulation of transnational capital, a site not of the "real" in Foster's sense, but of global capitalism. Her focus on the children thus works to shift the site from one inside the global system to one outside of it. This is because the brothel, for the children, is the site of political oppression rather than economic exploitation. Since they do not participate directly in the sexual economy of the red-light district, their abuse is seen to stem from the denial of their basic rights to education, health care and an adequate standard of living. The children are simply *born* into the brothel and are thus not responsible for participating in the economies that oppress them. By passing the task of representation to the children, the thorny question of false consciousness is ultimately avoided, and Kauffman and Briski are able to focus on their subjects' innocence, locating the children both inside the red-light district (and thus as reliable witnesses of the site) and outside of it (not participating in the sexual economies that produce the red-light district as a site of otherness).

Moreover, the children are outside of both the circuits of privilege and the eccentric use of power in a postcolonial nation-state. This is made clear in the contrast between Briski's initial images of the women sex workers and the photographs she takes of the children playfully leaning against a balcony or leaping from a doorway into the narrow street. Briski narrates,

> The brothels are filled with children; they're everywhere. And they were so curious. They didn't understand why this woman had come and what I was doing there. They were all over me. They wanted to learn how to use the camera. That's when I thought it would be really great to teach them and to see this world through their eyes.[9]

The photographs that the children take are strikingly different from Briski's: in the fray, on the street, the children catch the movement, lines and shape of brothel life. As additional case studies, Kauffman and Briski organize two photo expeditions that take the children away from the brothel, one to the zoo and the other to the ocean. Each expedition frames the imagined trajectory of the documentary, from captivity to liberation. At the zoo, the video's images of animals in their cages are metaphorically linked to the children's condition, and the children's reflections on the condition of the animals reflect directly their own entrapment. The expedition to the ocean features sweeping expanses, where the children run into the water and play, take photographs of each other and sing and dance in the bus on the way home. The movement between the zoo and the ocean mimics also the aspirational movement of the video's narrative.

In the narrative, the children's photographs mark an objective view onto the worlds that make up the Sonagachi district. The children are portrayed as victims not only of the perversion of familial bonds in the red-light district, but also of the inadequacy of the postcolonial state to provide for its citizens. In choosing such a perspective, Kauffman and Briski avoid the question of the mothers' radical alterity, which cannot be represented within the models of oppression that the film provides. Specifically, the sex workers cannot be understood within a classical model of labor exploitation since it is not simply that their labor is exploited (a question of alienation), but also that their bodies themselves are the site of value (a radical form of human capital). Further, their form of oppression (and the intimacy of subject and service in the transactions) is tainted by a moral valuation of their activities and livelihood.

From the children's position of oppression, however, Briski is able to locate her critique in the Indian state as an instance of failed modernity, where democratic rights and privileges are not extended to its most vulnerable citizens. The documentary is replete with instances that illustrate this critique, most notably in a scene where Briski attempts to gather all official papers necessary for the children to be enrolled in boarding schools. At the Ration Card Office, the system radically fails the children when the official is unable to properly inscribe the child's father's name on the ration card. He delays Briski numerous times, and her frustration is portrayed in scenes that break down her interactions with the system. She is figured riding in a taxi, a folder of official documents in her lap. She takes her head in her hands at the thought of returning to the Ration Card Office. To depict this despair, the camera tilts up the wall of the small office where piles of yellowed papers are stuffed awkwardly into small wooden cubicles. Against the forward motion of the photographs, the institutional arrangements are figured as regressive and "backward."

The oppression staged by the state apparatus is thus portrayed as something incongruous with the innocent world of the children; similarly, and although the threat of "joining the line" looms over most of the girls, the children are also outside the trade in sex that constitutes the brothel as a site of alterity. This difference is staged in the film by numerous scenes where the women of the brothel insult and abuse the children. For example, one child, Kochi, crouches to scrub a pot with newspaper and describes how she runs errands for a woman who lives upstairs: "For Geeta Masi upstairs, I do dishes, I bring tea, do errands." The camera pans across the room, and focuses back on the child. "She gives us money. I mop twice a day. The porch too." The video cuts to a woman applying lipstick. The child's voice-over continues, "In the evenings, if they want, I do shopping. Until 11:00 at night, if they want curry or rice, I have to get it." The scene ends with a close-up of the child against a dark wall: "I keep thinking if I could go someplace else and get education, I wonder what I could become."

Another child, Tapasi, is also crouched down, pouring water into a few buckets: "I never really think about being rich. Even if I were poor, I would have a happy life. One has to accept life as being sad and painful, that's all." The camera is high above the scene. At ground level, a woman stares down at the child. The video catches a close-up of water poured into the bucket. The woman speaks, "Pick up the bucket!" The child replies, "You do it. I don't have anything more to do." "You selfish fucking bitch," the woman retorts, "You can't even fetch water properly." The woman crouches to fetch water, "You worthless little cunt. Go tell your mother to get fucked." Through exchanges like this one, the women in the brothel are figured as part of the landscape of abuse that the children suffer, a site where not only are the rights of subjectivity or citizenship difficultly obtained, but also the affective relationships of families are shot through with the oppressive character of the brothel and the eccentricity of the local Indian bureaucracy.

Because the position of the children within the site of the brothel is figured as outside even center-periphery relations (a site of real alterity, or site of the "real" in Foster's terms), Briski's project seeks to transcode this reality into the language of human rights, subjectivity and citizenship. At this point, the Kolkata brothel is networked to a larger transnational institutional structure: the global art market, human rights organizations, news agencies and educational institutions. In one scene, Briski has organized an exhibition at Sotheby's in New York to auction off the children's photographs in order to fund the project. The children huddle together in a dark room and watch the live video feed from New York, giggling when their photographs come into view. In another, Briski organizes an exhibit at a bookstore in Kolkata so that the children may attend the opening. The children's images are valued for their representation of brothel life, but they also have purchase as capital that will fund the *Kids with Cameras* project (through the auction of photographs at Sotheby's in New York, or the use of the images by Amnesty International for their annual calendar publication).[10] The documentary itself benefits from this dual movement:

the photographs are artifacts, embedded within the fabric of the film, but through them Briski gains access to the reality of life in the brothel and circulates that reality through the vehicle of the documentary. The documentary's own representational practices are at a remove from the representations of the brothels, and their status as meta-representational recordings of Briski's project represses the fact that they participate in transcoding this seemingly outside space into the codes of a universal subjectivity.

The movement from outside a postcolonial modernity to within it, through transcoding by the West, is figured in the final scenes of the film, which follow the struggles of one child, Avijit, to get to Amsterdam. The World Press Foundation has identified Avijit as a child with "natural talent" and has invited him to Amsterdam to join children from around the world for an annual photography conference. Briski charts her efforts to obtain a passport for him, again facing the petty bureaucratic machine. At the same time, Briski learns that Avijit's mother is killed by her pimp—set on fire and burned to death. Avijit recedes from the photography class and seems to give up on traveling to Amsterdam. The documentary figures Avijit being pulled back, unable to escape the conditions of his existence. Nevertheless, once Briski is able to obtain a passport for Avijit, he is able to overcome this despair by arriving in Amsterdam. The movement through this first-world metropole shapes his vision of life back in Kolkata and his experiences—he attends the conference with children from around the world, walks along the canals wearing a big down parka, his camera close to hand, and attempts to ice skate. His return to India and his decision to accept a place at the Future Hope School confirms the movement of the documentary from a space radically outside the global system to one inside of it.[11]

Massumi's videos, on the other hand, foreground less obviously her own routes to New Delhi. Her representation of a New Delhi brothel, contrasting Kauffman and Briski's, is as an aporia, a space both radically inside and outside the space of postcoloniality. This is partly a result of their form; Massumi's installations are neither purely art not purely documentary. Documentary scenes are stitched to fictions, and re-creations mix actors and informants: a castration ceremony is reenacted by the hijra community; a former child prostitute in a New Delhi brothel and an Indian actor act out a sexual encounter between a child sex worker and a john; actors re-create a scene where a brothel madam beats her girls. Massumi's work is part performance, part reflection and part information. Her treatment of sexual violence does not figure a timeless oppressive practice or a purely oppressed subject, and as such, her installations are both ethically ambivalent and uncomfortable to watch.

Massumi's position vis-à-vis her subject exposes a weakness in Foster's argument regarding the artist as an ethnographer, a weakness addressed in critiques of his text by Renée Green, Jennifer González and Coco Fusco. Green and González both take up the striking presumption in Foster's text that the artist is distinct from the "other." Green notes that Foster's projected and imaginary artist cannot occupy multiple positions, either by "identif[ying] with a position of alterity which becomes mistaken for one's self" or by allowing for "a Levinasian awareness of otherness and the relativity and relationality of this concept."[12] González asks, "Who identifies *with* the Other but also who counts as Other, who is allowed to make representations of this Other, and who has the authority to enforce these representations[?]".[13]

For Fusco, the ethnographic turn is not only a symptom for a generalized "anthropological curiosity," but may also be a strategy for postcolonial artists. "Artworlding," a term used by Fusco to describe works by Latino/a media artists in the 1980s, signified not only a proliferation of perspectives, practices and objects, but also a social context for competing modes of approach. Thus, artists of color were able to resist the demand that they be "native informants" to the larger community and resist the demand that they produce authentic representations in the documentary genre. Fusco cites as an example Juan Downey, a Puerto Rican artist living in the United States, who created *The Laughing Alligator* (1979), a video about the Yanomami tribe of Venezuela. Downey used ethnography to critically interrogate the demand that he be a "native informant," even while he was received as a Latino artist working on Latino issues.[14] Green introduces the term "slippages" to render the binary global/local more complex within an "evolving transnational imaginary—the full scope of contemporary cultural production by which national identities of political allegiance and economic regulation are being undone, and in which imagined communities are being reshaped at both global and local levels of everyday existence."[15]

Perhaps most remarkable in this regard is how the visual economy in Massumi's projects manages the circulation not only of bodies, currencies and rites, but also of the figure of otherness. The castration ceremony depicted in *The Hijras* is both a mythical rite of passage and the entry of the child into a system of patronage, debt and association.[16] That the child might want to be castrated further complicates the forms of economic and social abuse suffered prior to and subsequent to the child's entry into the hijra community. From the viewer's perspective, witnessing the rite as a marked outsider also builds the kinds of relationality among incommensurable selves that Green articulates.

Both of Massumi's works—*The Hijras* and *A Kiss Is not a Kiss*—stress the imbrications of sexual trauma, ritual, capital, sustenance and exchange. In *The Hijras*, the castration rite takes place alongside two panels that represent how hijra communities sustain themselves, first through sex work and second through blessing births and weddings. Economic relations weave through forms of sexual violence and exploitation, as well as cultural rites. Massumi further raises questions about the economy of the image and hence about artistic production as an integral part of these exchanges. Take, for example, the third screen of *The Hijras* where a group of hijras bless a ceremony. The background is black and textured like painted celluloid. The top half of the screen has three small strips of images that run in different directions across the screen. These images too look like film strips; each image is a still frame, but because the viewer can see approximately nine or ten frames pass along the screen at a time, the images never resolve themselves into the flicker and tempo of film. The movement is not of the action in the film, but of the film itself, stroking the surface of the digital screen.

Below these strips of images, a larger window comes into view. In it, a group of hijras emerge from a glass door frame. The camera peers in voyeuristically, from above, across a garland of flowers. From below, the camera captures a man and a woman walking down a staircase decorated with hundreds of flower garlands. A woman dances in a red-and-pink sari, while behind her, a hijra claps and dances. In this last scene, a hijra dances for an older man dressed in a Western business suit. As the man waves bills above her head, she unveils and spins around, waving her hands in the air and sashaying her hips.

Represented here is a cultural tradition and a performance, but also a transaction, an encounter between traditional blessing rites and urban families in Western dress. The viewer is made explicitly aware of the economy of sight: the man must offer money to the hijra in order that she show herself and that the viewer, in turn, may see her. In the second screen also, where the hijra undresses before the camera, the viewer is placed in the position of the john and thus of having also paid in some manner to see the hijra undress. This exchange is all the more striking in the production context of *A Kiss Is not a Kiss*, where Massumi only gained access to the child sex worker who stages the sex act by buying time from her madam.[17]

The artist's—and accordingly the viewer's—implication in the economy of sexual exploitation is, however, far from liberatory. It is not so much that Massumi overcomes Foster's critique of the artist as ethnographer, but rather that her production process and the resulting work put into crisis his very notion of ideological patronage adapted from Walter Benjamin.

In "The Author as Producer," Benjamin calls for the artist to intervene in the means of artistic production, like the revolutionary worker. He argues that having political sympathy (Benjamin calls this a "correct tendency") only places the artist *beside* the proletariat, as a "benefactor" or "ideological patron." Benjamin thus asks for solidarity in material practice, not in artistic theme or political attitude alone, and thus for how the work stands *in* rather than *to* the relations of production of the time.[18] Foster argues, again via Benjamin, that the artist's identification with the cultural other (the worker in Benjamin's schema) further alienates the worker, confirming the gap between the two through reductive or idealistic representation.

Both *Born into Brothels* and *A Kiss Is not a Kiss* problematize the notion of the author as producer in Foster's and Benjamin's schema. For Kauffman and Briski, the founding of *Kids with Cameras* certainly involved a form of solidarity in material practice, since the photographs transformed the children into artists, and the filmmakers into documentarians and allies. The mode of artistic production, however, remained largely consistent with the channels of charity, international rights and documentary realism that supported the children's roles as native informants to brothel life. Kauffman and Briski's work is then reformist in attitude, but fails to confront the documentarians' position within the relations of production (both transnational capitalism and the sex trade) in the contemporary global system. By contrast, because *A Kiss Is not a Kiss* addresses specifically children who work in the sex trade, Massumi's work confronts head-on the unavoidable admission that the ties between her and the young women were not simply politico-ethical but also economic.

This acknowledgment highlights the contradictions in documentary representations of sex workers that I mentioned earlier, where the images themselves may reinforce the looks by which sex workers are eroticized, and further, the time taken up by the interview might more properly constitute labor time rather than leisure time, thus allying the artist with the john rather than with the sex worker. Massumi's acknowledgment of this contradiction is an admission that artworks engaging questions of sexual exploitation must do so on the grounds of the terms of production in the red-light district, including the hierarchies of the brothels, and thus recognize their participation in the women's sexual exploitation. To repress this fact is to forego the creation of a common ground that acknowledges the structural inequalities between artist and subject, and between global spectators and subjects. In discussing the ethnographic model in filmmaking, Trinh Minh-ha argues, "Interdependency cannot be reduced to a mere question of mutual enslavement. It also consists in creating a ground that belongs to no one, not even to the 'creator.' Otherness becomes empowering critical difference when it is not given, but re-created."[19] The ground of

Massumi's artworks is founded on the continuity, first, between the social relations of the red-light district and the global system itself, and second, between the sex workers' performances for their clients and their performances for the camera. For Benjamin, the single demand on the author is that of thinking about her position in the process of production. He calls such an activity a "mediated solidarity."[20]

Massumi's art projects figure the site of exploitation—the red-light district of New Delhi—not as a site outside the global system, but as a space of difference that displaces the center-periphery binary. Gayatri Spivak coins the term "decolonization" to reference this site, both outside the regulative logic of colonialism (including secularism, democracy, socialism, national identity and capitalist development) and outside the emergent postcolonial nation. This space "has no established agency of traffic with the culture of imperialism. Paradoxically, this space is also outside of organized labor, below the attempted reversals of capitalist logic."[21] For Spivak, the space of difference lifts the lid, so to speak, on a heterogeneity in the space of the other, a heterogeneity that belies the fantasy of a unified cultural or national identity, and hence of the "authentic subject of alterity" identified by Foster. This is precisely the site of subalternity figured by Massumi.

Let me return to the scene above where the hijras, invited to bless a wedding ceremony, dance for money at the house of an urban (Westernized) family. This scene would seem to confirm the notion of a specifically postcolonial Indian modernity, one where the spiritual resonance of the hijras coexists with the world of urban single-family households. In the space of the installation, however, the cycling image of the hijra undressing on another screen interrupts this staging of postcolonial modernity. These multiple figurations of hijras emphasize the heterogeneity of subaltern subjects, coded both within and outside of the logic of hegemonic national identity. This is also the case for the child sex workers in *A Kiss Is not a Kiss,* who exist both inside transnational capitalism (as exchange value) and outside it (as bonded labor). Whereas for Kauffman and Briski, the children's abuse stems from their being cast out from the global system (of privileges, rights, citizenship), for Massumi, violence and exploitation are thoroughly ensconced in its abiding logic.

The Space of Difference

The space of postcoloniality figured here by the sex worker's body is thus an aporia in Massumi's work, both within transnational capital (as superexploitation) and outside it (as bonded labor or the residual bonding of the sexual division of labor). The space of difference outlined by Spivak is most strikingly symbolized by the figuration of bodies as bonded labor (including the labor of prostitution). She argues,

> [I]n modern "India," there *is* a "society" of bonded labor, where the only means of repaying a loan at extortionate rates of interest is hereditary bond-slavery. Family life is still possible here, the affects taking the entire burden of survival. Below that is bonded prostitution, where the girls and women abducted from bonded labor or *kamiya* households are thrust together as bodies for absolute sexual and economic exploitation. [...] Woman's body is thus the last instance in a system whose general regulator is still the loan: usurer's capital, imbricated, level by level, in national industrial and transnational global capital.[22]

In both *The Hijras* and *A Kiss Is not a Kiss,* the sex workers' bodies are figured in a chain of exchange (in relation not only to the economy of the red-light district, but also to the production of the video images themselves). In *A Kiss Is not a Kiss,* Massumi focuses on two transactions: first, between a young girl's father and a trader who buyers her from a rural village, and second, between the john in New Delhi and the brothel Madam, who, upon receiving payment, summons a row of girls with a clap of her hands (Figure 2.1).

On the right-hand side of the screen, the viewer is introduced to the narrative of exchange, from father to mule to madam to john. This scene

Figure 2.1   Elahe Massumi, *A Kiss Is not a Kiss,* 2000. Courtesy of the artist

is primarily filmic, and the narrative takes place through a series of montages. On the left-hand side of the screen, three smaller frames show money and the child's body carried along the path of exchange. Each set contains two identical images, giving the effect again that this is a strip of celluloid. In this case, however, the images move in real time. Each set of images reveals simultaneously the three scenes described earlier in this chapter. One set shows the father trading his daughter, the second set shows the client and pimp negotiating outside the brothel, and the third set shows the negotiations between the client and the madam. While the right-hand side of the screen presents the scenes sequentially, the left-hand side of the screen does so simultaneously. Here, entrances and exits onto the scene are revealed and the minutiae are kept in the frame: the daughter and father engage in conversation; the father is shown running away after his daughter has been taken; the pimp is left at the foot of the stairs while the client has entered the building; the madam pinches saffron in her hand. These images are vivid—the colors are crisp and vibrant—in direct contrast to the grey-blue graininess of the central scene of action.

The scenes that reveal the child's entry into sexual exploitation map her movement through feudal and capitalist modes of production, from the traffic in bodies to the traffic in sex, from rural economies to urban ones. The split screens in Massumi's work both weave together these worlds and present them as disjunctive (symbolized by the separate screens on the left-hand side where the worlds remain separate, intact). The images themselves also call upon representational codes—filmic, digital, and videographic. These different codes figure the transaction through different times (the sequential montage versus the simultaneous juxtaposition). Through these prismatic strategies, Massumi represents the undecidable space where the child's body is both converted into exchange value and supersedes that valuation.

This also holds true for the following scene, where the john has chosen the young girl from a line and they retreat to a room. Here again, the scene is split. The filmic, blue-gray central scene occurs on the bottom half of the screen, while three brilliantly colored frames occupy the top half of the screen. The central image begins with the young girl reclining naked on a bed. The client lifts her legs, and the camera zooms in on her face and naked breasts. The image then rolls vertically, much as in early video experiments with frequency modulation, and in the new screen, the client is forcibly trying to kiss her.[23] She pushes her face away as he continues to wrestle with her. The images are shot in close-up, grainy with high contrast, and they exemplify the project's title, asserting vividly that a kiss is not a kiss. As with the other screen, the top frames give more information and its images are more explicit. The young girl is undressed and then pushed back on the bed. The client caresses her breasts and climbs on top of her. He tries to kiss her as she moves her head back and forth in an attempt to resist him.

The relationship between the upper and lower parts of the screen is ambiguous and more ambivalent than the image of the hijra sex worker in Massumi's previous project. Yet as with *The Hijras*, the filmic scene is more circumspect—it does not fully reveal the forced sexual act that the young child endures, a scene that is explicitly represented in the upper half of the screen. Here, though, the more explicit content does not simply invite a voyeuristic mode of looking. The upper screen instead invites the viewer to watch the sex act voyeuristically while the lower screen reminds the viewer of the prohibition: a kiss is not a kiss. This juxtaposition not only sets up a disruption in the representational field of the video—what the viewer sees is deceptive—but also firmly links the violence of the sex trade to sexuality, eroticism and pleasure, just as it links exploitation to human sociality. This is not the site of false consciousness (informing the girls' participation in the sex trade) or of pure oppression (the child as purely a victim). Massumi does not repress the economies of desire that both constitute the site of the child's exploitation and supersede her participation in the global system. Massumi's figuration of women's bodies is doubly coded, then, both by the loan (as a general regulator) and by the image (in its eroticism).

In this context, Kauffman and Briski's documentary acts as a counterpoint: unlike Massumi, these filmmakers often repress the ambivalence in the coding of women's bodies. As I argued earlier in this chapter, *Born into Brothels* situates the site of exploitation or human rights abuses outside the circuits of international humanitarianism or postcolonial modernity. The children are coded as both the subjects of victimization and the site of resistance, which holds insofar as they do not participate in the economies of sex in the red-light district. The prostitutes and mothers in the brothels, on the other hand, are figured as both the subjects of victimization and the site of abjection. They are difficult victims because they constantly blur the boundaries between violence and pleasure, exploitation and intention, erotics and ethics. Kauffman and Briski in fact repress the difficulty of witnessing sexual exploitation in the red-light district—that making it visible results in the unavoidable presence of eroticism.

A symptom of this repression, which irrupts in multiple scenes, is the women's vulgarity. Take for example Tapasi's retort to the woman cursing her—"you know how to use your filthy mouth alright"—which ties together the vulgarity of the women's language with the (unrepresentable) vulgarity of their work. This dynamic repeats itself numerous times, most strikingly when a fight breaks out between women in the brothel. The scene presents a mother dragging her young son across the courtyard, hitting him. The women begin to curse at each other, ordering the woman to "beat that son of a bitch," impugning her reputation ("If we are sluts, what are you? You are twice the sluts we are. Do you hear me? Or do you have a dick in your ear?").

The mothers become in effect part of the landscape of the brothel, signifiers of the environment in which the children suffer. Their reticence to rescue their children from "the line" is often figured as false consciousness, as when the grandmother refuses to let her granddaughter enter the boarding school because, she claims, she never makes an important decision on a Thursday—the day her own mother died. In all these scenes, the vulgarity of the women's language is played out not only in relation to the sex acts they perform but also through their use of expletives in addressing their children, through insulting each others' mothering, or through the women's accusations that other women in the brothel are "giving out all the time in [their] room."

The breaking apart of the family as the site of affective relations constitutes a clear site of horror in the video, where the brothel is in fact the space where the family is broken and deflected. For Kauffman and Briski, the family unit's destruction not only makes the mothers monstrous but also destroys the first site of sociality for the children. While the women's abusive relation to their children is striking, it is important to understand that children are often born into the brothel as a result of sex with clients. The inscription of the female body—through pregnancy, as mothers—is economically as well as affectively coded. Thus, exploitation may create monstrous relations between mothers and children, but it may also figure new sites of collectivity where civil society does not have to be assumed in order to posit struggles for social justice.

Massumi's *A Kiss Is not a Kiss*, on the other hand, does not back away from the graphic depiction of sex work that represents the daily life of the children in a New Delhi brothel, and thus sympathizes more fully with the intertwined affective and economic dimensions of sex work. More than this, though, her use of a split screen, presenting both the eroticization of the child's body through the perspective of the brothel client as well as the child's perspective on the sex act, raises the question of the erotic in social documentary. This is all the more poignant in *The Hijras*, which presents a radically other space for affective coding. Such viewing practices seek to make visible the erotics-ethics binary at the social and communal levels. The familial bonds of a particular hijra community are a tangle of interest payments, material solidarity, identification and desire. These communities not only produce new forms of ethical relations, but also break open the family structure (which Spivak calls a "machine for the socialization of the female body through affective coding").[24]

While the connection to the erotic here might not be clearly evident, Massumi's representation of the hijra prostitute undressing in a hotel room for her client refigures the possibilities of desire (both for the hijra herself and for viewers of the video). Employing the familiar layering mechanisms present in Massumi's work, the staging of this scene is more traditionally filmic. The scene begins with a shot of cool greenish-gray folds of fabric, unfolding into a background and foreground. The fabric becomes translucent, as if it is a thin scrim. Behind this scrim, a hijra stands in a silk sari before a mirror. The viewer sees her back and her reflection in the mirror. As the camera reveals more of the anterior scene of the hijra before the mirror, she places a hand on her hip, turns to look at the camera, and gives a coy smile. She leans forward, throws her head back and laughs. In the foreground, a small window in the top-left-hand corner reveals the same scene but in a vivid red light. This small screen moves slightly faster than the slow, measured pace of the background scene.

This scene develops in two lights and two times. Each frame reveals the scene of undress, the relay of looks and the action at different paces. On the left-hand side of the screen, the hijra undresses, taking off her bra and revealing her small breasts. A third screen, also bathed in red light, appears below the first, this one panning up and down her body, showing at once her face and torso, and then her thighs. As the cool black-and-white background depicts a modest scene of the hijra undoing the buttons on her blouse, the two red windows show graphic and fragmented images of the hijra's body: her breasts in the first frame and her genital area in the second. These are not subtle images, but rather graphic fascinations with the ambiguous markers of the hijra's sexed body. From the prostitute's gyrating hips, the camera zooms in obscenely close to her genital area, revealing the scar that simulates a vulva. A fourth window emerges, filling the left-hand side of the screen with three frames bathed in red light, panning again up the hijra's body, showing her face, torso and genitals. The scene is cyclical, the images of seduction interchangeable: a glistening thigh, her genitals, her breasts and her actions, unbuttoning her blouse, sashaying up to the camera, leaning on the bed, flipping her long hair back. This form of erotic seduction is tropic, engaging with the gestures of erotic representations—but the content troubles and fascinates the penetrative gaze of the camera, conveying the different temporalities and dimensions of the hijra's subjectivity, and opening up the space for identification (Figure 2.2).

This scene is intriguing as much for its ambivalence as for its erotic content. First, the scene shuttles between cinematic and digital modes of representation. The general scene's large scale—its graininess, its colors and its slow pace, as well as its monocular perspective on the undressing

Figure 2.2   Elahe Massumi, *The Hijras*, 2000. Courtesy of the artist

prostitute—refer to the staging of Hollywood cinema. This frame is constantly interrupted by pop-up windows, however, which render the numerous screens that make up the vision of the hijra in the hotel room more like a prism than a screen. Through diffraction, the frames deconstruct the boundaries between exploitation and sociality (sex work as the basis for her placement in the social order of the hijras and as a form of exploitation), and between violence and pleasure (symbolized by her castrated genitals). The ethics are here, in the erotic register of the hijra's body, in her pleasures and in the effulgence in the space of a "lack" represented by her castration. Such prismatic visions serve to break apart the singularity of her gendered representation, allowing a space for a whole field of discontinuous states to constitute her subjectivity. One only understands the hijra's subjectivity through this erotic relation, through her own desires and identifications, which organize the scene Massumi stages.

Ethics-Erotics

Bill Nichols's important text, "Axiographics: Ethical Space in Documentary Film," posits a central distinction between the concerns of Laura Mulvey regarding the affective dimension of narrative (and its concomitant creation of an "imagized, eroticized concept of the world") and the institutional discourse of documentary, which does not "support," "structure" or "reward" voyeurism, fetishism or narcissism.[25] Erotics versus ethics: desire, simply put, sublimated into desire for knowledge. Nichols argues that it is precisely the indexicality of the documentary image and the relation between the subject of the documentary, the documentarian and the viewer that thwarts the forms of visual pleasure outlined by Mulvey in her essay "Visual Pleasure and Narrative Cinema."[26] *The Hijras* obeys the theorization of neither erotics nor ethics. On the side of the former, the schema of the "male gaze" and "woman as image" is disrupted by the ambiguously gendered figure of the hijra as well as by the clear demonstration of castration (as a site of erotic pleasure).[27] On the side of the latter, indexicality itself is a trap: to represent the act is to engage a taboo erotics, a visual code that repeats the desire that gives birth to the trade in sex itself. Further, indexicality is a trap because the "reality" of sexual exploitation does not in fact lie in the act itself (although it partially does), nor solely in the structural and social conditions of brothel life; it also lies in the register of fantasy, a fantasy in which the visual medium participates—through advertising (licit and illicit), travel literature, pornography and so on. What is real, then, about the forms of exploitation discussed here cannot simply repress (or sublimate) the erotic register.

We might conclude that the erotics-ethics divide needs to be vigorously maintained for it to hold. It is in this way that the ethical dimension of documentary usually must repress the erotic to make its stand or uphold its (neutral) gaze. The threat always exists that the gaze might linger too long on its object. Thus Nichols, in examining documentary treatments of death, argues that "psychopathologies of desire may infiltrate any ethic, coloring the gaze with undertones of voyeurism, sadism, masochism, or fetishism."[28] *Born into Brothels* sheds light on the labor involved in cementing this erotics-ethics divide. In the opening scenes of the documentary, the contrast between the still images of the sex workers and the vivid, buoyant camera work depicting the children signals the documentary's shift from an uncomfortably voyeuristic gaze to a documentary gaze. The children become powerful proxies, speaking to conditions in the brothel while effectively marking the ethical-erotic boundary. Of course, the camera's look is not simply resolved in this choice of subject. The possibility that the children will "join the line" threatens not only the children's lives and livelihoods, but also the representational regime of the film (where the women engage in sex work and the children suffer the consequences of that life). Further, as mentioned earlier, the depiction of the women working in the brothel is both phobic and fascinated. The women are monstrous, coarse, violent and loud, and while they capture the camera's look, they often remain caricatures.

It may be that *The Hijras* and *A Kiss Is not a Kiss* cross the erotics-ethics divide *because* they stress the imbrications of trauma, ritual, pleasure, capital and exchange. The child prostitutes and hijra sex workers make visible how violence, far from being simply a human rights abuse, is itself also constitutive of sexuality. Similarly, the pleasures that the sex workers exact are always already difficultly obtained in social relations that are exploitative. This close imbrication of pleasure and labor cannot be adequately represented in the narrative structure of *Born into Brothels* because of its failure to account for the sex workers' own subject position.

With regard to the vacillation between erotics and ethics raised by Nichols, Laura Marks argues that many artists have of late been exploring the tactile or haptic qualities of video, pushing beyond the simply aural or visual. This longing for the tactile is especially pronounced in video, since its images do not have the depth and detail of film, but also since video artists are working within a broader cultural dissatisfaction with the "limits of visuality."[29] She concludes that "this denial of depth vision and multiplication of surface, in the electronic texture of video, has a quality of visual eroticism that is different from the mastery associated with optical visuality."[30] According to Marks, such visual eroticism has two effects: first, it questions cinema's illusion of representing reality by focusing the viewer's look back to the surface of the image, and second, it enables an embodied perception. The video becomes another body, its screen another skin.

The first purpose of haptic visuality, the return to the surface or skin of the image, raises epistemological and formal questions: rather than its contents (surely an important question in the revelation of political or social injustice), a focus on the image's surface considers not only how it filters light, but how it refracts it, emanates it. Marks draws the term "haptic" from Gilles Deleuze and Félix Guattari, who imagine visuality as a smooth space, like "navigating an expanse of snow or sand."[31] Marks suggests that this close bodily contact with the image, the tension between distance and intimacy, produces "a particular erotic quality, one involving giving up visual control."[32] She notes that haptic images are "erotic regardless of their content, because they construct a particular kind of intersubjective relationship between beholder and image."[33] This erotic surface seems inappropriate to a politics of visibility, however, particularly when the content speaks to human rights abuses. Yet it is precisely this skin that is repressed in the distinction between erotics and ethics posited by Nichols.

The surface of the image, and certainly its erotic valences, are often repressed or disavowed in order to lend weight to the representation of sexual oppression and exploitation. Such a distinction, and its application in documentary genres, render *A Kiss Is not a Kiss* and *The Hijras* particularly shocking to their viewers. Not only do strips of images stroke the surface of the screen, but each frame comes alive with its own series of vivid, colorful and erotic images: the skin of a hijra's thigh, the weave of a red and gold veil, the fluttering eyelashes of a child's eyes. This formal quality jars with the content: a violent sex act with a child prostitute or a child's castration. Massumi then plays between the visuality of the cinematic image—the slow seduction of the hijra sex worker undressing, the surface of the child prostitute's naked body—and the fragmented spectacles of body parts, in discontinuous and non-narrative motion. The hapticity of the image is thus a question of form but also of content, of erotic regimes and of modes of viewing.

Both works are troubling not only because the scenes mark social and sexual transgressions, but also because the formal experimentation appears transgressive and excessive. The trouble in depictions of abuse and exploitation stem from the fact that the transgressive potential of the image is mirrored by a more nefarious transgression—the sexual violence that constitutes abuse and exploitation. While the sexual acts themselves are transgressions (of legal, moral, social and bodily codes), documentary accounts of them must repress erotic valences in order to both evidence the abuses and lend weight and objectivity to the visual document. What such an approach elides, however, is that the image's transgressions (in their graphic or titillating depictions of the sexual) are indispensable to the sense of outrage such images elicit.[34] Massumi's work seeks to link pleasure and outrage by demonstrating the transgression of child prostitution or castration through a transgressive (erotic) representation. The eroticism of the video's surface, then, summons up the close relation between the erotics of sexual transgression and the outrage such images might provoke.

The second purpose that Marks outlines for haptic visuality is its transformation of video into another body or another skin into an intimate contact zone. The effect of video's hapticity is that rather than being subjected to the presence of an other, "the body of the other confers being on me."[35] This close bodily contact creates an erotic relationship with the surface of the image, rather than with what is represented. I argued earlier that the scene of seduction, the hijra undressing before her client, shuttles back and forth between a distanced, filmic perspective and a haptic, digital mode of viewing. Neither side of the screen resolves itself into the other. Rather than repressing the question of the erotic—the necessary condition in a politics of visibility, particularly in relation to sexual violence—Massumi emphasizes their ineluctable eroticism. Because the images are haptic and engage the viewer intimately, however, the viewer has to question the invitation to be intimate, both with the screen and with the bodies which appear. Such a strategy is perhaps constructive in imaging relations of visibility (specifically around sexual exploitation) that struggle with the very question of proximity.[36] A retrospective of Massumi's works was exhibited at the *Telefonica Foundation* in Madrid, Spain, in 2004. In the show's catalogue, the curator notes that in Massumi's installations, "the spectator gets literally inside the story since his or her body becomes integrated with the screen as a projection surface."[37] Such envelopment is a function not only of the multiple projections, frames and subjects, but also of the circular time of the installation. Massumi's play with the spatial and temporal schema of the installation makes the viewer feel the envelopment, the close proximity of her body to the skin of the screen, the skin of other bodies on screen, the textures of fabrics, façades of buildings, passing strips of celluloid or a sharp razor's edge. For James Clifford, participant observation itself involves a "continuous tacking between the 'inside' and the 'outside' of events: on the one hand grasping the sense of specific occurrences and gestures empathetically, on the other stepping back to situate these meanings in wider contexts."[38] Such shuttling involves both a spatial movement and a methodological shift between the two poles of experience and interpretation. Whereas early ethnography secured the authority of the participant observer by tipping the scales toward experience (the outsider entering the culture and creating a rapport), later ethnography focused on what such an experiential bias left out, namely textual transcription and translation, as well as the role of interpreters and privileged informants. Culture, then, became "an assemblage of texts to be interpreted."[39]

Massumi's organization of scenes in both video installations moves between outsides and insides, foregrounding barriers, cuts in the narrative flow, voyeuristic modes of viewing and various framing devices. In *The Hijras*, the viewer's position in the staging of the castration ceremony is complex. At once barred from the rite by the garlands of flowers, the camera also captures multiple angles, displays a total and particular view simultaneously and maintains a tight frame around the young child. Massumi's wide-angle view over the room resembles the paintings of Jean-Léon Gerôme, evoking older colonial visions of ethnographic rites.[40] At the same time, while this tableau forms the background to the scene, the proliferation of windows emphasizes a multiple, nomadic viewpoint, which might offer a privileged vantage point but might also particularize and fragment the close-up views of the ceremony itself. This emphasis on different modes of vision—painterly, colonial, postmodern, digital—are in conversation with the modes of viewing offered in the other screens of this installation, specifically the juxtaposition between filmic and digital mises-en-scène. The distance of the camera from the scene, as well as the long depth of field, further emphasizes this distance. Massumi makes the viewer conscious of "looking in," and such unease is productive in highlighting the spatial relations of the artist to her subject (outsider-insider) and of the viewer to both (limited to seeing through the eyes of the artist, but without the mobility to move between these separate spheres).

Clifford notes that the experiential pole of ethnography (and hence the "insides") required a feel for the foreign context. Massumi's use of a short depth-of-field, as well as her emphasis on the surface of the child's skin, or indeed the film's skin, stands markedly against the contextual-interpretive schema characteristic of documentary, the wide-angle shot or slow pan. In this sense, Massumi's approach is the antithesis to the ethnographic turn that Foster identifies. Massumi is largely conscious of the ethnographic authority she holds only tenuously, in complex engagements with the subjects of her work. *Born into Brothels* also admirably disperses the authorial position among Kauffman, Briski and the children who participate in the photographic workshop, and the viewer is made aware of the partiality of vision through shaky hand-held camera work or scenes with low lighting. Such devices, however, also serve to grant the viewer a sense of immediacy with—and immersion in—Kauffman and Briski's vision of the children's lives in the brothel. In contrast to *Born into Brothels*, Massumi defamiliarizes the position of the viewer, treating the sites of sexual exploitation and survival as uncanny spaces. The viewer of Massumi's work is thus literally beside herself, both affectively, in relation to the content unfolding, and formally, through the four projections that encircle the viewer in the installation space.

*   *   *

By way of a conclusion, I would like to return to the question of scale, responsibility and relationality with which I opened a comparative discussion of these video works. *Born into Brothels* had a broad distribution and viewership, and garnered awards at film festivals around the world.[41] Its accessibility is important in bringing to light questions of sexual exploitation; however, because it by-passes the very conditions of sex work, and of the red light district in Kolkata's relation to transnational capitalism, globalization and postcolonial megacities, it largely places audiences in a "charitable" relation vis-à-vis the children born into the brothels. In this regard, Pooja Rangan's detailed reading of the *Kids with Cameras* website concludes "The visitor to [the Kids With Cameras Web site] is hailed as a node in a global humanitarian apparatus who can, to borrow the slogan of the eponymous Web site, 'save the world one click at a time.'"[42]

Conversely, Massumi's installations have depended on the institutional supports of galleries and museums (and thus are much less widely available than *Born into Brothels*), and yet they provide a vision of the very contradictions of visualizing sex work, of the visual currencies in which cultural producers trade. I argued earlier that Kauffman and Briski take for granted the boundedness of the Indian state as the site of children's sexual exploitation and locate their liberation within international (and universal) structures. Massumi, by contrast, examines how sexual exploitation is both thoroughly entwined in the global system—as constituted by capitalism and the "freedom" of trade—and violently cast out of it, as a space of difference where bonded labor defies models of election and agency that underpin mainstream economic subjectivity. Each work's conclusion informs this distinction of inside and outside: Briski sees hope through Avijit's return to India from Amsterdam (his travel to the World Press Foundation and enrollment in the aptly named Future Hope School), and the film's images locate him within the circuits of transnational capital.

Massumi's *A Kiss Is not a Kiss*, on the other hand, ends with a child lying sick in an empty hospital room.[43] This final panel actually contains four images of the same scene taken at different focal lengths. These sepia-toned images roll vertically from one to the next. The first image is of the child's face, the next of her head and shoulders in bed. A further image incorporates the whole bed, and the final image is a wide-angle view of the room with rows of empty cots alongside her. Down the right-hand side of the screen, the strips of images replicate the same series of images in full color. When the main screen shows the close-up of the child's face, the strip of images passes over her mouth like a gag (Figure 2.3).

Most notable, however, is the repetition of the images across all the frames. It is as if, at this moment, there is no repressed story (hidden by the framing of the camera). In her illness and possible death, all that can be made visible is the child's ailing body. The position of the children and hijras depicted in these works has consequences for a politics of representation. Both of Massumi's video works comment not only on sexual trauma, bodily integrity, various flesh trades and cultural rites, but also on the project of representation and visibility, the forms that mediate representations of sexual violence and the (implicated) viewer who watches them. *The Hijras* and *A Kiss Is not a Kiss* figure the impossibility of getting at the real subject of oppression and thus do justice to the reality of oppressive practices, both inside and outside the circuits of the global system, constituted both by material relations and by the workings of desire. The visual document takes on the risks of repeating the codes by which the child or the hijra is eroticized and exoticized. But it is only through this that

Figure 2.3   Elahe Massumi, *A Kiss Is not a Kiss*, 2000. Courtesy of the artist

the fetishization itself is theorized within the subjective experience of prostitution, rather than in the gaze of a spectator whose position is suspended in the narrative space of the cinematic text. The position of the subject—within filmic space as well as within larger social economies—is important not only in situating the solutions proffered by artistic and documentary works, but also in evaluating the visual currency of representational regimes themselves and their negotiations of ethics and erotics.

3

Discontinuous States: Palestinian and Israeli Border Imaginaries

How does one critique the border as the space of a violent determination of movement and stasis by the nation-state and at the same time voice one's firm commitment to statehood as an articulation of communal belonging?[1] In "Reflections on Exile," Edward Said notes the paradoxical drive to overcome what he terms the loneliness of exile, "without falling into the encompassing and thumping language of national pride, collective sentiments, group passions."[2] In the articulation of powerful (and often imperialist or neo-imperialist) national formations, feminist critiques of hegemonic masculinity can sometimes be allied with the emancipatory politics of subjugated communities. When nationalism and demands for statehood are themselves articulated from within counter-hegemonic struggles—as is the case with the demands for Palestinian statehood—critiques of nationalist discourse may undermine struggles for emancipation or very real demands for territory, rights or recognition. Smadar Lavie and Ted Swedenburg, for instance, argue for the political necessity of essentialism when a group or culture is faced with radical effacement: "Hybridity [...] does not appear to be a viable strategy in the struggle for Palestine—a case of an exilic identity demanding to return to its historic territory."[3]

The experimental media under consideration in this chapter speak to the predicament of emancipatory claims to Palestinian statehood by visualizing the transitional, hybrid and differential nature of national identity. Focusing on the contested territories of Israel-Palestine, the artworks foreground border zones specifically as sites of teeming semiosis, producing powerful fantasies of collectivity, belonging and unbelonging. In these liminal spaces, racial, ethnic, religious and gendered differences form the armature of an imagined (and imaged) body politic. The transformation of the landscape of the West Bank and Gaza Strip through a series of checkpoints and barriers, the construction of the West Bank Separation Wall and, indeed, even the solutions for peace brokered through international bodies and third-party states are all signs of the breakdown of spatial and social arrangements across varying scales. While globalization has entailed a hand-off between more traditional state (and interstate) systems of governance and new transnational technologies of governmentality, the increasing militarization of the border and the reproduction of borders throughout the Palestinian territory signal a crisis not simply of the state system, but also of rights-based structures at both national and global levels.[4] Although it is likely that these questions emerge in other contexts also, whenever conditions of exile are framed around collective demands for statehood, the questions that emerge point to a specifically "Palestinian model" of border art. The border space is a coded landscape, a repressive message for those who seek to pass, made up of checkpoints, soldiers or guards, barbed wire, flags or walls.[5] This landscape of signs is maintained and bolstered by cultural formations (languages, state apparatuses) and by a series of abstractions (photographs, maps, charts, etc.). All of these representations become narrative structures that frame the abstract space of the state (to one side) and the globe (to the other), working to erase the complex "borderlands" that exist in the liminal territories between these geographic and discursive fields.[6]

In this regard, the border art that shapes this analysis is markedly different from the art of the 1980s and 1990s on the U.S./Mexico border. In that instance, artists were more committed to performative crossings that either undermined the border itself (in its role as a differencing machine, with all of its concomitant xenophobia, racial and racist binaries) or highlighted its repressive mechanisms at the level of Latino/a subjectivity. The work, for example, of Guillermo Gomez-Peña was more critically playful and performative than the work I consider here.[7] Indeed, Smadar Lavie argues that the discourses of borderlands and hybridity offered on the one hand by Gloria Anzaldúa and on the other by Homi Bhabha are inadequate for dealing with the borders in the case of Israel-Palestine. Whereas Anzaldúa celebrates the borderland as producing a non-essentialized, counter-hegemonic identity (and sees crossing the border as displacing the "Euro-USA center"), Lavie notes that in the case of Israel, "the Israeli center keeps usurping, as its own frontier, the border zones between European and Arab, Israeli and Palestinian, and Ashkenazi and Mizrahi."[8] The artworks that I examine in this chapter are both a counter-argument to the syntax of the border's repressive topography and actions that restage social relations and mediate between competing practices. Through strategies of refraction and diffraction, they not only represent and defy the mythical signs of nationalism, but also enact and produce social space. This last point is of critical importance to Palestinian artists, for whom the question of space is invested with forms of communal belonging, statehood and recognition. The productivity of space engages not only geographical imaginaries but also subjective space for hybridized identities. For Lavie and Swedenburg, hyphenated identities open up a space, "charted in the interstices between the displacement of 'the histories that constitute it' [...] and the rootedness of these histories in a politics of location."[9] Similarly, Alarcón, Kaplan and Moallem refer to the *spacing* (the "becoming-space of time or the becoming-time of space") between "woman" and "nation" that interrupts the exclusionary and totalizing rhetoric of nationalism.[10] The artists whose works I consider are all engaged (to a greater or lesser degree) in negotiating the complexities of differential identity within the imaginative dimensions of radical claims to statehood. Nevertheless, each artist works from a different context and location and articulates a specific topography for the discontinuous states he or she experiences: Mona Hatoum's sculptural installations respond to the violence embedded in abstract imaginings of the world map, as well as to the relation between these abstractions and the lived reality of city streets in the Palestinian territories. She strives in her work to deal with processes of safety and danger, inviting modes of identification that move beyond the specific reality of Palestinian experience (in Palestine and abroad). Michal Rovner's works both raise questions about the affective force of borders in Israel's national imaginaries and posit spaces whose cardinal points have been removed, articulating the possibility of free flows of movement above and outside the constraints of nationalism and globalism. Akram Zaatari unpacks photographic archives by returning to the landscapes depicted in a key ethnographic text, including historical visions of the desert and Bedouin life, the topography of Beirut during the Lebanon War in 1982–1984 and the possibility of travel and movement in the West Bank and Jordan during the Israeli invasion of the West Bank in 2001–2002. Emily Jacir's conceptual artworks and video installations articulate the multiple ways in which the borders and checkpoints in the Occupied Territory are experienced by Palestinians on a physical, affective and subjective level, and articulates the various and varied modes of Palestinian belonging in the Occupied Territories.

The artworks examined here open up sites for a critical interrogation of the relation between topography, sociology, economy and desire, and contain both a critical and an imaginative dimension. Thus, on the one hand, they are engaged in a deconstructive project: they pry open the representational strategies for stitching together language, traditions and places, demonstrating the repressive strategies by which a homogenous topography is produced. In doing so, these artistic practices take head on the representational tools of national cartographic imaginaries— principally here, the map and the photograph—and demonstrate vividly the relation between these sedimented visions of the world and the flows of people, ideas and goods that pass across them (licitly or illicitly). On the other hand, many of these artworks are also constructive, seeking to articulate the imaginative bases for models of statehood. In defining and visualizing a "third time-space" (the "borderzone between identity-as-essence and identity-as-conjuncture"), the artworks under consideration ally themselves with Chela Sandoval's call for a differential oppositional consciousness, a method of "daily living and surviving," of "negotiation and renegotiation of positionalities," of "capturing the fragmented, rapidly shifting registers and modalities of the forces that shape everyday life."[11] The critiques of abstraction, alongside the profoundly situated and embodied visions of sites of contestation, give form to complex differential visions of community and belonging within specific historical and geopolitical contexts, and thus provide models for Chandra Mohanty's call for a feminism without borders:

> It acknowledges the fault lines, conflicts, differences, fears and containment that borders represent. It acknowledges that there is no one sense of a border, that the lines between and through nations, races, classes, sexualities, religions and disabilities are real—and that a feminism without borders must envision change and social justice work across these lines of demarcation and division.[12]

In exposing the strategic and differentiated use of inside/outside distinctions in nationalist discourse, many of these artworks expose not only the manner in which exclusions are lived in daily life, but also the risks of articulating interiority in a totalizing and ahistorical form, relying often on the figure of woman as symbolic of the domestic sphere.[13]

In the following sections, I trace three strategies that these artists employ in critiquing nationalism's repressive cartographies. First, I examine how specific artworks critique the abstraction of space necessary to the production of two-dimensional maps. Some critiques contrast mapping practices with multi-sensory and mnemic representations of social space, others juxtapose different spatial schemas (international, local, national, global) to show their contradictions, and still others highlight the costs of crossing between cartographic landscapes. In doing so, they denaturalize and fracture the current state of affairs and highlight how active hegemonic processes mask their own labor in creating "self-evident" representations. This remains largely a critical and deconstructivist project. Second, I examine how artistic practices expose the effect of border crossings within the circuits of transnational capitalism and the global system. Rather than seeing borders in opposition to the flows of a deterritorialized, global world, such works emphasize that the violent determinations of totality and division occur largely *within* the global system. The border's fixity may thus actually result from and regulate increasing exchanges across national boundaries. Finally, I explore how artists shift the scales of dominant cartographies to open up space for unexpected critical sites of belonging. These strategies often rely on an embodied camera to show how the movement of bodies through places is actually productive of space. Representations that actively tie diasporic communities to the imaginary dimensions of nationhood territorialize those desires by locating them in city streets, in the wide expanses of the desert or within the discontinuous spaces of exile. In these cases, video is fundamental to articulating fantasies of home that are politically grounded in specific memories, locations and experiences.

Defying Abstraction

In 1996, at the Anadiel Gallery in East Jerusalem, artist Mona Hatoum staged a large-scale installation called *Present Tense*, which covered the gallery's bare floor. Over 200,000 blocks of olive oil soap produced in Nablus were arranged to form a square, and embedded in the surface of the soap, lines of tiny red glass beads were laid out in what appeared to be an abstract series of patterns. As one approached the surface of the installation, the lines became recognizable as outlines of the territorial concessions contained in the Oslo Agreement (1993/1995), specifically the small fragmented pockets of land that were to be returned to the Palestinian Authority as a result of the Agreement. In this highly coded landscape, the West Bank was divided into small islands, all floating in a "security zone" established by the Israeli state. The Gaza Strip was more holistically organized in the Agreement, except that islands of Israeli settlements dotted the territory and a heavy security zone guarded the eastern and northern borders. Between the two areas were a series of "safe passage routes" and, within the West Bank, a series of Permanent Israeli Check Points and Crossing Points. On what basis could statehood be understood in the fragmented pockets of territory ceded to the Palestinians?

How might the state of emergency signaled by the refugee camps dotting the landscape be ossified into the land grants of a new Palestinian state? The Oslo map's strikingly violent cartography in all respects sanctified the state of emergency as a permanent (and yet ultimately precarious) solution.

In the Oslo Agreement, the border itself became a state of emergency because its regulative function (its negotiation of national and global spheres of activity) had broken down. This points also to a contradiction at the heart of border spaces: ideally, borders should be non-sites whose regulative function is naturalized as a product of spatial paradigms. Such a view of the border masks how it produces (gendered, ethnic) social relations as much as it represses particular individuals. Increased militarization, the affective force of a gendered nationalism and the figuration of victims of displacement all mean that the border generates differential gendered, ethnic and religious identities *in space*. It becomes a machine for generating national identities, and is not then simply the site where rights are difficult to guarantee. The border's hyper-articulation in the Occupied Territories signals then its failure to articulate nation/globe relations and indexes in its very build-up the impossibility of state-based or global solutions.

Hatoum's installation highlighted the violence of abstract territorial negotiations by transforming the map's sterile abstraction into a more material (and sensory) experience. The glass beads reflected the light at the surface of the small soap bars, and the bars themselves constituted an uneven patchwork on the floor of the gallery. Further, for Palestinians entering the room, the scent of the soaps provided the first powerful impression of the substance of the landscape. The olive oil soaps made according to centuries-old processes recalled the city streets and open marketplaces of Nablus. To further emphasize this point, a series of photographs hung on the gallery walls that showed "the textures of daily life, of produce and cooking and shopping traditions that [shored] up some bit of the eroded sense of relations between identities and land."[14] These photographs taken in marketplaces called upon an embodied and immediate sense of place, which stood in sharp contrast with the map on the gallery's floor. Yet both elements of the installation confounded the relation between the abstract and the material. On the one hand, the floor's abstract patterns emphasized the violence of abstraction in cartographic imaginaries, but those patterns were embedded in a fragrant tactile medium (the Nablus soaps). On the other hand, the photographs called upon a rich sensory experience, but the sights and smells that figured there were abstracted by the medium of photography. In both cases, access to the spaces figured on the map were firmly mediated by cartographic and photographic technologies, as if to highlight that the artist's own fantasy of locality was also abstracted, that even sensory memories of space are representable only through proxies. Jaleh Mansoor stresses, however, that the soap's signifers slide depending on their audience. Israelis from Tel Aviv who attended the exhibition's opening made associations between the soap and concentration camps, an association Hatoum stressed "couldn't have been further from [her] thoughts." Mansoor concludes from these disparate responses that the movement of the signifier across differential audiences testifies to "the overlap between the shared and the restricted among two groups bound by enmity. Both associated the soap grid with the terms of biopolitical limits; both are exiles in a perforated space. The political task for each viewer would be to acknowledge this shared exile status and relinquish the violence brought to bear precisely by a set of abstractions: identity, citizenship, and mapped territory."[15]

Hatoum was born in Beirut in the early 1950s after her Palestinian family fled to Lebanon during the early years of the Arab-Israeli conflict. In 1975, Hatoum traveled to London for a visit, but had to remain there when the outbreak of war in Lebanon prevented her from returning home. Her performance, video and installation works focus on the relation between the body (both her own and the viewer's) and the spaces she produces. In many of her works, domestic appliances or household furniture are made to appear threatening and strange. Many times, the most intimate or banal objects suggest the possibility of physical danger. Sometimes, her work gestures toward generic institutional spaces—a dining room, a prison cell or an archive—and at other times, she locates strangeness (and strain) in particular geographical conceptions of the world, and specifically in the abstract territorial negotiations around Israel and Palestine.

In creating the installation *Present Tense*, Hatoum was inspired by her initial shock at the irreconcilable gap between her experience of daily life in the Palestinian-Occupied Territories (the rich colors of spices and fabrics, the scent of the soaps produced in Nablus and the sounds in the streets and alleyways) and the patchwork of territories that made up the Palestinian state under the Agreement. Hatoum says of this work,

> On my first day in Jerusalem I came across a map divided into lots of little areas circled in red, like little islands with no continuity or connection between them. It was the map showing the territorial divisions arrived at under the Oslo Agreement, and it represented the first phase of returning land to the Palestinian authorities. But really it was a map about dividing and controlling the area. At the first sign of trouble Israel practices the policy of closure, they close all the passages between the areas so the Arabs are completely isolated and paralyzed.[16]

Hatoum initially thought to drive nails into the landscape of soap, retracing the demarcations of the Oslo Agreement, but saw this gesture as overly "aggressive and sad."[17] For Hatoum, because the soap was produced traditionally in Nablus over centuries, despite the drastic changes that had occurred in the area, it served as a symbol of resistance. She was also interested in the fact that the soap was a shifting material, that it could change shape or dissolve entirely. The glass beads were thus embedded in a mobile medium, one that refused to hold the beads permanently in their current configuration.

The piece's title, *Present Tense*, carries (like many of Hatoum's titles) a double meaning: it indicates both a temporal framework (a grammatical tense) and a diagnosis of the current moment (i.e., that the present is in a state of tension). The title energizes the work and makes the viewer interpret the beads as a contingent arrangement, threatening to collapse at any moment. Given Hatoum's play with objects that are both compelling and dangerous, this piece comes into relief as an artificially frozen arrangement within a larger set of mobile and active forces. By adding this tension to the work, she foregrounds the precariousness of contemporary states. Further, Hatoum makes the point that stasis is itself part of an active containment policy, a discursive and material practice that includes maps, treaties, borders and checkpoints. The abstraction required in order that the Oslo Peace Accords be drawn up is exposed as a fictional stasis, and a violent one at that.

In *Present Tense*, the contingency of the world system is infused into the static cartography of the Oslo Peace Accords through a tension between the two-dimensional map and the experiential space of Nablus, between the lines on the map and their subtension by the materiality of Palestinian life, the soap into which they are violently embedded. In another piece, Hatoum focuses this contingency not solely on the claims of statehood, but also on the global system's structure. This work, entitled *Map* (1998), was produced first for a one-person exhibition occupying the entire top level of the Kunsthalle Basel.[18] Here, Hatoum created a world map out of 3,000 pounds of clear glass marbles, covering the floor of the space in a 25 × 48 foot installation. As viewers entered the space, not immediately recognizing the world map on the floor, some tripped over the formation, walked gingerly around it or took time to decipher the landmasses and the negative floor space of the oceans. The marbles were not fixed to the floor, rolling around whenever someone approached the work (Figure 3.1).[19]

The possibility that the marbles might shift emphasized for the viewer first the precariousness of the configuration of states and continents, and

Figure 3.1 Mona Hatoum, *Map* (1998). 14 mm glass marbles; dimensions variable. Photo: Christian Mosar. Courtesy of Casino Luxembourg and The White Cube Gallery

second the existential chasm of spatial change. In walking into the room, a viewer might disrupt entirely the cartographic formations laid out on the ground. Hatoum explains,

> In contrast to the map in Jerusalem, [*Map*] was a world without any borders. But the map was very fragile: as soon as one set foot on the parquet, the marbles on the floor started moving. At the same time, the work was very menacing. I like it when things are attractive and forbidding at the same time – both seductive and dangerous. The marbles made the floor hazardous, because you could slip on the glass balls and fall down. I've done quite a few works which destabilize the ground you walk on.[20]

It is thus important to read *Present Tense* and *Map* together, to see the ways in which Hatoum theorizes the precariousness and violence of both nation-state formations and visions of a world "without borders."

In *Map*, the discourse of borderlessness is as threatening as the mass of internal borders contained in the Oslo Agreement. Borderlessness is also an organization of space and a powerful imaginary. It points to histories of people who are, in James Clifford's terms, "variously empowered and compelled."[21] Hatoum describes how, as a reaction to her own personal history in embattled areas, she made a map that, denies all political borders. But this map is so unstable that even the geographical delineation of the continents cannot be fixed, since the simple movement of those walking across the floor will shift parts of it and threaten to destroy it. At the same time, it renders the floor surface treacherous for viewers as it destabilizes the surface they walk on. So there is this double aspect of fragility and danger.[22]

The dual character of both *Map* and *Present Tense*—both fragile and dangerous—radically revisits images of a stable international order and of an interconnected global system. *Present Tense* makes clear first that the international system—the basis for human rights collaborations, refugee solutions and United Nations' development and aid programs—is a provisional formation. Regional conflicts are difficult to solve by carving out pockets of national territory in a field of contestation. Second, the piece highlights the fact that, under a binding topography, multidimensional and multisensory experiences of space by (collective and individual) subjects have a resilience that supersedes territorial boundaries. The laborious process of pouring the olive oil soaps by hand into large vats and stirring them according to customary practices that have been repeated for centuries works under the radar of bureaucratic decisions, checkpoints and national anthems. In embedding the map in the soap, therefore, Hatoum's work crosses between public and private domains, between the domestic and the national, between daily life and states of emergency.

By staging an opposition between the sensual and mnemic experience of Nablus and the cartographic imaginary of the Oslo Accords, Hatoum also asserts the importance of memory and fantasy in the constitution of place. Whereas the maps of the Oslo Accords are two-dimensional, depersonalized and detached from the lived experience of space, Hatoum's insistence on the experiential, sensory and imaginary dimensions of place highlights how the peace treaty—conceived under Oslo—is in fact uninhabitable, impossible in relation to the psychic attachments to Nablus and other cities and neighborhoods by Palestinians living in the Occupied Territories or abroad. While this appears to set up a contrast between objective and subjective dimensions of social life, such a contrast neglects the register of fantasies of statehood and collectivity in Hatoum's work. Alongside the constitutive function of memory, fantasy introduces a third category into the opposition between reality and illusion, that of structure. According to Jean Laplanche and Jean-Bertrand Pontalis's reading, a Freudian understanding of fantasy as structure "permits the analysis of the dialectic relationship between fantasy productions, the underlying structures, and the reality of the scene."[23] The soaps' materiality—their fragrance and tactility—thus represents the grounds of a powerful collective imaginary, a territory that is affectively charged and materially present, even as it remains metaphorical.

Map also highlights the fragility of interconnectedness. The global system (so pervasively bound by transnational capital, cultural translations and migration) could easily scatter into exchanges, conflicts or cooperation that are international, intra-national, inter-ethnic or internecine. Such a scattering has both liberatory possibilities (critical interventions in the worlding of the world) and repressive ones (mimicking the "scattered hegemonies" of postmodernism, neo- and postcolonialisms and transnational feminisms identified by Inderpal Grewal and Caren Kaplan).[24] Like *Present Tense, Map* defies the very solidity and boundedness of the international and global systems, where fragility serves to make room for other processes—just as the soaps may dissolve the lines that divide segments of Palestinian territory, so too the continental shifts of viewers might refigure the global landscape. Both of Hatoum's installations thus work critically to deconstruct the border as a site of affect, nationalism and control, but they also make visible the tension in the contemporary organization of space, as well as the precariousness of daily life for Palestinians.

While much of this work derives from Hatoum's own experience of exile and dislocation—from her sensitivity to the tricky transmutations between danger and safety, between homeliness and the uncanny—these kinds of destabilizations also occur, conversely, for those *inside* closely guarded national territories. In this regard, Michal Rovner's work also emphasizes the precariousness of the national/global system, but this time from within Israel. Rovner was born and raised in Israel; her father settled there in the late nineteenth century from Russia, and her mother came to Israel from Germany in 1933. While Rovner moved to New York in 1987, she continues to travel back and forth between Israel, Europe and the United States to produce her works and exhibit them, and lives part of the year on her farm in the Valley of Ayalon, on the road between Tel Aviv and Jerusalem. Her photographic images and site-specific installations open up the question of the ties between geography and Israeli national identity, and specifically of the border as the site of nationalist affect. To do this, she uses various techniques of defamiliarization, techniques that either remove information from the plane of the image or add signs to an already condensed visual field. In the former case, Rovner works through a process she calls *reduction*, photographing and re-photographing an image until only a blurred figure remains against an indeterminate background. The landscapes she depicts are, as a result, both familiar and strange, encapsulating the *Unheimlich*. In her early career, she photographed a farmhouse in Israel starkly against a blurred landscape. The house appears abandoned and isolated, and the image hovers somewhere between suggestion and impression. Her photographic practice makes the relations between figure and ground in her works appear strange and estranged, prying open the image through a kind of deliberate unbelonging, without in any way dismissing the affective charge of the image.

Rovner also defamiliarizes spaces through addition. In 1996, Rovner created two site-specific installations that, to a certain extent, presage her later video *Border* (1997).[25] In the first of these, *Dilemmas: The Good Fence* (1996),[26] she hung 44 flags above an electric fence at the border between Israel and Lebanon. On each flag, Rovner photographed and re-photographed human figures until they formed only a blurry "X" shape. In the second, *Edge-Tower* (1996), two banners (each almost 200 feet long and printed with anonymous figures) stretched from a guard tower across the boundary.

Rovner intended for the installations to engage the curiosity of patrolling soldiers and residents on both sides of the border.[27] This additive strategy resists the naturalization of the border, drawing attention to the fences and watchtowers. By doing this, Rovner asks viewers to pay attention to the border's status as a contested—even enigmatic—message. The temporary installations negate both the illusion of transparency (that the border simply is) and the power relations that produce that transparency.

The piece also stresses the liminality of the border space as a place rather than as a line, where the figures that walk along the border itself do not fall under either side's jurisdiction. Moreover, the reduction of the figures to slim archetypes means that they cannot so easily be coded through the logic of same/difference, self/other. Such a practice highlights by negation the (gendered, racial, ethnic and religious) differences that are produced by the border's inside/outside logic. The figures that walk the border are neither Jewish nor Muslim, neither Israeli nor Lebanese; they are stripped of gendered or racial markers. And yet, their tenuous travel along the border line does not grant them access to the universal category of human rights subject that is the very basis of the international (the space outside both the local and the global system). Rovner's work thus emphasizes the effect on a subjective level of passing from one rights regime to another, and specifically the empty spaces between those regimes where one is caught between states, outside the structures that grant rights-based subjectivity.

The Good Fence and *Edge-Tower* thus highlight the border's status as a site of national affect and mobilize estrangement as an ethical act. The desire for homeliness is not eliminated, but is articulated in relation to an underlying estrangement, and a persistent questioning of the sites of propriety. Irit Rogoff calls this mode of being an "uncanny geography," the experience of the *Unheimlich*, a search for an alternative set of relations in which it is not scientific knowledge or the national categories of the state which determine both belonging and unbelonging, but rather linked sets of political insights, memories, subjectivities, projections of fantasmic desires and great long chains of sliding signifiers.[28]

The logic of reduction Rovner employs also pushes abstract space to its limit: on the ground, these well-laid plans do not actually exist. The border is both a site of unending semiosis (brimming over with the symbols of barbed wire, watchtowers, guards and tanks, walls, sandbags, identification controls, etc.), and is quite literally not there. The border is a "voided entity" in Rogoff's terms, a liminal space of statelessness between two states.[29] This is especially true at the time of the installation, when Israel's occupation of Southern Lebanon meant that this "buffer zone" was neither here nor there, an occupied space that constituted neither entirely the state of Lebanon nor the state of Israel.

If moving populations and shifting borders signal the crisis of both the nation-state and the international order, the artistic practices of Hatoum and Rovner are meant to simultaneously highlight the artificiality of national boundaries (exposing them as contingent formations) and interrupt repressive visions with the lived experience of space and the potent fantasies of homelands. In both cases, the artworks themselves do not so much retrace the lines of other maps, but rather engage in practices that hold in tension the very borders and demarcations of those maps. This is accomplished either through shifts in the medium of map-making or in the addition of contrasting signifying systems. Through the artists' representational practices, the borders between states are rendered unstable, tense or contingent.

Part of the strategy of the works discussed thus far involves a scale shift from national to local imaginaries. Hatoum and Rovner question how modes of subjectivity are either territorially bound or violently deterritorialized, examining the relation between statehood's closely guarded borders and the fantasy of a world without borders. Similarly, artist Emily Jacir comments explicitly on the clashes of scale that are responsible for the very violence of displacement and occupation for Palestinians. Her installation *Memorial to 418 Palestinian Villages That Were Destroyed, Depopulated and Occupied by Israel in 1948* was created in 2001 during the Second Intifada, and during Jacir's residency at PS1. The piece consists of a large refugee tent, raised in the installation space. Embroidered into the inside and outside of the tent, by Jacir along with 140 others she recruited through email and listservs, are the names of the 418 Palestinian villages destroyed, depopulated and occupied by Israel in 1948. Drawing from Walid Khalidi's book, *All that Remains: The Palestinian Villages Occupied and Depopulated by Israel in 1948* (1992), Jacir ties together the 1948 war for Israeli statehood, the expulsion of over 780,000 Palestinians and the production of the "problem of protracted refugee situations."

The installation's refugee tent serves as a recognizable icon for the international human rights community, referencing the United Nations Relief and Works Agency (UNRWA) areas of operation that are the only sites of Palestinian territorialization visible in UN maps of the disputed territory. The tent in Jacir's installation houses not the people who have taken flight, however, but an entire state of villages, histories and locations. Such a device shifts the subject of refugee politics from the populations in states of emergency to the more specific question of statehood. The installation articulates a landscape of belonging and the material connections between villages, people and naming that are somehow lost from the UNRWA's refugee solutions.

The piece is also committed to the practice of naming as an act of remembrance, both in the title of the work (a title that constantly fights forgetting, metaphorical interpretation or a formalist aesthetic) and in the names embroidered with great time and labor into the tent itself. Geographical naming typically represents the desire of ownership, power or dominance; yet, in this case, the names of the villages are excavated from the archive and, rather than imprinted on the terrain on a map, are intricately woven into the fabric of the refugee tent. This act of naming situates the diasporic Palestinian community in both a real historical location and an imagined landscape. The incommensurability between the site of the installation and the lost villages referenced by the work locates collective belonging in a space of memory, even as the imaginary landscape sewn into the tent's fabric becomes the basis for Palestinian political demands.

Staged at the Queens Museum in 2002, as part of the "Queens International" showcase of the diverse national origins of artists living in the New York borough, a second installation of *Memorial to 418 Palestinian Villages That Were Destroyed, Depopulated and Occupied by Israel in 1948* juxtaposed specifically the incommensurable (local, national, global) scales by which Palestinian displacement is constituted. In his careful archaeology of the Queens Museum, John Menick notes that in researching the site, Jacir discovered that the museum had served both as the temporary home of the United Nations in the 1940s (and particularly, on November 29, 1947, when the UN General Assembly Resolution 181 to partition Palestine was passed) and as the site of the 1964/1965 World's Fair. Jacir therefore decided to include in the exhibition of the work two new elements: first, in vitrines on one side of the tent, Jacir displayed reproductions of the photographs taken during the partition meetings in 1947; second, Jacir made available reproductions of pamphlets distributed from the Jordanian Pavilion during the 1964/1965 World's Fair, which contained a poem that detailed the suffering endured by Palestinians as a result of the international community's decision to partition Palestine. These pamphlets became a site of major controversy in New York, and Jacir was forced to modify their contents.[30]

By placing the installation at the site of both the UN's partition of Palestine and the site of the 1964/1965 World's Fair, Jacir brings into contact the overlapping scales of the universal, national, international and transnational, rereading the specific site through those various structuring paradigms. The critical force of Jacir's work here is that it subverts the common understanding of the problem of protracted refugee situations. By placing the tent on the site where the UN General Assembly Resolution partitioned Israel, she notes that the problem of refugees lies in the very national and international system itself that—through its rigid immigration laws, border politics and colonial and neo-colonial formations—proliferates forms of displacement, dispersal and occupation. At the same time, the landscape of the tent's fabric has a double resonance: on the one hand, the state of Palestine is itself a refugee; the tent houses a landscape of villages. On the other hand, the tent refigures contemporary forms of Palestinian belonging in the experience of producing the names, remembering villages, excavating a history and so on. The work also has a transnational dimension because of the various communities that participated in embroidering names into the tent.

The work then critically interrogates each spatial paradigm by putting it into friction with another spatial logic. The problem of displacement is a result of state-making, and yet statehood is exactly what has also been lost. Jacir's articulation of Palestinian experience is located in an impossible place, both displaced into the refugee tent itself and irremediably lost even as it is recovered in the historical practices of Khalidi's text. The tent itself is also a critique of the remedies of internationalism (the structure of the refugee tent sitting atop the space where Partition took place), and at the same time, the fact that an international community of participants stitched the names into the tent highlights new forms of collective articulation on the plane of the international.[31] Finally, the disenfranchisement to which the installation refers produces a committed critique of the universalism of human rights discourse (since even as it enforces a population's rights, it may disenfranchise others), and yet it still connects a global diasporic community through the production of an imaginary landscape, the topography of Palestine transcribed onto the surface of the refugee tent.[32]

These artistic interventions in border spaces reconceptualize the relation between ensconced nationalisms and the global system, and particularly the place of representation in making visible the repressive apparatus of the border (and its negotiation of passing/non-passing). In Hatoum's, Rovner's and Jacir's works, cartographic and topographic imaginaries are contrasted with a subjective (and often collective) experience of place. Such contrasts serve to show how mapping practices aim to divorce representation from social and subjective processes, to present a naturalized and material agreement about territorial boundaries, purportedly removed from questions of the attachment to place, territorialized memories and fantasies of belonging. By reinserting social subjects in the very abstracted landscapes from which they have been violently erased, works like *Present Tense*, *The Good Fence* and *Memorial to 418 Villages* emphasize the inadequacy of interstate solutions to the contestations in Israel/Palestine.

Nevertheless, these works are largely characterized by a deconstructive and critical project—to denaturalize borderlands and highlight the incommensurability between spatial schemas or the tenuousness of the world system. Their representational practices are thus bound to the abstractions by which hegemonic national formations are imagined and imaged. As the next section makes clear, these representational interventions form only a subset of the larger processes of imaging explored in this chapter. While in some cases, the works also open the space for new forms of movement or engagement (for example, Rovner's positing migratory spaces outside the national/global framework), they do not necessarily serve to produce new sites from which claims to statehood may be imagined and articulated.

New World Borders

Border sites especially are founded on complex systems of exchange (both social and capital), and are thus both the product of social relations as well as a catalyst for the staging of conflicts, Manichean oppositions or distancing tactics. As such, artists' interventions in borderlands emphasize that the border is caught up in a whole set of transnational systems. In 1999, Rovner was invited to create a video for the windows in the new wing of the Stedelijk Museum in Amsterdam, entitled *Overhanging*. The installation stretched along two sides of the 130-foot gallery, consisting of 18 floor-to-ceiling sections that could be seen from indoors during the day and from outdoors at night. In it, nondescript shadowy figures shuffled slowly through snow and heat. In one segment, a figure beat the ground until the screen turned red. In 2000, Rovner repeated the installation, which she entitled *Overhang* in this instance, at the Chase Manhattan Bank in

New York City.³³ This would seem to mark the installations as mobile site-specific works, symbols of the globalized art world and of the movement of artworks at the speed of transnational capital. Rovner's statement that the work is about the dynamic interplay between things, however, shifts how one reads the work's own circuit of travel, as well as the movement it displays in the city streets of global urban centers. Particularly in relation to *Overhanging*, Rovner's work seems to critique discourses of globalization themselves, and the collapse of signs, bodies and objects with the movements of transnational capital. The figures in this piece walked slowly across 17 windows of the Chase Manhattan Bank branch at 410 Park Ave. and 55th Street, visible from sunset until 2:00 A.M. for one week in March 2000.³⁴ Their slow movement served as a counterpoint to the perceived speed of exchange under transnational capitalism, signaled by the Chase Manhattan Bank, the site for the installation.

The movement of these two works (like many of her other video installations) implies something of the slow shuffle of migrations: their time virtually geological, punctuated by clusters of more dramatic action. Rovner argues that her video installations are less about movement per se than about "dynamics": "Movement happens from one place to another. Dynamics happen between things. The term refers to their relationship, to the forces that play the game."³⁵ For example, in *Field 1*, a single-channel version of *Overhanging* prepared for the 2000 Biennial Exhibition at the Whitney Museum of American Art in New York, figures continued their slow shuffling across the screen. At the same time, on the front of the screen, a frenetic activity was noticeable. Michael Rush argues that such movement has the effect of aging the video, making it seem grainy or electronically raw. He explains that, to achieve this effect, Rovner overlaid footage of swarms of insects onto the video image, creating "an impression of dense, restless movement."³⁶

Rovner makes use of a process she calls "reduction" in constructing the video images of thin wispy black figures against a white empty background, comparing this representational strategy to a slingshot:

Yes, a slingshot. This is a frequent weapon used now in the conflict in Israel, by the way. Let's say the slingshot is a point of reality. I always start from reality. I record it, and then, little by little, I pull the image away from reality, and then the image gets blurrier. It loses definition. It becomes about something else. It goes here, it goes there. When I release it, it goes through reality and past it, to another place. [...] I am not trying to get away completely from a situation that has to do with reality, but I take it, break it, restructure it—I make another reality.³⁷

The slingshot metaphor powerfully joins the aesthetic strategy of refraction I have been marking throughout this study with the political, historical and cultural context in which experimental media intervene in transnational circuits. These images do not counter the flows of globalization with a local antidote, the markers of localism or nationalism, the specificity of a particular landscape. And yet, the landscape is not simply abstracted either. The multiplicity of figures and their slow trajectory across the windows reference forms of nomadism, tribalism and other trajectories of movement, but these are far from the deterritorialized subjects who travel freely along the routes opened up by the global system. Indeed, the frenzied buzz of insects at the surface of the image might more readily represent the vision of routes in contemporary discourses of globalization than the slow shuffle of people. Their movement points to historically entangled processes of dwelling and travel, which are never experienced in a separate or pure state.

Further, Rovner's play with "pulling the image away from reality" should not be read as an act of deterritorialization, but rather as a complex negotiation with the production of space and familiarity. This has a double resonance in the context of Rovner's own Israeli identity and her critical examination of modes of belonging. First, her defamiliarization of familiar places may be read as an important political project, a questioning of the modes of belonging incumbent upon nationalisms' claim to territory. Second, her use of the metaphor of the slingshot positions her own representational practice alongside the tools of protest for disenfranchised Palestinian youth: the slingshots poised to defend against Israeli tanks. Aligning herself with these signs of protest means that her project of "reduction" resists the contraposition of the freedom of movement with the fixity of national markers. In the spaces of transnational capitalism (New York, Amsterdam), the relation she stages is not between globalism and nationalism, but between the contemporary world system (with its articulation of nations and transnational formations) and these more archaic and enigmatic forms of movement: the patterns of insects, the migration of birds and the shuffle of populations.

Rovner's work provides an index to the national and global imaginaries of the structures of international governance, and particularly to the crisis in securing a stable landscape that adequately controls the flow of bodies across territories. In the introduction to *Routes: Travel and Translation in the Late Twentieth-Century,* Clifford argues that "contemporary capitalism works flexibly, unevenly, both to reinforce and to erase national hegemonies."[38] Thus, the nation-state system and what we have come to call "globalization" both operate, on the one hand, to regulate the increased mobility, flexibility and speed of travel, and on the other, to articulate a series of (symbolic, material, cultural and economic) boundary markers that enforce particular forms of stability and sedimentation. Such a view has broad effects on the vision of the border in the global system. While, as Clifford argues, borders have paradoxically gained centrality in contemporary critical theory, this has often been because they have been viewed as lines of division (between state boundaries and the global system, between "us" and "them" more generally). If, however, the system of nation-states and processes of globalization are sides of the same coin (and may thus trade—albeit often unevenly—in common currencies), the border instead becomes charged with the task of articulating modes of governance at the intersection of the national and the global. Not simply repressive, the border is also immensely productive (of space, situated subjects, culture, social relations, exchange, translation and, ultimately, power).

Emily Jacir's *Change/Exchange* (1998), completed while in residency at the Cité International des Arts in Paris, foregrounds the productive status of the border in terms of the costs it exacts on those who cross. In the work, Jacir began with US$ 100 and traveled to approximately 60 currency exchange offices, exchanging the American dollars for French francs and then back for American dollars, and collecting the receipts (which registered the loss of a small sum in the transaction). She performed the operation until no money remained of the original $100. Menik argues that "it is easy to see in the work's frantic migration, its crisscrossing of borders, the plight of Palestine. And isn't something here lost as well, albeit not as precious as land or human lives, but perhaps as in the case of Palestine, as frustratingly irreclaimable?"[39]

Jacir was born in Bethlehem, but grew up in Saudi Arabia and Italy, and has lived in the United States, Palestine and France. She currently lives in both New York City and Ramallah. Her living between cultures and the mobility she has always experienced profoundly influences her work. Such displacement should not be read, however, through the lens of a new global cosmopolitanism; Jacir's installations themselves make this very clear. *Change/Exchange*, for example, demonstrates several kinds of violence: first, the exploitative relations at the center of international capital's circulation (the loss involved when one is a consumer of transnational capitalism's systems of exchange). More abstractly, the piece demonstrates the violence of abstraction and exchange, of the conversion of value from one system to another. Translation itself is not free, and it entails a loss for the subject crossing a frontier. Finally, the piece expresses metaphorically the violence of loss as one crosses borders, moves from one site to another or between different rights regimes, or crosses from rights-bearing to non-rights-bearing subjects.

Clifford's sense that "travels and contacts are crucial sites for an unfinished modernity" exposes how multiple borders in the world system negotiate fluidity and fixity. For Clifford, cultures are constituted as much by travel and displacement ("routes") as by stasis and fixity ("roots"). Histories of contact, exploitation and collaboration long precede the contemporary forces of globalization, and, while it is likely that the world has become more connected, this does not mean that it is more homogenous or harmonious. Borderlands point specifically to those spaces where fantasies of belonging are thoroughly dependent on the phobic constitution of an alien otherness.

Clifford's routes/roots dialectic thus helps us understand how, at each site of a contested terrain, the relation between fixity and movement is played out both as a discourse of rights (permitting passage) and an articulation of desire (defining belonging). In each space, the relation between routes and roots determines modes of belonging and unbelonging, how individual subjects articulate themselves in relation to group ideals and how fantasies of autochthony inform the spaces through which one travels or lives. This is made clear not only by the jurisdictional apparatus of the border (its systems of checkpoints, permits, taxes and policing), but also in the larger visions of international and transnational forms of governance, and particularly how rights-based claims (whether they be local or global) must tack back and forth between the nation and transnationalism in controlling human populations on the move. In this way, Rovner's and Jacir's works raise the question of translation and exchange, particularly across various scale-making and epistemic fields. Their attention to the dynamic relation between things reinterprets figure/ground relationships; movement does not happen by subjects moving through space, but rather through the dynamic interplay of forces (with their own tempo and patterns), which produces the space of their interaction.

Traveling Subjects

While the representational strategies described thus far have wrestled head-on with the transparency of maps and systems by reproducing them in alien media, artists have also sought to create alternative visions of social space. In an interview, Emily Jacir described how "a lot of my work is not so directly about Palestine, but about me wandering through space and time, and about borders and crossings, and exchanges."[40] Resonating with Said's attention to the "discontinuous states of being" that make up Palestinian experience, Jacir's comment sheds light on the representational strategies that artists employ to articulate common experiences, memories and histories.[41] Throughout this study, I have focused on how video art and experimental documentaries not only expose political realities, but also engage in signifying practices where self-images and subject positions are inscribed in ideology, and where they reproduce specific social imaginaries. In examining such videographic experiments, I have drawn from Teresa de Lauretis's understanding of "processes of imaging," to articulate the prismatic nature of the media under consideration.[42] In the case of the discontinuous states of being that bind diasporic Palestinians in a common experience of exile, imaging's materialization of specific social imaginaries is all the more important, since it makes visible modes of belonging and homeliness that are incomplete, fractured and displaced, except in powerful fantasies of statehood or collectivity. Thus, while prismatic processes serve to inscribe social subjects in space, here they serve to define a (national) space as a potent collective fantasy of home.

Prismatic strategies here specifically express how images serve to articulate desires for statehood from the very tension between critiques of nationalism and demands for territorial recognition, referencing the powerful fantasies of home that go beyond territorial debates by peacemakers and government officials. They rely on sensual and embodied apprehensions of place, even as they represent localities as unfinished projects rather than imagined totalities. The commitment to refraction and diffraction as representational practices rests on two key assumptions: first, it maintains that the border is not simply repressive—not simply the nation's limit point—but also contributes to and entrenches varied nationalisms (at the affective as well as the geopolitical levels). Second, it counters nationalism's mythologies, and particularly the nation's historical narratives that tie collectivities of people, language, culture and territory together as an *a priori*. Nationalism hides the scenes of its own production, and the border is not the site of its negation but the generating force of that naturalization. As such, Clifford argues,

> nationalisms articulate their purportedly homogeneous times and spaces selectively, in relation to new transnational flows and cultural forms, both dominant and subaltern. The diasporic and hybrid identities produced by these movements can be both restrictive and liberating. They stitch together language, traditions and places in coercive and creative ways, articulating embattled homelands, powers of memory, styles of transgression, or ambiguous relations to national and transnational structures.[43]

The homogeneous spatial and temporal framework of the nation thus masks a field of contestations, and imaging processes struggle to hold open this multiplicity in the face of the strong pull of such seamless and smooth spatial categories as nation or community.

Prismatic media here also convey the imaginative dimensions of imaging, the manner in which images articulate meaning and desire for viewing subjects, relying on unconscious productions—memory and fantasy—to articulate an imagined and still politically and communally salient image of home. In this regard, Laplanche and Pontalis's understanding of fantasy is again indicative:

> Fantasy [...] is not the object of desire, but its setting. In fantasy, the subject does not pursue the object or its sign: he appears caught up himself in the sequence of images. He forms no representation of the desired object, but is himself represented as participating in the scene although, in the earliest forms of fantasy, he cannot be assigned any fixed place in it [...]. As a result, the subject, although always present in the fantasy, may be so in a desubjectivized form, that is to say, in the very syntax of the sequence in question.[44]

Collective articulations of belonging must deploy fantasy in this way to assert a bounded and territorialized image of cultural cohesion (Palestine as a committed imaginary), while simultaneously critiquing ethnic or religious nationalisms, the violence of state power and its concomitant exclusions. The notion that fantasy is the ground of desire rather than its object shifts the cardinal points on which belonging is mapped. Not located in specific objects (a line in the sand, the heritage of certain cultural traditions or codes), fantasies of home involve a setting where disparate personal and collective experiences might be staged. As the analysis of the videos that follows should make clear, it is far less the territorial negotiations that resonate for the artists, those they represent and those who view their images, than it is the sites of memory, the recollection of sights, smells and tastes and the appeal to common experiences (even the common experience of exile and the communal longing for Palestinian statehood). Prismatic media thus stage a ground for the figuration of a collective fantasy of home, while challenging the repressive apparatuses of state power that are the very cause of displacement and exile.

Prismatic strategies also highlight the commitment within feminist critiques of nationalism to betweenness. Alarcón, Kaplan and Moallem argue that the space *between* "woman" and "nation" is the space where we can deconstruct these totalizing categories to render them "more historically nuanced and accountable to politics." For the authors, the space of betweenness refuses the priority both of feminism over nationalism (as in the discourses of global feminism) and of nation over woman (in nationalist discourse). Instead, between signals "a peculiar form of temporality, a 'suspended moment,' a moment of simultaneity and mutual inclusiveness or the spatiotemporal interval of *différance*."[45] The active form of imaging is meant to articulate the struggle for culture, staged across different territorial scales and by differently situated subjects, exposing rather than resolving Said's emphasis on discontinuous states of being. Jacir's video and photographic works largely focus on the liminal zones in her transition from one state to another. Shooting as she walks through checkpoints, Jacir visualizes space not as an abstraction or an *a priori*, but as a practiced place. This is a strikingly different strategy from that of Hatoum's and Rovner's works discussed above, which seek to pull apart repressive cartographic imaginaries on a conceptual level. Jacir's focus on an embodied and mobile camera instead not only creates a vision of space as the product of social exchanges, but also disrupts the field of those relations by passing through it. A central strategy for enacting these other spaces is the use of an embodied camera angle, tying tightly together the embodied experience of specific charged and contested spaces with the military, political and economic strategies by which certain marked bodies gain (or are denied) the right of passage in space. These artworks contrast the bird's eye view of well-laid plans with the more limited, shifting and mobile perspective of the traveling subject. This section considers such works by Emily Jacir, along with those of Michal Rovner, Mona Hatoum and Akram Zaatari, and examines how they put into motion the border's repressive apparatus and, in doing so, expose its productive as well as repressive functions. It is not simply that the border denies rights of entry; the border also engenders militarized and national masculinities (in the figure of the border guard, for example), or marks certain bodies as suspect or alien through pat-down procedures.

The vision of the traveling subject is coincident with Henri Lefebvre's writings on the production of social space. For Lefebvre, production (in its broadest social sense) imposes a temporal and spatial order onto a set of related operations. This chain of activities and exchanges carries with it a whole series of materials ("stone, wood, bone, leather, etc.") and *matériel* ("tools, arms, language, instructions and agendas") caught up in the productive process.[46] Social space is thus both the result of a series of past actions and what "permits fresh actions to occur, while suggesting others and prohibiting yet others."[47] Space thus results from social practices— the social relations of movement through a public square, for example, or the designations of usefulness by which whole populations move through thoroughfares at given times of the day—and does not preexist them. Such a view allows us to see how Jacir and others use video to make visible not simply the border's topography, but also its (repetitive and repressive) practices. These social relations are productive not of the limit point of the nation-state, but of the state itself in its dialogical relation with other states, on the one hand, and the global system, on the other. In these artist videos, the border is less a line than a machine, producing national and global spaces through its military artillery, system of verifications, identifications and regulation of the movement of people and goods. It is an active space of emergence and repression, of the regulation of trade routes and the negotiation of cultural roots.

Jacir's use of the time-based medium of video serves to make visible how the movement of bodies across such militarized borders produces space. In carrying a camera through a contested landscape, Jacir makes the viewer constantly aware of her visual trespass into an occupied terrain. The viewer senses her body in space, her location secured through the camera's point of view, even as the distinctions between one location and another become indeterminate or uncoded. The viewer is also trapped in the "real time" tempo of the tape's progression, the slow progress through border zones. This is especially true of *Crossing Surda (a record of going to and from work)* (2002), a two-channel installation project that records Jacir's crossing through a checkpoint every day in her travel to and from Birzeit University and her home in Ramallah. She comments that the production of the piece came to her from the outside, from her own experience of crossing the checkpoint:

> I was simply walking without intending to do an "art piece." I was walking across this checkpoint every day to get to Birzeit University from my home, and I just wanted a recording of it for myself. And then I had this horrible experience with the Israeli soldiers when they saw me filming, they held me at gunpoint for three hours, they confiscated my tape, they threw my passport in the mud [...]. When I went home, I thought we need to have a record of this, we must have a record of this. Then I cut a hole in my bag and filmed my daily commute to work for eight days. This came directly from this horrible experience.[48]

The resulting installation consists of two screens: a large 132-minute projection on the back wall of a darkened installation room and a 30-minute video on a monitor in the corner opposite the projection. The projection is dizzying, the vision jolting. A car door opens, and Jacir walks out, weaving between cars stopped at the checkpoint. Because the camera is in Jacir's bag, it is low to the ground, swaying as she walks. The camera moves in and out of focus as it captures the road ahead in real time (Figure 3.2).

On the soundtrack, one hears the hum of stopped trucks, car horns and people shouting. There is never a clear view of the road because cars, taxis and a mass of legs block the view. Jacir advances through the checkpoint, the camera pointing to the right and left. As Jacir emerges from the stopped cars, she captures a large Israeli tank in the background. Sometimes the day is clear and bright, and the mass of people move here and there, between

Figure 3.2   Emily Jacir, *Crossing Surda (a record of going to and from work)* (2002).
Two-channel video installation, with text. Dimensions variable. © Emily Jacir.
Courtesy of Alexander and Bonin, New York

stopped cars. Other days, the rain muddies the road, and people trudge
through the dirt. In one scene, the camera lens itself is wet with raindrops,
obscuring the view of the street ahead. Scattered along the side of the road
are markers of the border zone: an Israeli flag painted on a large cement
wall and tanks stopped by the side of the road.

The monitor-based video installed in the adjacent corner also contains
a mobile and embodied camera, but its vision of the checkpoint is of a
different order. The tape is slowed down, advancing at an oneiric pace.
The horizon line is high in the frame; the image captures the long dirt
road ahead and, toward the top of the screen, a sign written in Arabic.
Two Israeli soldiers stand near the sign in the top right-hand corner of the
image. The sun (which is not in the frame) casts two beams that divide
the screen into four images: the sky in the top left-hand corner, the dirt
road in the center images and the soldiers and checkpoint in the top right
corner. As Jacir advances, one of the soldiers moves forward. They are both
carrying prominent semi-automatic weapons. One soldier stands at the
sign, his rifle at eye level. The other advances, his weapon pointed at a
young man walking toward the checkpoint. Jacir stands between these two
figures, her camera moving back and forth as they advance toward each
other. In another section of the video, the camera moves right up to the
side of an Israeli tank and slowly scans the mud-caked wheels, moving in

and out of focus as the slowed tempo of the tape doubles the image over and over again. As she passes the tank, an Israeli soldier stares at her, his gun held close to his chest. In the bottom of the frame, the viewer sees Jacir's shadow, extending across the dirt path. The soldier continues to look at Jacir as she passes, staring almost directly into the camera.

In the whole of the installation, the viewer feels carried along through the border space and across the checkpoint.[49] The camera's unstable vantage point, as well as the collapsed horizons or long stretches of road, produce the border space as a lived reality, one whose representations are obtained with a great deal of risk for the artist. The viewer is also sandwiched narrowly between the two screens, replicating in their doubled vision the multiple internal checkpoints through which Palestinians must travel, even within the West Bank. The artwork *Crossing Surda (a record of going to and from work)* thus has both a documentary and a performative function. While the installation is more resilient and open to a broader viewing public than her recording of her passage across the checkpoint, the action of crossing the checkpoint (and recording her passage) is also important. The video not only comments on the landscape of signs that combine to form a veritable syntax of repression, but also records an engagement and—through the embodied intimacy of the video's perspective—reenacts the border's political order. In passing through the checkpoint, Jacir demonstrates the repressive and productive function of the border in relation to her specific body. In taping the encounter, however, she challenges the discourses of security, regulation and control that govern the border spaces for Israeli soldiers. The viewer is made aware that the fractured and displaced spaces through which Palestinians must cross on a daily basis are not abstract but material, reenacted in the micro-operations of power between Israeli soldiers and Palestinians traveling to and from work.

It is important also to see how *Crossing Surda (a record of going to and from work)*, as it travels through the global art system, inserts the militarized border into the seamless circuits of the art market. The piece's exhibition in the traveling exhibit *Made in Palestine* (originally staged at the Houston Museum in Texas in 2003, followed by the *Global Feminisms* exhibit at the Brooklyn Museum in 2007, the Guggenheim Museum in 2009, and several international biennales) may both deterritorialize the border and reenact it as a friction point in the global circulation of culture. Indeed if, as Lavie and Swedenburg argue, "the Israeli center keeps usurping, as its own frontier, the border zones between European and Arab, Israeli and Palestinian, and Ashkenazi and Mizrahi," the very circulation of Jacir's work implicates broader audiences in this border that crosses over and into, and usurps, transnational sites of cultural community.[50]

Akram Zaatari's *This Day* (2003) similarly highlights the intimate relation between spatial and temporal practices in its complex visualization
of contemporary Beirut. Unlike Jacir, Zaatari's video was created during
a time of relative peace and stability in Lebanon, reflecting back on the
historical effect of the Lebanese Civil War, the Israeli air strikes he witnessed as a teenager in Beirut and the occupation of Southern Lebanon
by Israel. Zaatari's oeuvre seeks to make connections between several historical eras (the colonial period, the Lebanese Civil War and the present
moment), excavating the Lebanese archives (both private and public) to
shed light on alternative historical narratives and experiences. His work is
concerned with the traces of Lebanon's difficult history in the present, but
he ties his archival practices to the contemporary moment—as, for example, when *This Day* turns from contemporary Beirut to Amman, Jordan,
during the Israeli invasion of the West Bank in 2001–2002.[51] While these
differences mark a distinction between the artistic practices of Jacir and
Zaatari, their works are also united, not only by the question of Palestine
that ties together the state of emergency in the Occupied Territories and the
protracted civil war in Lebanon, but also by the mass of internalized borders that constitute daily life in Beirut or Ramallah, as well as by the effect
of the protracted refugee crisis in the region. Both Jacir's and Zaatari's artistic strategies actively seek to represent communities and collective visions
of history from below, territorializing those visions by locating them in
city streets, in the wide expanses of the desert or within the discontinuous
spaces of exile.

Zaatari's *This Day* also highlights the intimate relation between spatial and temporal practices in its complex visualization of contemporary
Beirut. In the second part of the video, where he moves from a consideration of the desert as a site of Arab culture to present-day Beirut, Zaatari
passes from a sweeping pan across the city to a series of video stills taken
from the inside of a moving car. In the former scene, the soundtrack is
drawn from the radio in the 1980s, during the time of the air strikes
on Beirut. The tape begins with an ABBA song, followed by the radio
announcer listing a series of warnings regarding locations in and around
Beirut: the surrounding of the Kuwaiti Embassy, the National Stadium,
Sabra, Chatila, Bir Hassan and others. In the latter scene, Zaatari points out
these same landmarks around Beirut. The viewer sees underpasses, busy
roads, stoplights, the city skyline, hotels and office towers as the camera
moves through the city. The scene is both photographic and videographic,
presenting a series of video stills that move the viewer through the city
haltingly. The movement resembles more closely time-lapse photography
than video, shuttling the viewer through a fractured, stop-and-start voyage
across Beirut. As if to reinforce the tension between stillness and movement

(there is no movement in a frame, only across the sequence of frames), Zaatari includes stills of a succession of traffic lights, flashing from red to green as the viewer moves from one image to the next. This complex formal experimentation highlights how the protracted civil war micro-regulated movement and timing across space or between places. Like in Jacir's *Crossing Surda (a record of going to and from work)*, here the relation between fixity and movement is constantly being negotiated at each site of a weighted landscape, although in 2003 Zaatari is able to travel through a city in the process of reconstruction and stabilization. Such a staging of space serves to create a series of analogies between the 1980s and the contemporary moment, to see the continuing traces of the protracted civil war not only in archival photographs and radio broadcasts, but also in the landscape of the city itself.[52]

In her consideration of borders, Rogoff argues that a heavily armored and barricaded border contains a paradox: on the one hand, it is "a border whose integrity must be kept at all costs, and those who attempt to pierce or contravene it pay a bitter price."[53] Contested borders are in this case overdetermined with guards, patrols, security fences and surveillance technologies. On the other hand, this border "is not really there, it is the suspension of both the entities which have been kept apart and as such it is a voided entity."[54] The border thus signals both a complex repressive apparatus and a failure of stabilization. In its ideal form, the border itself would instantiate rights of passage or blockades.

Rogoff is also keenly aware that this overdetermination of the border has a psychic dimension. She argues that "links are set up between the border as a psychically internalized concept of boundaries crossed and repressions breached and the external traces of a containment which holds one in, which does not allow for that very breach."[55] Given this psychic resonance, it is no coincidence that Freud describes the act of resistance in analysis with the difficult progress of advancing troops in times of war.[56] Similarly, we view Beirut in 1982 through the keen archival impulse of Zaatari as a young teenage boy who seeks to manage his fascination and fear during the air raids. The viewer's travel through the archive of Zaatari's personal photo albums exposes not only the visible evidence of war, but also the affective charge of making visible the shifting landscape. In her staging of the affectively charged encounters of the system of checkpoints in her work, Jacir likewise draws out the force of the border in subjective and (national) collective imaginaries, the charge of the soldiers' actions and her own position as a "foreign body." She is thus recording not only an encounter and exchange, but also the affective charge of the nation being produced *through* the contested territory, and indeed through a phobic (xenophobic even) reaction to her very passing through the liminal site of the checkpoint. Her act of taping the border not only records its repressive apparatus, but also opens up a path for trespass. For Zaatari, the tension between the border's overdetermination and its invisibility is especially marked by the ghostly presence of the Lebanese civil war in Beirut in 2003. In this case the border is and is no longer there.

The affective stakes of this social relation are the very subject of Mona Hatoum's *Corps étranger* (1994). The work, originally installed at the Centre Pompidou in Paris in 1994, relied on two medical imaging processes, endoscopy and colonoscopy, which both use fiber optic cameras (passed either through the throat or the anus) to inspect the digestive system. The resulting images were projected onto a large disc on the floor of the installation space: the movement through the body, teeth, cilia, the throat cavity and the intestines. Above the floor, Hatoum installed a cylindrical wall with two small apertures through which the viewer entered the installation. The viewer stood against the wall, at the perimeter of the image. Movement was severely restricted, and viewers engaged not only with the screen, but also with other viewers who blocked exits and entrances, and with the soundtrack in the space—a track of Hatoum's own breath and heartbeat that filled the narrow installation space (Figure 3.3).

The work clearly raises the semiotic slippage between strange and stranger, and the gendered dynamics of this elision in the body and the body politic. There are many foreign bodies in this work: first, the penetrative camera, what Hatoum calls "the ultimate in the invasion of one's boundaries," is a foreign body inside Hatoum, subjecting her body to inspection. Also, though, the resulting image is irreducibly foreign, situating the viewer at the edge of a sinking trajectory through a long body tunnel. While *Corps étranger* is readily viewed politically as a commentary on racism and xenophobia in European capitals (and in the art world also), the image's indeterminacy fights a simple resolution of the shifting nodal points of alienness. Hatoum is clearly visualizing a body that is utterly alien, but at the same time, the insides of the body cannot evoke the gendered, racial and ethnic markers by which difference is produced and upheld. Since this body is both completely alien and completely indeterminate, it can never be reduced to the self/other relations that form the basis of xenophobic attitudes and indeed of the very imaginary that constructs the national body politic.

Hatoum argues that this work resulted from her observation of the system of surveillance technologies in London (a response, importantly, to the threat of terrorist acts by the IRA). The work repeats the violence of that panoptic gaze with a vengeance, but it also paradoxically makes visible the object of dread in the center of an institution for public culture in Paris. Since the work is videographic, it demonstrates the intrusion of the gaze

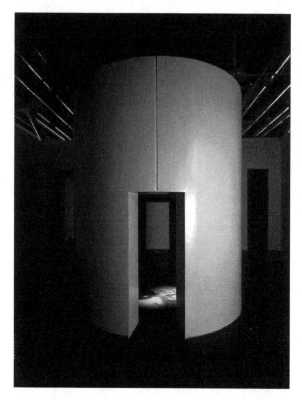

Figure 3.3   Mona Hatoum, *Corps étranger* (1994). Video installation with cylindrical wooden structure, video projector, player, amplifier and four speakers. 137 13/16 × 118 1/8 × 118 1/8 in. Photo: Philippe Migeat. Courtesy Centre Pompidou, Paris and the White Cube Gallery

into the body and at the same time a whole alien topography that becomes the other body. Like Jacir, Hatoum is also seeking to activate and make visible the affective force of the familiar and the strange. The threat of the work itself is clearly visible in an interview Hatoum gave with John Tusa at the BBC:

> *Tusa*: So is it also trying to de-mythologize our fear and our ignorance of the body?
> *Hatoum*: To activate those fears and ...
> *Tusa*: To get rid of them?
> *Hatoum*: To question them.
> *Tusa*: Yes to ...
> *Hatoum*: To question all these things yes, to question them, yeah.[57]

While Tusa is clearly committed to managing the uncanny affect the work produces, Hatoum prevents him from taming the work's affective charge. For Hatoum, *Corps étranger* lays bare the foreigner's body, but the resulting image also functions as an uncanny eye, looking back at the viewer from the space of its most violating inspection. The body is objectified and still objectifies the viewer; the screen is both a map and an eye. As the camera travels throughout the channels of the body, it creates a map of the human form from the inside, moving further and further into the colon, for example, or down the throat. And yet, even as the camera offers a sadistic and scopophilic gaze taken to the *n*th degree, it cannot simply objectify the body for the viewer. Partly, this is because the image's scale and the installation's staging of proximity prompt the viewer to feel under the gaze of the hole being presented, rather than in the space of a privileged viewpoint.

Hatoum's installation thus reverses (albeit ambiguously and only momentarily) the terms of surveillance and inspection normally directed against the foreign body, seen as trespassing into the space of national identity. *Corps étranger* might then serve as a tool for reading the potential subversion that Jacir's and Hatoum's works perform. This is especially the case for Jacir's *Crossing Surda (a record of going to and from work),* where her camera looks back even as she is most vulnerable to inspection. Partly, the subversion of the border systems stems from making visible its repressive operations, but it also emanates from the very vantage point of the embodied subject to challenge the spatial regimes that the border secures.

In both the production of the videos and in their installation, they are thus much less a document of borderlands than an active production (and thus reiteration or rearticulation) of those sites. Artwork is always conceived as a social interstice: it stages the articulation between social relations and spatial practices in its very representations. The tropes of this production—a mobile embodied camera, the attention as much to the figuration of time as of space and a commitment to the question of value (the production of the image for exchange, the translation of subjects and objects as they move between discursive and spatial frameworks)—pry open the intimate relation between the documentary prerogative (evidencing an *a priori* notion of space) and forms of nationalism (in this case, Israel's commitment to a territorial articulation). In the following section, I will examine further the spatial imaginaries that the videos articulate, and specifically their commitment to articulations of statehood, even as they are refracted through conditions of displacement, alienation, repression and loss.

Imaging a Prismatic Collectivity

How might one imagine and represent the desire for statehood not from the location of culture or nation, but from the discontinuous states of being that constitute the lived experience of Palestinians around the world? In *Routes*, Clifford finds a provisional solution to culture's "mixed blessings" by locating displacement at the heart of culture, rather than in its constitutive outside, arguing that "[p]ractices of displacement might emerge as *constitutive* of cultural meanings rather than as their simple transfer or extension."[58] The spatial metaphors of this insight are especially suited to the committed articulations of belonging from positions of exile, and thus to the demands of culture *within* discontinuous states. Many of the videos accomplish this through a search for sites that deconstruct the national/global opposition, but stay committed to the intimate relation between social and spatial practices.

Zaatari's *This Day*, for instance, illuminates a complex set of views of the desert as the site of a pre-national mode of Arab belonging in West Asia. Zaatari's process, in this work and others, involves mining photographic, audio and artifactual archives to reveal the staging of a particular vision of culture as "authentic" (and authentically documented). The artwork is divided into three parts: the second and third sections relate to the contemporary conflict in West Asia between Israel and its neighbors, and within the Occupied Territory; the first involves a historical and archival analysis of the Syrian Desert and Bedouin life. As a guide, Zaatari uses *The Bedouins and the Desert* (1995), a text by the Orientalist scholar Jibrail S. Jabdur, who studied and photographed Bedouin life. *This Day*'s first section is presented as a quest narrative, exploring, on the one hand, the photographic evidence gathered by Jabdur, and on the other, Zaatari's own travel through the desert in search of those people captured in Jabdur's images.

The travel through the desert is staged in two different manners. At first, Zaatari shoots from the back seat of a car, including in the frame the front windshield (which itself frames the desert scene before the viewer) and the reflection of the driver in the rearview mirror. Toward the end, Zaatari shoots out the side window, producing a long panoramic view of the desert. In each, Zaatari reveals multiple representations of the landscape: when the camera is recording the space ahead, the video more properly locates the desert as the location for the journey, the object that drives the narrative forward; when the camera points out the side of the car, the landscape is transformed into a panorama, a flattened image.

The first movement through the desert is informed largely by the search for Abu Saad, a camel herder. Norma Jabdur, Jibrail Jabdur's granddaughter, makes clear the object of this quest: her grandfather often photographed camels as a symbol of the desert, which she sees as the whole context of Arab civilization. The quest to make the camels visible becomes symbolic of the desire to represent the desert. The video, however, labors over their representation. In one section entitled "Waiting for Bassel to Imitate the Voice of the Camel," a young boy sits on a camel, looking shyly down and away from the camera. A man holds a microphone in the corner of the screen and the boy looks up tentatively. People offscreen encourage him, "Just do it!"; "Bassel, there are no more girls here. Don't be shy!" Bassel looks down, laughing uncomfortably, but he won't imitate the camel's voice. The video records this scene for several minutes, waiting as those around encourage Bassel to make the sound. At another point, as they are driving through the desert, Zaatari must choose between recording the camels and risk getting trapped in the sand. In each case, the symbolization itself is a vexed process, exposed as a complicated series of negotiations and enticements.

At the end of the segment, the camera is pointed out the side of the car. The foreground's blurred landscape gives way to the desert topography clearly visible in the background. A truck occasionally passes by in the rightmost lane, obscuring the view. Every few seconds, Zaatari places a figure from Jabdur's book into the landscape: for example, the image of a Bedouin woman or a camel flashes for a second unnaturally in the landscape. Over the unfolding scene, Norma Jabdur gives an account of her grandfather's research:

> He believes that Arabic culture stems from the Bedouin life and that they are linked to understanding something that is vanishing, the source of this culture, because as they vanish then also will the understanding. You have a living lens to understanding what the sources of a culture is [sic], and they are what remains of the Bedouins, and their ways.... And their ways, their way of life, their way of speaking. Their mores are the basis of Arab civilization. And there's something whole and noble to them.

The camera stops and rewinds the footage backward, scanning the desert in reverse. Following this, Zaatari creates a montage consisting of a black-and-white image of two women artificially superimposed on a video still of the desert landscape. Norma Jabdur explains that the photographs themselves are a reconstruction of her grandfather's impression of Bedouin life. The two women in the photograph turn out to be not Bedouin women at all, but Norma Jabdur's grandmother and aunt Hoda, dressed up in the clothes of Sheikh Shaalan's wife. Norma Jabdur explains, "they look like they're children trying on clothes and if you don't know them you have no idea that that's what it is."

Zaatari's experimentation with the images in Jabdur's text (as well as his own tapes) makes clear that images of the desert are not so easily decoded; their transparency is often cast into doubt. In the final moments of the segment, Zaatari freezes the image of the landscape and superimposes the image of Jibrail Jabdur's wife and niece on the desert landscape. The color digital still of the landscape shot by Zaatari then fades into the desert images taken by Jabdur himself. Jabdur's photographs of the desert, however, do not become more authentic representations than Zaatari's. Instead, Zaatari plays with figure-ground relations in Jabdur's photographs: the images of the landscape—dotted with camels and rocky protrusions—become the background on which rest cut-outs of all the figures that appear in Jabdur's text. Bedouins, camels, a man on horseback, a British Orientalist whose jeep has broken down, a young woman balancing a clay jug on her head and Jabdur's own wife and niece dressed as Bedouin women all slide across the screen as in a magic lantern show. The figures move laterally across the flat surface of the foreground, and the figure-ground relations appear artificial and detached (Figure 3.4).

This segment complicates the desert's role in the imaginary of Jabdur, Orientalists, contemporary scholars and Zaatari himself. Rather than

Figure 3.4   Akram Zaatari, *Desert Panorama* (2002). Video. 9 min. Based on photographs by Manoug and Gibrail Jabbur, taken in the Syrian Desert in the 1950s. Courtesy of the artist and Sfeir-Semler Gallery, Beirut and Hamburg

constituting a space of liberation, an unscripted place in the spatial politics of contested borders, the desert is caught up in the complex desire for origin stories, for wholeness, on which nationalism itself rests. The video's experimentation also undermines a too-quick celebration of nomadism as resisting territorialized identities. Zaatari visibly disrupts the archive, unmooring figures from their backgrounds, and stitching the photographs together into an unending panorama. The viewer is not sure which figures are matched to their background, and indeed at one point a cut-out of a camel travels over its own image in the frame. The desert is a potent fantasy for both Jabdur and Zaatari that, far from denying its importance, rather signals its central role in setting the stage for a form of collective desire that ties belonging to place and to the figures that are bound to that place, even if they are available only in representation.

Jacir's *from Texas with love* (2002) also stages the complex relations between desire and the space of the desert, signaling more forcefully the displacements made necessary by the state of the Occupied Territories. While in residency in Marfa, Texas, in 2002, Jacir was struck by the long stretches of highway she could travel on for miles on end. She notes, "I was in West Texas for a residency, and the piece was about being in a place so incredible and beautiful and being able to drive freely and to listen to music, and at the same time wanting to cry, because this cannot happen back home."[59] In response, she interviewed Palestinians around the world and asked them what songs they would listen to if they could travel 50 miles without being stopped or blocked by checkpoints and borders. The 51 songs on the list included Arab and American pop songs, national anthems and other songs. For the final installation of the work, Jacir screened the video on a small monitor, which displayed the scenery she shot from her car window as she drove for one hour in Texas without stopping. From a set of headphones, the visitor can listen to all 51 requested songs. The work thus highlights vividly the displacement even of the fantasy of unimpeded movement, the gap between the stretch of road in Marfa, Texas, and the mass of internal barriers that prohibit free movement for Palestinians in the West Bank and Gaza Strip. Jacir thus rematerializes landscape as the site of intense negotiations of social space.

Jacir's and Zaatari's imaging processes mediate social relations in space, creating actions that both articulate a critique of the abstractions of various nationalisms and simultaneously make fierce demands for statehood.[60] Both Zaatari and Jacir approach the desert as a space for the articulation of a (collective and individual) desire to locate Palestinian belonging and the unique sources of Arab culture. At the same time, however, the multiple photographs, footage, soundtracks, interviews and viewing positions acknowledge that the desert is a space of fantasy. The desert does not become solid, uncontested, a romanticized space of liberation. Instead, the very demands of cultural rootedness are made visible, even as their vexed eclipsing of routes is raised. Zaatari's desert is the space of a kind of historical longing, signaled by Jabdur's photographs but also by Zaatari's own quest to uncover the social life that produced that representational practice. For Jacir, the desert is the site of a displacement, since she shoots not in West Asia but in Texas, where the desert becomes quite literally a fantasy.

To say the desert is a fantasy is, of course, not to deny its importance or reality. In Jacqueline Rose's *States of Fantasy*, where she recuperates fantasy as important to the political understandings of statehood, she argues rather, "like blood, fantasy is thicker than water, all too solid—*contra* another of fantasy's more familiar glosses as ungrounded supposition, lacking in foundation, not solid *enough*."[61] If fantasy is the *mise-en-scène* of desire, rather than its object, then the desert takes on a different resonance in the representational practices of Zaatari and Jacir. Not the totalizing fiction against which artists defied mapping practices (which I discussed above in relation to Hatoum's *Present Tense* and Jacir's *Memorial to 418 Villages*), the desert becomes the setting of desire rather than its object. It does not take on the mystical quality of the thing that defines culture, that produces roots without acknowledging routes. In other words, the desert is the location from which collective modes of belonging might be imagined. In this view, statehood has less the character of an object than of a medium or vehicle. The effect on representational practices is clear: they become the medium for the articulation of desire—they spatialize it *in relation* to the complex images of the desert. In all cases, the very space represented is the space of displacement and desire: a discontinuous state *from which* articulations of belonging (and longing) are formed.

In Laplanche and Pontalis's definition, the subject cannot be assigned a fixed place in the fantasy; she or he is in fact "caught up in the sequence of images." This description describes succinctly the relation between the displaced subject and the desert: neither Jacir nor Zaatari actually figures in the frame of the image directly. Thus, in *from Texas with love*, the road appears, unfolding before the viewer. Jacir is the producer of the images, but the work actually displaces both the space represented and the driver himself or herself. The road in Texas stands in for both the desire for unimpeded movement, the freedom of travel by Palestinians, and the wish that such an open vista might be located in Palestine, elsewhere than where she is taping. Further, her own space at the wheel is a proxy for a whole series of impossible positions, signaled by the songs chosen by Palestinians who, in fact, cannot take up Jacir's position. The viewer is thus caught in the spaces between the articulation of the desire and its (forestalled) satisfaction. It is precisely this space that makes clear Palestinians' experiences of displacement and the necessity of binding together this disparate and diasporic community in images that inscribe the experience of exile at the heart of fantasies of home. This contradictory representational practice, which makes clear how exiled social subjects are bound together by "memory, expectations, decisions, pain and desire," exemplifies what I have been describing specifically as a process of prismatic mediation, a mode of imaging where subjects are tied to images and inscribed in space in order to make claims for statehood while still acknowledging the routes (the complex histories of "travel and translation," in Clifford's terms) that inform all claims to rootedness.[62]

The viewer also becomes caught up in *This Day*'s process of instating through the montage of figures, detached from the ground and floating through an endless but constructed panorama of the desert. Zaatari's detachment of the figures from the ground of the desert unmoors the viewer's space from the field of vision, positioning the subject—through a strategy of refraction—in a fantastical space, a space of fantasy. Through such refraction, Zaatari's video, along with the works of Jacir, Hatoum and Rovner, instate new visions of collective belonging from the very tenuous states that situate and shape the artists as individual and collective subjects. Their commitment to representation is not simply a commentary on the geopolitical realities of border politics in West Asia; their works produce specific spatializations and locate subjectivity within those representations, and within representation itself more generally. Less governed by evidentiary modes than by imaging practices, these videographic works articulate subjectivity and statehood from a position that is, to return to Said's formulation, discontinuous—discontinuous but still committed, inflected by a desire that is constitutive of social space, and of one's emplacement in it.

These modes of representation are governed by systems of exchange that confront directly the presumptions of globalization.[63] The specificity of the subject's position *in* and *as* representation raises also the question of what kinds of exchanges, translations and transformations are productive of social space (at both the local and global levels). Jacir's work in particular seeks to resist the modes of exchange by which the current global system is figured, the seamlessness of transnational capitalism. For example, *from Texas with love* is organized, as its title suggests, through the logic of a gift. Jacir offers her visualization of the Texan desert to Palestinians around the world. Of course, Jacir is well aware that the freedom of movement cannot be offered but only experienced. *from Texas with love* thus represents the impossibility of representing movement for another body. Both the necessity and the inadequacy of the notion of proxy are at stake in the work; she cannot stand for those she seeks to represent. The work embodies a keenly aware slippage between two forms of representation—*Vertreten* and *Darstellen*, proxy and portrait—to articulate the impossibility of her project and to question its adequacy in the transaction of social space.

* * *

I would like to end by examining another of Jacir's works that explores modes of exchange, a photographic installation entitled *Where We Come From*, exhibited in Palestine in 2002 and New York in 2003, and finally at the Istanbul Biennial that same year. For the project, Jacir asked Palestinians living in Palestine and around the world, "If I could do something for you, anywhere in Palestine, what would it be?" She then used her American passport to cross checkpoints and fulfill the desires of people who could not (and still cannot) gain access to those areas of Palestinian territory. In text, photography and video, the exhibition documents the requests as well as her attempts to fulfill them. One person requests that she visit his mother, another that she play soccer with a Palestinian child in Haifa and another that she put flowers on a grave in Jerusalem. The work attempts to make visible the proliferation of checkpoints, borders and boundaries throughout the Palestinian territory, not by making them visible directly, but by making visible their effects on Palestinian community and culture. It is important to note also that the work itself would be impossible to recreate in the contemporary moment, due to the construction of the separation or Apartheid wall, the Israeli-imposed separation of Gaza, the denial of entry to Palestinians even with foreign passports and tighter Israeli restrictions more generally (Figure 3.5).

Figure 3.5 Emily Jacir, *Where We Come From* (2001–2003). Detail (*Rizek*). American passport, 30 texts, 32 c-prints and 1 video. Text (*Rizek*): 9 ½ × 11 ½ in. Each photo (*Rizek*): 5 × 7 in. Photo: Bill Orcutt. © Emily Jacir. Courtesy of Alexander and Bonin, New York

The images she takes to fulfill the gathered wishes all embody a singular point of view or sharp perspective. For example, to fulfill the wish "Go to Bayt Lahia and bring me a photo of my family, especially my brother's kids," she exhibits four images. In one, a photograph of the nephew is taken as he passes almost immediately in front of her. She is thus looking down at him, catching him walking as he passes by. The viewer becomes immediately aware of Jacir's position in the field of the image. At the same time, Jacir herself often appears in the images in a deflected manner, either as a shadow cast into the frame, as a hand in the image or in silhouette from behind. The ambiguity of her own subject position is meant to show the ambivalence of her position in relation to the parameters of the project. The representational strategy is meant to highlight the impossibility of its fulfillment, the nonsensical nature of her *representing* another's wish, much less fulfilling it.

This failure in the work is also the success of the work, its constructive dimension. In making visible the frustration of desires by Palestinians, she also creates the space for an articulation of a common culture in this displacement. She thus says: "I was more excited about the people in the West Bank and Gaza reacting to the requests of their people in Lebanon, Syria and America. They wanted to know what did those outside Palestine want me to do?"[64] She also maintains that the work is not conceived for non-Palestinians, that in fact she felt uncertain about others "being entertained by our sorrows and dreams."[65] She thus used formal strategies to target particular audiences, to differentiate the spectatorial position of the viewing subject. For example, she chose to display a letter written by a Palestinian to the Israeli occupiers of his family home in West Jerusalem only in Hebrew, so that those who could read Hebrew would take on the responsibility for the position of the occupier.

By demonstrating the force of the proxy and other modes of affective exchange, Jacir highlights economies that are not so easily capitalized on and that are also difficult to value. These supplementary modes of exchange are both beneath the global system (including the nation-states that regulate movement) and constitutive of it. They are not meant to be outside the national or global system, but speak from a discontinuous state within those formations. This is of critical importance also to the production of artworks as traveling cultural forms. Clifford argues that culture is both repressive (in that it erases "unruly" processes that might challenge its holistic aesthetics) and enabling (in order to support and recognize systems of meaning and difference). He concludes that culture is a "profoundly mixed blessing."[66] The ambiguity of the economies Jacir exposes both makes visible the demands of culture and raises its vexed histories. This involves a profound acknowledgment of the double edge of diasporic longing.

Prismatic media here serve to visualize and imagine a global system that is in a constant process of routing and rooting, where states fragment, become independent, are the object of committed fantasies or the fodder for repressive intolerance. Aesthetic strategies foreground active social relations and fields of contestation. Unlike the nation, the state often floats above the fray (or beneath the radar) as a more humble geo-political formation, the terrain of bureaucrats, politicians, border guards and military commanders, rather than a more powerful affective category. The affective charge of artworks made from sites of exile, and particularly their capacity to articulate forms of collective belonging in the materiality of these installations, both highlight the force of statehood (its repressive apparatus or right to sovereign power) and at the same time resist its descriptive nature, the stillness of the social relations that produce it. Imaging does not (in this vision) simply dream of a return to normative models of nation-states and collectivities.

In the post-war period, Theodor Adorno argued that "it is immoral to feel at home in one's own home."[67] There is, in the radical forms of imaging articulated by artists, writers and activists, a commitment to strangeness, to the uncanniness of belonging and unbelonging. They experience the violence entailed by assertions of belonging, as well as their necessity. Politics of instating always create anchor points even as they unmoor other attachments, putting in place a contingent and fervent subjectivity. In this way, instating works to open up the space for critique within the space of subjectivity and sociality, from a position that is (often violently) displaced. Building upon de Lauretis's complex understanding of imaging—"the process of the articulation of meaning to images, the engagement of subjectivity in that process, and thus the mapping of a social vision into subjectivity"—prismatic media bind together, engage and enact political subjects, spectators and social visions in the face of violent personal and political prohibitions.[68] The prismatic visions traced here and throughout this book are the product of the shifting ground under these subjects in process.

4

Diffracted Mediations: The Framing of Gender in the "War on Terror"

In wrestling with the imagery of Abu Ghraib and Guantanamo, Anne McClintock posed the question, "How do we insist on seeing the violence that the imperial state attempts to render invisible, while also seeing the ordinary people afflicted by that violence?"[1] What she identifies is a paradox of visual culture in conflict zones: that an exposure of the spectacle of wartime media coverage may render a more grounded perspective impossible and—less obviously—that the converse might also be true. Historically, grounded visions have sought to flesh out the cost of war and the immediacy of conflict, and have played an important role in shattering the singular views of the war presented on either side of the conflict. Multiple and fragmentary visions on the ground of conflict zones may work to counter the consolidation of wartime power (which draws heavily on iconic images and mythical forms of speech), demonstrating acts of solidarity with nascent resistance movements and drawing transnational attention to local political actions. Such visions may also confirm (and allegorize) the binary oppositions within a conflict zone, however, and thus contribute either to a resurgent nationalism (on either side) or to the rendering of absolutist subject positions. The immediacy of grassroots media, and their distribution through the networks of new media platforms, may electrify distant (and differently) located publics just as they may repeat the mythical speech of top-down media forms. What critical tools exist, then, to parse the expanded field of visual culture and, particularly, its role in visualizing contemporary conflict zones?

Visual culture studies have drawn the connections between the spectacular violence of military campaigns (with names like "Operation Enduring Freedom" and "Shock and Awe") and the spectacle of wartime media coverage—the "liveness" of events unfolding on television screens and the destructive vision from the perspective of so-called smart bombs, the spectacle of light combined with the utter obscurity of the bombing campaign's effects on the civilian population. Robert Stam, for instance, argued in relation to the first Gulf War that TV news gave viewers an "exhilarating sense of visual power," combined through the reach of cameras deployed around the world, the direct transmission of images and sounds through satellite and the apparatuses of military simulation and a surveillant gaze.[2] The iconic images at the onset of the U.S. war in Iraq and Afghanistan contrasted the visibility of U.S. power with the invisibility of the enemy, both in the elusive nature of key figures (such as Saddam Hussein and Osama Bin Laden) and in the iconoclasm of the Taliban.

Specifically, the binary of visibility and invisibility served to prop up the U.S. regime's distinctions between "freedom" and "terrorism." In this context, the Taliban's "iconoclasm" was figured in Western media through, first, the images of women forced to wear the burqa under the Taliban regime, and second, the March 2001 shelling of the Buddhist statues in the Bamiyan province. As compensation for these visual prohibitions, images of both the Bamiyan Buddhist sculptures and of Afghani women became icons in the Western imaginary for a country "out of time with Western modernity, by referencing an existing discourse in which image destruction indexed the inherently medieval nature of Islamic culture."[3] Since September 11, 2001, this particular imagery has been bolstered not only by the depictions of "Islamic terrorism," but also by a re-codification of self and other across newly articulated racial, gendered and ethnic boundaries. Central to this was the attachment of discourses of freedom to the specific image of Afghan women's unveiling.

The images of Afghani women came into view in Western media through a quite striking mythological sleight of hand, one where they became transformed (and naturalized) as icons of Afghanistan's suffering at the hands of the Taliban. In her unpacking of the particular tropic value of icons, Cornelia Brink finds that (a) they are indexical (in religious terms, they imply a direct causal relationship between the copy and the original image); (b) they are symbolic (in other words, they "condense complex phenomena and represent history in an exemplary form"); (c) they rely on their reproducibility and the image becoming canonized and (d) they rely on separation. The effect for Brink is that iconic images "make a moral claim to be accepted without questioning."[4] Top-down media thus *reveal* graphically to us (explicit in the doctrine of "Shock and Awe"), but also conceal and mediate our relation to war, providing what Brink calls a "protective layer." These images inure their audience to violence; they are dehistoricized and decontextualized, distancing the viewer from the events unfolding.

Similarly, anthropologist Lila Abu-Lughod has reflected critically on the myriad invitations she received post-9/11 to speak on news programs about the "plight of Muslim women." She noted that the questions were not only hopelessly general (they asked questions in the format of "Do Muslim women believe 'x'? Are Muslim women 'y'? Does Islam allow 'z' for women?"), but also resorted to a notion of "cultural difference" to explain the attacks of 9/11, rather than seeking political or historical explanations. She argued: "Instead of questions that might lead to the exploration of global interconnections, we were offered ones that worked to artificially divide the world into separate spheres—recreating an imaginative geography of West versus East, us versus Muslims, cultures in which First Ladies give speeches versus others where women shuffle around silently in burqas."[5] This iconography was indelibly drawn for the (conservative) American public by Laura Bush's radio address on November 17, 2001, in which the monstrous figure of "The Taliban and the terrorists" (uttered under one breath as a hyphenated identity) sought to "impose their world on the rest of us," while—by contrast—U.S. policy rescued women from being "imprisoned in their homes." She concluded her address by arguing that "The fight against terrorism is also a fight for the rights and dignity of women."[6]

Official media channels (on the left and the right) relied on a discourse of visibility—within an ideologically constrained channel—to present Western viewers with a kind of offer that cannot be refused: the retributive might of the United States in avenging the wrongs of 9/11 embedded in the moral rectitude of a discourse of freedom and a civilizing narrative that has its roots in the mantra identified by Gayatri Spivak, "white men saving brown women from brown men." Such an analysis, however, has not yet dealt with the proliferation of images, tapes and leaked documents that have also constituted the media culture of conflict in the twenty-first century. Images taken with cell phones, the work of embedded journalists, viral videos on the Internet and independent reportage by journalists and NGOs have increased the visual rhetoric of the war, in support of both the war efforts and opposition movements around the world. Such new visions—relying on more grainy, amateur production equipment, as well as alternative channels of distribution and reception—have also shifted the vantage points on the war from the spectacular heights of smart bombs or the iconic portraits of rescue to the more grounded perspective of the desert road, the city street, the inside of an advancing tank or a secret school.

Optimistic accounts of the expanded field of visual culture have emphasized the potential of these media forms to challenge the hegemony of cable media channels. The grounded perspective employed by soldiers, reporters, documentarians, artists, activists and civilians suggests a kind of democratization of images of war, not only because the number of actors recording their experiences has multiplied, but also because the images are channeled through not only traditional news media, but also blogs, email campaigns, YouTube and other viral avenues. At times, this footage relies on representational conventions to indicate the immediacy of the action taking place (a shaky camera, for example, or the sudden disappearance of a recorded image), but such conventions also render certain subjects and certain forms of seeing impossible, even as they cloak themselves in the guises of a new form of objectivity.

Yet there is a need to parse more carefully the important structural connections between top-down and bottom-up media forms within a given image environment. How do media frame events and subjects? What are the thresholds of visibility? And how are these thresholds critical to the politics of representation under feminism? The key question here is whether new media reflect dominant iconographies across the field of visual culture, or whether they *diffract* such visions, implicating multiple perspectives, media and visual languages. Donna Haraway has argued that reflexivity might be an impoverished framework for critical practices because, in her terms, it "only displaces the same elsewhere," rather than attending to the interference patterns created as cultural producers travel through different media and channels.[7] The transparency of certain figurations thus may take the place of various labors of communication across cultural, racial, gendered and class differences. Diffraction, on the other hand, contains the possibility of attending to the interference patterns that mediate our relation to the visible world—be these technological, economic, political or ethical. How might one parse the different forms of media and their interconnection, attending to the processes of reflection and diffraction in representations of conflict zones?

In the service of examining this complex field of visual representations, I would like to propose a schema that perhaps simplifies its dynamics, but one that may contribute to expanding the conceptual tools for analyzing the field of visual culture. This Greimasian semiotic square takes as its central opposition the relation between visibility and invisibility in contemporary representations of the wars in Afghanistan and Iraq, and overlays this binary with the distinction between top-down and bottom-up media (Figure 4.1).

The top set of terms traces the relation between, for example, the "frenzy of the visible" presented by "Operation Enduring Freedom" and the forms

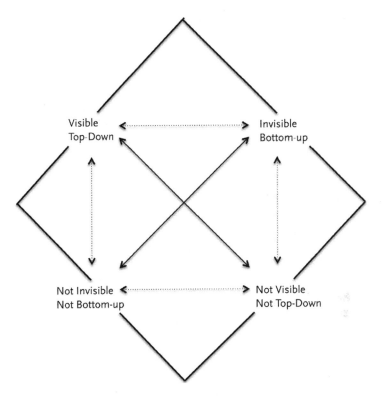

Figure 4.1 Greimasian Semiotic Square

of new media emanating from a grounded perspective of the conflict. While works taken on the ground seem to provide an immediate, first-hand account of the theater of war, the experiences they reveal are often coded within the very terms of the iconic images of war, and thus confirm the governing logic of that conflict. Such works make use of the immediacy of a grounded perspective without the appeal to the "grassroots." An example of this form of media is a video recorded by a Canadian soldier serving in Afghanistan, Glen Villa. Villa shot footage of his base camp, the battlefield and his unit patrolling villages, all through a small camera attached to his helmet. The footage was picked up and edited in a longer reportage piece entitled "Fighting Ghosts," which aired on the Canadian Broadcasting Corporation's news program, *The National*.[8]

The footage paradigmatically exemplifies the liveness of the war from the ground. As Villa repositions himself, the viewer feels the camera's moving and shaking, sees the dust kicked up and the frenetic panning of the horizon and hears the gunshots ringing out in space. The video thus participates in the extension of visions of the war, from mainstream news media coverage to amateur footage by inside sources. What is particularly interesting about this footage, and the title *Fighting Ghosts*, however, is how the perils of the war against the Taliban are particularly articulated as a failure to see the enemy, and hence the figuration of a "shadowy enemy." In presenting the Taliban in this manner, such footage reinforces the tropes employed by the U.S. administration and Laura Bush's radio address, and serves to associate invisibility with a threat to security, the oppressive and secretive regime and the abuses against women in Afghanistan and against American citizens on 9/11. It also serves to secure the relation between invisibility and women's oppression, and thus affirms U.S. rescue narratives by "shedding light" on women's oppression, but also by "bringing them into visibility" as a metaphor for the granting of universal rights. The very vividness of the footage captured, therefore, lies in what it fails to represent: the Taliban fighters, the human contact that should ground the experience of war on the ground. At the same time, this failure of seeing is precisely what the footage represents as the vulnerability of war. Hence, the invisibility of the enemy guarantees in some ways the immediacy of this alternative media form. The grainy aesthetic of night-video and of satellite reportage through cellphones by embedded journalists works as a kind of aestheticization of grassroots imaging within the terms of the mainstream media. The form signifies a groundedness that masks the more normative channels of war's visual culture.

In Villa's footage, the struggle to identify the location from which he is being fired upon reconfirms the rhetoric of ghostly apparitions at play in official government statements—for example, in George W. Bush's statement that "we do not know who the enemy is, but we know they are out there," or former Attorney General Gonzalez's statement that "we face an enemy that lies in the shadows."[9] Thus, the prevalence of camera phones and video cameras, like the practice of embedding journalists with army units, might extend rather than challenge the iconicity of war, mobilizing a grounded vision to reinforce the indisputability of the events unfolding before the camera. It is worth noting also that the footage dehumanizes the enemy not only because it presents it as a target one cannot see, but also because the effect of the camera mounted on Villa's helmet reproduces the figuration of identity in video games and—more importantly—in army training videos. Thus, the reality effect is closer to the simulated energy of game culture than to the complexity of combat on the ground.

A useful contrast to Villa's grainy footage is the experimental film by Cyrus Frisch, *Why didn't Anybody Tell me it would Become this Bad in Afghanistan?* (2007). Frisch shoots the entire film on a camera phone, and mostly from within the confines of his apartment in Amsterdam. The film is intended to represent the experience of a soldier who returns from Afghanistan in shock, and examines the increasing tensions and xenophobia upon his return. The aesthetics of the camera phone certainly provide a fragmented vision of the scenes unfolding below Frisch's balcony—an aesthetic that copies the liveness and authenticity of Villa's footage. But Frisch is conscious of the rocky terrain on which artistic producers travel in representing the war in artistic and documentary forms. Rather than reproduce the "liveness" of wartime footage, Frisch places the shaky footage and grainy images in the service of a kind of "aesthetics of boredom."

Further, while Frisch presents the viewer with an acutely voyeuristic perspective, such voyeurism is frustrated by the lack of clarity of the medium (the use of a camera phone), and accordingly, it is a voyeurism that doesn't have a precise target, and that doesn't obey the rules of scopophilia. Instead, the viewer is presented with a kind of detached and wandering view of the street below. In emphasizing the pixilated vision produced by the camera phone's low resolution, Frisch foregrounds in the work *itself* a scopophilic mode of looking under threat, one that challenges both the penetrative gaze of the "Shock and Awe" campaign and the frustrated visions presented by Villa. The work thus questions the force of iconic representations, and involves modes of looking bound by the very prohibitions of visibility.

In using a Greimasian square to open up the binary visibility/invisibility to its negations, the emergence of a more complex vision of the production of the enemy complicates the representation of conflict zones, if only through an exposure of the mechanisms of power in dominant visual culture. Thus, the forms of media characterized as "not invisible" and "not bottom-up," for instance, might constitute an irruption into public view of what would have remained hidden, a return of the repressed—both in the sense of the bodies, desires and affects rendered invisible in the conflict zone and in the sense of the modes of disenfranchisement produced out of the occupation of a foreign country (and the institution of a weak governing structure). The photographs at Abu Ghraib thus testify, in McClintock's terms, not only to the desire to produce the enemy as a "legible enemy," but also to codify and represent a "phantasy of domination."[10] The dazzling omnipotence of the "Shock and Awe" footage of air raids also might reveal what is beneath—and co-extensive with—its logic: heterogeneous enactments of domination on the ground (forms of domination covered over with the discourse of "bad apples").

A semiotic square might seem like a blunted instrument for prying open the field of new media, especially given its static and ahistorical appearance. Yet it remains a useful tool for at least two reasons: first, there is a tendency to associate new media with new developments in technology, and thus to see the opening of new communication spaces in the light of narratives of progress (the promise of democracy, access, expansion, the freedom from hierarchy and the absence of authoritarian or monopoly control). As Saskia Sassen insists, however, "electronic space is inscribed, and to some extent shaped, by power, concentration and contestation as well as by openness and decentralization," and thus challenges the progress narratives that underwrite forms of technophilia.[11] Second, a structuralist model allows for an examination of the processes of *mediation* between levels or instances of visual culture, an understanding of the interdependencies in a larger structure and, most importantly, a foregrounding of the sites of foreclosure or the *aporias* within that structure (in this case, heavily inflected by gender, race and ethnicity).

Fredric Jameson argues that Greimas's schema should be viewed as "a set of categories to be explored, rather than as a forecast of the shape of the results of analysis."[12] What appears to be a static analytical scheme organized around binary oppositions can then be reappropriated for criticism by, in his terms, "designating it as the very model of ideological closure."[13] Feminist analyses of new media must accordingly pay particular attention to these sites of ideological closure and to mechanisms through which certain figurations of gender, sexuality, ethnicity and/or class are upheld. As mentioned in the Introduction, the gender system within each culture is a "symbolic system of meanings that correlates sex to cultural contents according to social values and hierarchies."[14] Gender is the product of social technologies, institutionalized discourses and symbolic processes. The representation of gender, therefore, is deeply rooted in a semiotic apparatus, as well as in a sociocultural system. Accordingly, the semiotic square proposed here not only maps the manner in which new media might support or critique normative models of sexual difference, for example, but also presents methods for a critical feminist media practice.

The final quadrant in the Greimasian schema outlined above classifies a form of media that engages with the iconicity of the image without counter-posing it against the immediacy of a grounded vision. This final level of analysis points to some of the inadequacies of certain figurations of gender within this field of visual culture and, specifically, to the manner in which their mobilization of iconicity repeats the dehistoricizing gesture of top-down media. In this regard, the Afghani-American artist Lida Abdul's *White House* (2005) serves as an interesting critical example. *The White House* was produced while Abdul was an artist-in-residence in Kabul in 2005, and has circulated broadly in international contemporary art circuits.[15] In the work, Abdul approaches the ruins of a large neoclassical building in Kabul that has been turned to rubble. Armed with a can of white paint and paintbrush, she endeavors to paint the entire ruin white, down to the smallest stone. At one point, a man emerges in

Figure 4.2   Lida Abdul, *White House*, 2005. © Lida Abdul. Courtesy of the Giorgio Persano Gallery

the scene, and he too is painted with a broad brushstroke across his back (Figure 4.2).

The work engages the status of the icon (the iconic nature of the ruin, but also the reification of everyday life through the artistic process) and its relation to the artistic performance. Because the work presents a decontextualized image of ruin, however, the ruin itself transcends the historical and geopolitical specificity of contemporary Afghanistan. This is true not only of the excising of the contemporary history of the ruin in Afghanistan (most of the bombed buildings in Kabul are a result of the war against Soviet occupation and point perhaps to the ongoing devastation of the country, caught in the crosshairs of the Cold War), but also of the nostalgia of ruin, which Andreas Huyssen has identified as a nostalgia for modernity itself.[16] The relation between Abdul and the man who steps into her sculptural tableau may refigure the art historical conventions of the masculine creative act and woman-as-image, but it does so only through a reversal that does not question the structures of gender ideology at play across the U.S. and Afghani contexts, as well as across the different sites of the work's display (the nationalist residual imaginaries of the Venice Biennale, or the appeals to a "global feminism" in the exhibit at the Brooklyn Museum).

This example serves not simply to elucidate the models of ideological closure within the structure of the semiotic square outlined above, but also to articulate how the structure itself works against multiplicity, difference and diffraction. Accordingly, strategies within media cannot simply expand their reach to those subjects that do not appear within the system, since the system itself guarantees their very invisibility (often by narrowly defining political subjectivity). Within existing media structures, the politics of representation often lead to largely metropolitan (and usually Western) audiences being invited to witness abuses, which are always conceived as occurring elsewhere. These structures of visibility reinforce the terrain of the other as a visible field, open for inspection or revelation. Attention, then, to the structure of ideological closure by cultural producers opens the possibility of rupturing received frameworks, attending to issues of cultural difference and scrutinizing the translation of images as they travel across contexts, classes and historical realities. Centrally, such strategies at least hold open the possibility of registering difference at the level of both the subjects invoked in media and the viewing subject.

The Expanded Field of Visual Culture

How then might these larger structures of ideological closure function in relation to grassroots media? A key example of grassroots feminist media in the case of Afghanistan is the Revolutionary Association of the Women of Afghanistan (RAWA). RAWA was founded in 1977 and has acted as a public voice, initially for women's rights in Afghanistan and subsequently against the Soviet occupation, the Taliban's rule and the United States-led war after 9/11. They have been central in voicing social justice issues in Afghanistan and organizing access points for basic human rights (creating hospitals and schools, teaching nursing courses and promoting literacy and distributing basic food and medicine). Since 1992, they have recorded incidences of human rights abuses and provided them to human rights organizations and the news media. More recently, since 1997, RAWA members have been posting footage on their own website to disseminate records of abuses under the Taliban, by the Northern Alliance, and as a result of the United States-led war. Most of the videos and photos posted on the site have been taken by RAWA activists with a hidden camera and have used the structure of invisibility imposed by the Taliban on women (specifically the mandatory requirement that women wear the burqa) to subvert the Taliban's ban on image production more widely. The footage is largely unedited; it is posted soon after recording to a YouTube gallery that overflows from page to page.

Perhaps the most-well-known video recorded by RAWA is the footage of the execution of a woman, known simply as Zarmeena, accused of murdering her husband. The video shows her being brought to the national football stadium, before she is publicly executed by a Taliban soldier in front of a cheering crowd. While the Associated Press reported the execution, cable and broadcast media outlets such as the BBC, CNN and ABC refused to air the video. RAWA states, "We were told, 'as the footage is very shocking, Western viewers can't bear it, so we are sorry that we can't air it.'"[17] After 9/11, however, these same media channels aired the footage repeatedly (Figure 4.3).[18]

What emerges from the lifecycle of this footage is a path across the categories outlined in the Greimasian semiotic square above, from the bottom right-hand corner to the top right-hand corner. As the piece moves along this path, the forms of visibility shift from a form of invisibility sequestered away from the mainstream media by censorship to a form of invisibility that parallels both the vision of the Taliban as a "shadowy enemy" and the violence of its purported iconoclasm. Although RAWA has made strong critical statements against the war, the U.S. support for the Northern Alliance and the diminishment of women's rights since the overthrow of the Taliban, their transnational interventions have had to negotiate the complex relation between their isolation from the Bonn Accords, for example, and their media presence on Oprah Winfrey and in *Glamour* magazine

Figure 4.3 Revolutionary Association of the Women of Afghanistan, *Afghanistan Execution of Zarmeena* (November 17, 1999). Courtesy of RAWA and World Picture Network

(where they were named "Women of the Year" in 2001). The debate surrounding RAWA's critique of the Feminist Majority Foundation (a Western feminist organization that has supported RAWA's fundraising efforts and helped put a stop to a secret oil pipeline deal between the Taliban and U.S. multinational Unocal) signals the complex emergence of RAWA in the Western press, and its efforts to resist enclosure within the wartime field of visual culture.

Thus, it is important for critical media studies to trace a given media text's function within the larger structure of media culture, to trace the mediation of the tropes of visibility and invisibility as objects move through the system. Specifically, feminist experimental media are tasked with highlighting the disjunctions between media platforms in the field of visual culture, and thus with mapping the diffraction—the interference patterns—within that system and between the actors they call upon and interpellate. This is especially pertinent for a transnational feminism without borders, where the transparency of certain figurations may take the place of various labors of communication across cultural, racial, gendered and class differences. Diffraction is therefore a politics that attends to the differences between and within women, and may be materialized through such strategies as experiments in narrative form, departure from evidentiary tropes and the weaving of archival documents with fictions, so-called unreliable witnesses and partial visions. This signals that it is not enough to "make visible" as a rights-granting mechanism, since the terms of visibility are already predefined by a sociocultural system and semiotic apparatus that brings only certain subjects into visibility and exclusively on specific terms. Cultural producers must, instead, examine *in media* the manner in which framing devices limit the rights-bearing subject herself, often in ways that disable differences not simply between cultural systems but also within them.

Diffracted Media

While media such as RAWA's activist footage are diffracted across the expanded field of new media, experimental media may themselves mediate among such media objects, refracting them through a broader filmic or documentary project. The aesthetic strategy of diffraction traced throughout this book thus gains greater currency in mediating the movement of grassroots and official media through various channels. Diffraction highlights not only the processes of mediation internal to the artwork or documentary, but also the effects of various media objects in the context of their production and reception.

The strategy of diffraction is central to engaging a politics of representation in the context of media cultures. In relation to this chapter's topic, diffraction breaks open the repressive binary of visibility/invisibility posited in relation to the wars in Afghanistan and Iraq. I noted above that the binary itself appropriated feminist discourse as an alibi for war, using narratives of "unveiling" to reference women's rights after the overthrow of the Taliban. In this case, strategies of diffraction serve to interrogate the equation of visibility with rights, to expose the very risks of exposure alongside those of invisibility, without renouncing the emancipatory aims of rights-based claims.

I turn to three examples of cultural works that take up diffraction as a central strategy in visualizing women's experiences under the Taliban. The first, reporter Saira Shah's documentary *Beneath the Veil* (2001), is the only work produced prior to 9/11, the U.S. war against Afghanistan and the overthrow of the Taliban. It therefore negotiates more immediately the ban on visibility and representation under the Taliban. The second and third works were produced several years after the onset of the war, following the overthrow of the Taliban (at least in Kabul, where both these works were produced). The first of these is Siddiq Barmak's *Osama* (2003), the first film to be shot entirely in Afghanistan since 1996, when the Taliban regime banned the creation of films and burned film stocks in Afghanistan's archives. The second, Sandra Schäfer and Elfe Brandenburger's *Passing the Rainbow* (2008), is an experimental documentary filmed over several years in Kabul, consisting (among other things) of interviews with the actors in Barmak's film, footage from the film set of *Osama* and experimental "stagings," dramatizations of everyday life performed by the women in the film to reflect on contradictions between constructed images and the reality of life under the Taliban and in the contemporary moment. Each work employs diffraction to highlight the mediation of social life both under the Taliban and today, particularly for women and girls.

Documentary Diffractions: Beneath the Veil

The possibilities and limitations of diffraction as an aesthetic strategy are evident in Saira Shah's documentary *Beneath the Veil*. Although the documentary repeats some troubling tropes of groundedness and immediacy, it also reveals how the field of visual culture might itself be framed *in media*, and in some ways *in medias res*, in the thick of that system, without positing a space outside. The documentary was produced by Hardcash Productions, an independent production company known for "filming in difficult foreign places" and reputed for a series of "undercover" productions they created in Britain.[19] The "undercover" trope has been extended since 9/11 to a series of "unveiling" documentaries, including *Lifting the Veil: Zarmina's Story* (2002), *Islam Unveiled* (2004) and *Afghanistan Unveiled* (2007). *Beneath the Veil* is of particular interest because it was produced in early 2001, prior to 9/11. After 9/11, the distribution of Shah's documentary shifted its location within the Greimasian semiotic square to consolidate the binary visibility/invisibility, airing on heavy rotation on CNN's "CNN Presents," serving to support the rhetoric of Afghanistan's "barbarism" and aligning it with Channel 4's "Unveiling" series. In the contemporary context, the documentary holds in tension a vision of Afghanistan prior to its coding within the context of the "war on terror" with the deployment of U.S. wartime rhetoric.

Two elements in the film elucidate especially the struggles of cultural producers to visualize the mediating force of visual cultural regimes, pointing to some partial successes in the possibilities for diffraction as a feminist media tactic. The first involves Shah's use of the RAWA footage of the execution of Zarmeena, and the second, the foregrounding of segments of tape within an expanded field of visual culture. The footage of the execution in the football stadium actually frames the documentary, appearing prior to the opening titles, and is accompanied by a strangely factual and doubling voice-over, whose rhetorical style is quite literal, made up of sentence fragments that lack verb structures: "Veiled women, hunched in the back of a pick-up truck. A football stadium in Afghanistan. A place of entertainment turned into an execution ground. Secret pictures showing medieval barbarity the country's rulers want to keep hidden. We're trying to uncover the truth beneath Afghanistan's veil of terror." The footage fades to black before the execution takes place, and the viewer is then transported to the Pakistani-Afghan border, and subsequently, to a RAWA protest in Pakistan. The first quarter of the film takes place in Pakistan, and it is here that the viewer is introduced to RAWA, to their stock of cameras and tape stored in their secret headquarters. The documentary makes clear that it is RAWA who will assist Shah in entering Afghanistan and grant her access to the conditions of life under the Taliban.

The second time that the documentary presents the RAWA footage of the execution of Zarmeena, Shah heavily mediates the viewing experience, cutting back and forth between RAWA's tape and the documentary crew's footage of the empty stadium. She invites the viewer to enter into the stadium and to remember the scene that unfolded there two years prior. The montage works to suture the viewer to the scene, to invite a form of identification with Shah and, ultimately, with the RAWA members who recorded the footage. At the same time, Shah's mediation interrupts the immediacy of the scene of execution, through her commentary, certainly, but also through several formal devices: the fade-to-black that fragments the montage and the view of the camera crew, captured as shadows on the pitch, when the camera approaches the goal posts in the stadium. Through these strategies, the apparatus of production is exposed, disrupting access to the event one is asked to recall.

Similarly, at the moment when the RAWA footage reveals the scene of Zarmeena's execution (the scene that was not fully unfolded at the beginning of the documentary), Shah's prior voice-over complicates the viewer's relation to the scene. The voice-over emphasizes that the stadium itself was financed by the international community. Zarmeena's execution, therefore, is located in an arena that was literally, materially, supported by the West. The Western viewer's complicity with the Taliban is further emphasized at the end of this scene by the interview with the Taliban foreign minister, who argues that the West should build a separate stadium for executions if they want Afghanis to play football in the existing stadium. The statement thus highlights the West's complicity with the devastation in Afghanistan, with the destruction of buildings and infrastructure, with the failures of international aid structures.

When distributed in a Western context, what does the documentary's mediation accomplish? On the one hand, one might see the intercuts of the empty stadium as the film's guarantee of the immediacy of the crew's presence in Afghanistan. A reporter for *The Guardian* noted wryly that "downtown Kabul must be packed to the minarets with Western journalists secretly filming the goings-on there." He says further, "One suspects that half the people covered from head-to-toe in veils, lurking in ramshackle marketplaces and on street corners, are actually camera crews and intrepid reporters intent on exposing what the Taliban has done to Afghanistan."[20] While his suspicion about the heroism of reportage done from "the most dangerous places on earth" and the immediacy and truth value such rhetoric produces is of critical importance, many reviews of *Beneath the Veil* note specifically that the most moving footage in the documentary belongs not to Shah's crew but to RAWA's activism.[21] This is not only because the documentary so carefully foregrounds the social relations between the crew and RAWA, but also because the documentary itself jumps haltingly between multiple media formats as it moves into Afghanistan and through the various sectors of Afghani society.

The documentary shifts between official interviews, high-resolution cameras, hidden cameras, found footage and refracted visions. Shah often has to film surreptitiously through the windows of the van in which she travels, transforming it into a veritable camera obscura. At times, a hidden camera is placed in a bag, and the awkward angles and framing indicate the negotiations of visibility/invisibility in specific contexts. The most overdetermined refractory mechanism in the film is Shah's donning of the burqa to record the work of RAWA in Kabul. The footage of the execution of Zarmeena, in fact, marks the point in the film where Shah leaves behind her crew and follows RAWA, hiding under the cover of a burqa, to record the conditions of life for ordinary Afghanis. On the one hand, the footage shot through the burqa consolidates the very binary of visibility/invisibility proposed by the U.S. language of women's rights. The viewer is invited to occupy the position of veiled Afghani women as the camera moves through the city, and the obscuring of vision does much to confirm the association of invisibility with oppression.[22] On the other hand, Shah chooses *not* to shoot through the burqa, but with the same hidden camera placed in a bag, the edges of which frame the scenes of private life in Kabul. The viewer is thus provided the same surreptitious view in the private sphere as in the public, not a view "beneath the veil" but the view of the undercover reporter. Further, as is the case with RAWA, what Shah uncovers beneath the veil is accessible exclusively because Shah can remain invisible under the burqa. This overturns the colonial fantasy inferred by the phrase "beneath the veil," providing not the uncovered female body (as outlined by Malek Alloula, for instance), but women's activism to address the conditions of starvation, lack of access to medical care and education and the deep disenfranchisement felt at the level of the entire community.[23]

As the camera switches from official to unofficial, from barely visible to hidden, the documentary records the transition, capturing the camera's efforts to focus on its object, the overexposure of footage as it moves from the interior of the van to the street, the swiveling of the frame as the camera shifts from one window to the next. In one instance, Shah notes, "We try to film it, and again it seems we're in trouble." The camera zooms forward quickly, shifts into focus, then back out of focus and zooms in. Cutting to a hidden camera (accompanied by the notation "hidden camera" in the bottom left-hand side of the screen), the scene depicts the cameraman conversing with a Taliban member who asks, "So, is there a problem?". Then the crew is marched into a derelict building and in front of a Taliban security chief and other Taliban security officers; this scene is shot from the low angle on the floor, where the bag containing the hidden camera has been placed. Next, the viewer sees a narrow view of two large weapons resting on the floor, accompanied by the voice-over noting that the Taliban themselves ask to be filmed. The documentary switches to a high-quality, wide-angle view of the room, as one Taliban leader digs under a sofa to retrieve a video cassette recorder. Shah explains, "The head of security wants to show off his collection of confiscated cassette players. I now realize we are guests of the very same people who arrested us in Kandahar. This time, far from detaining us, they take us on a tour to boast about their rigid control of the city." These are certainly tropes of immediacy, confirming the riskiness of Shah's undercover reportage, but they are also an aesthetics of process, of the diffracted transition of one visual regime to another. More importantly, these diffracted mediations highlight the shifting visual codes that signify for the viewer the different points of access and censorship in Afghanistan. While the semiotic schema outlined models the ideological closure that supports the binary of visibility/invisibility, these moments in Shah's documentary point to a complex mediation of the boundaries of visibility and invisibility in Afghanistan and in the West. Such diffraction in the documentary across the field of official and unofficial channels, between the protection of official interviews and the access points of activist networks, destabilizes the presuppositions voiced in the United States and Europe that visibility equals rights.

Diffraction Across Fiction and Documentary Genres

Shah's reportage at times risks reconfirming the binary structure of visibility/invisibility, and particularly overlaying this binary onto the binary West/Middle East (as per the United States's wartime rhetoric). The narrative form of the documentary—undercover reportage—and the emphasis on the Taliban's control of image production squares in many respects with a popular imaginary of "Islamic iconoclasm," an iconoclasm that signals hostility to Western modernity. Finbarr Flood cautions that such essentialist tropes do not acknowledge the historical context of representational politics: "It not only obscures any variation, complexity, or sophistication in Muslim responses to the image but also a priori precludes the possibility of iconoclastic 'moments' in Islamic history, which might shed light on those complex responses."[24] Shah's documentary principally marks the threshold between visible and invisible, top-down and bottom-up, stressing the multiple contexts in which her crew negotiates access to the conditions of life under the Taliban. As such, and although the documentary sometimes reverses the presumptions of privilege in the different poles of media production (particularly in emphasizing the Taliban's willingness to represent their own hold on power), it primarily passes between the different poles of media production within the field of visual culture outlined above, rather than prying open its forms of ideological closure.

The two other instances considered here, Barmak's *Osama* and Schäfer and Brandenburger's *Passing the Rainbow,* emerge out of a different context. While they largely examine the conditions of life under the Taliban, they are produced after the overthrow of the regime and in the context of the United States's "global war on terror." For this reason, these works appear more attuned to the field of visual culture and the contested terrain of representational politics in the post-9/11 era. Each work focuses specifically on a figure of crossing—the character Osama in Barmak's film—thus allying the diffraction of media with questions of gender and ideological structures of sexual difference.

Osama *(2003)*

Osama tells the story of a young girl living under the Taliban who is forced to dress as a boy in order to gain employment. Because her father and uncle died during the Soviet invasion and ensuing civil wars—and because her mother is unable to work at the local hospital following the Taliban's rule—the multi-generational family of women is destitute. The young girl, who takes on the name Osama, is scooped up in a sweep of neighborhood boys and must attend a religious school. While she attempts to pass as a boy in the classroom and playground, she is eventually discovered when she begins to menstruate. Tried by a Taliban judge who spares her life, she is nevertheless forced to marry an old Mullah, who has three wives. The film ends on her wedding night, where the Mullah offers her a choice of lock for her room, and then retreats to her quarters, subsequently emerging to perform his ablutions in the courtyard.

While *Osama* is an international co-production (Afghanistan, The Netherlands, Japan, Ireland and Iran), and garnered awards at Cannes, the London Film Festival and the Golden Globes, it also clearly articulates itself as an Afghan film. The director, Siddiq Barmak, is Afghani and headed the Afghan Film Organization from 1992 to 1996, when the Taliban came into power. Film productions since 1996 were frequently shot on Afghanistan's borders and directed by Iranian filmmakers (particularly Mohsen Makhmalbar). Barmak, by contrast, chose to produce *Osama* in Kabul, using only local amateur actors. Its main character Osama is played by Marina Golbahari, a young woman whom Barmak discovered begging in the street. The film is thus, in Hamid Naficy's terms, "situated but universal," articulating itself as both an international production and a form of national cultural production in contemporary Afghanistan.[25]

Particularly interesting in relation to analyses of strategies of diffraction is the treatment of the alternatives of neorealism and cinematic formalism within the film itself. The use of amateur actors, and especially of street children in key roles, certainly allies *Osama* with the genre of Italian Neorealism. The film begins with a young boy addressing the camera directly, offering incense—which, he claims, "keeps all misfortunes away" and "saves you from the Evil Eye"—in exchange for an American dollar. He exhorts the filmmaker, "Rich man, be generous. Give me one dollar." The filmmaker extends a hand into the frame and gives a dollar to the young boy. The boy and the filmmaker are then suddenly caught in the midst of a large demonstration of women, wearing burqas and holding up signs asking for work. The young boy acts as a translator, informing the filmmaker about the women's demonstration and the Taliban who are approaching to break up the demonstration. As the Taliban approach and begin firing into the sky, the filmmaker runs with the women to escape. The viewer feels caught up in a frenetic moving sea of purple, as the shot is hand-held, grounded and close-up. The young street boy tells the filmmaker to run or he will be killed, and the women run in all directions, past the camera, alongside it. This footage is intercut with context shots, pans and zooms taken with a stationary camera. The foreign filmmaker's camera follows a young girl and her mother (the young girl is the character Osama), before being blocked by a closed door and returning to shoot in the street, where the demonstrators are being detained in a large cage. A Taliban soldier approaches the filmmaker and strikes him on the head, and the camera swivels to the sky and then goes black.

A review of the film stresses that *Osama* draws from Neorealist precursors such as Roberto Rossellini's *Rome, Open City* (1945), where "Italians donned German uniforms to portray their decamped oppressors as a way of exorcising that oppression—not just of communicating it to the world."[26] Although this review does not mention Gillo Pontecorvo's *The Battle of Algiers* (1966) specifically, the opening scene resembles in key respects the scenes of demonstrations therein, allying *Osama* with not only neorealism but also anti-colonialism. It is clear that Barmak's production process entails the reliving of events by amateur actors shortly after the overthrow of the Taliban regime, and thus that the stunning reenactment that opens the film highlights the force of neorealism in rendering the reality of everyday life under conditions of duress.

This same review notes that the director has "contrived here, not to trick his audience, but instead to broach the integral subject of vision: of what is or is not seen and whose eye, whose lens, in fact does the seeing or spying."[27] The opening scene—with its juxtaposition of the language of illusionist cinema with the hand-held immediacy of the foreign filmmaker—engages the question of the portrayal of actuality. This form of realism, in André Bazin's terms, is "profoundly aesthetic," living off the contradiction that one arrives at "that extraordinary feeling of truth" through the selection and aesthetic rendering of reality.[28] The opening of *Osama* thus echoes the revolutionary humanism of Neorealist film, its concern with the representation of reality in contraposition to the mobilization of realism as a political symbol (as, for example, in Socialist Realism).

What is striking, then, is that the hand-held immediacy of the opening scenes is, quite literally, arrested in the film. When the filmmaker is detained by the Taliban, so too is his camera work, and a formal cinematic language governs the remainder of the film.[29] The film then presents, centrally and immediately, the foreclosure of a bottom-up perspective of the reality of life under the Taliban (and, more particularly, of the aesthetic of groundedness mobilized by Glen Villa and others). Moreover, the foreclosure of this bottom-up perspective is also a foreclosure of models of invisibility and their association in Afghanistan with the question of veiling. The scene of the women's demonstration is remarkable not only for the groundedness and immediacy of the camera work, but also for the impenetrability of social life—the unindividuated mass of women demonstrators, the filmmaker's dependence on a young street urchin to negotiate the event and the filmmaker's exclusion from the house where the young girl and her mother take refuge (a scene to which the viewer has access only through a careful contrast of perspectives).

The remainder of the film is more properly situated in the formal languages of *auteur*-based cinema, where the expanded field of contemporary Afghan visual culture is frequently repressed in favor of the film's narrative drama. Interestingly, the two central scenes where questions of visibility are addressed diegetically concern questions of sexual difference and gender binaries under the Taliban. In the first, the young girl, working for the first time disguised as a young boy in a small shop, looks fitfully out at the street life. The view of the street is obscured by the condensation that has formed on the vitrine from the boiling milk she stirs continuously. She pauses from her work and draws the outline of a female stick figure on the window. The figure is not only a projection by the young girl of her disguised identity, but also a means through which she gains a limited but unobscured vision of the street traffic (see figure 4.4).

This hastily drawn female figure provides the conditions of possibility for vision to overturn the sequestration of women as visible subjects but also as viewing subjects. This scene makes clear that it is the very position of the female subject in the Taliban regime that provides a unique vision on conditions of life at the level of society as a whole.

Indeed, while the young girl's masculine disguise permits her to enter the public sphere (and thus earn a meager wage and walk in the street unaccompanied by a male relative), in the film it is her female perspective that provides a defamiliarized view of the effects of the Taliban's repressive regime on the rituals of *masculinity*. The figure sketched on the shop

Figure 4.4 Siddiq Barmak, *Osama*, 2003. Courtesy of Barmak Films

window thus becomes an allegory for her own mode of viewing in the film—a mode whose clarity of vision is dependent on the distance between her (female) identity and her (masculine) disguise. In fact, the film's subject matter largely circles around Osama's privileged access across public and private spheres and feminine/masculine domains. The second half of the film takes place after the Taliban sweep the neighborhood, gathering up all the young boys to bring them to a religious school. It is here that Osama faces the greatest estrangement, being unable to tie a turban or read from the Koran. The young girl is also unable to enact the rituals of play in the courtyard, and is bullied incessantly for being weak and feminine. In one of the most striking scenes in the film, Osama witnesses from behind a sheltered doorway as a Mullah instructs the boys in the rituals of ablutions following nocturnal emissions. The viewer identifies with her estranged and distanced perspective, one that sheds light on the effects of gendered ideologies across Afghan society.

Osama's subject position is allegorized by her grandmother's story about a young boy passing under a rainbow, repeated twice in the film:

Once upon a time there was a good looking boy whose father had died. He went to work and came home exhausted. He was tired of working. He wished he could be a girl so he wouldn't have to work. One day, the wise man told him that if he passed under a rainbow, he would become a girl. "What's a rainbow?" he asked. "It's a souvenir left to us by Rustam, the great hero, to free us from pain and misery. Boys turn into girls, and girls into boys."

The young girl resists her transformation into a boy, both in mourning her lost femininity (she plants one of her cut braids in a pot and waters it with an IV drip left over from the closed hospital) and because of a fear of being discovered by the Taliban. Her disguise is clearly grounded in material necessity: "You'll be a boy. They won't suspect you're not a boy. People always believe their own eyes. My dear, we'll starve to death if you don't work." The grandmother also views the transformation as functional: "Men and women are equal. My hair grew white, but I saw no difference between men and women. They both work equally hard. And they are equally unfortunate. A shaved man under a burqa looks like a woman. A woman with short hair, a hat and pants, looks like a man." The effect of this discursivity surrounding Osama's transformation is to articulate a structural framework for examining the effects of power in Taliban society, and thus also to secure a passage for the viewer across its different domains, a passage that is further guaranteed by the film's strategies of montage.

A striking example of this is a scene when Osama, returning from working in the shop as a boy, is asked to dress as a girl in order to assist her mother in serving at an illicit wedding celebration. A young boy warns the celebrants that the Taliban is approaching, and the women quickly don their burqas and face the wall, performing the act of mourning to trick the Taliban officials into believing it is a funeral rite. The camera is positioned in the doorway, behind the women, who rock back and forth, mourning in the dimly lit room. The film then cuts abruptly to a scene in the religious school of the young boys in a row, in daylight, facing the camera and reciting from the Koran (see figures 4.5 and 4.6).

Figure 4.5 Siddiq Barmak, *Osama*, 2003. Courtesy of Barmak Films

Figure 4.6   Siddiq Barmak, *Osama* (2003). Courtesy of Barmak Films

The formal contrast between these two opposing scenes recalls Sergei Eisenstein's montage of opposition. In Eisenstein, Gilles Deleuze argues, the totality of the social world represented finds its internal law "in the golden section, which marks a caesura-point and divides the set into two great parts which may be opposed, but which are unequal [. . .]. The opposition serves the dialectical unity whose progression from the initial to the final situation it marks."[30] The articulation of a cinematic language of dialectics is not meant to represent empirical reality from the outside, but rather "the way in which dialectical reality constantly produces itself and grows."[31] In *Osama*, montage thus serves to render the dialectical nature of social reality under the Taliban, to attend to the dynamic production of difference and to articulate the social and material effects of such differences across the fabric of Afghan life.

The figure of the young girl who crosses between femininity and masculinity negotiates the dialectical force of the film, moving between separate spheres and their differential orders of power by passing between visibility and invisibility, and between masculinity and femininity. In its framing of this movement, the film breaks apart the ideological structure of visibility/invisibility outlined above through the Greimasian semiotic square. It is for this reason that the most recognizable instances of women's rights abuses in transnational feminist discourse are largely repressed from *Osama*'s narrative: the mass of veiled women demonstrating is captured only by the foreign filmmaker who is arrested; a European woman doctor is detained at the beginning of the film, and then sentenced to death by stoning at the end, but remains markedly peripheral to the filmic world.

In this regard, it is interesting that Bert Cardullo's review of the film in the *Hudson Review* conforms more properly to the schema of ideological closure outlined above than to the film itself:

> For women in Afghanistan under the Taliban, recognizing one's own image took on a different, and even more basic meaning. Hope or happiness for them, in a sense, was the day they would be seen by, or see themselves in the eyes of, the outside world, and thus the idea of vision—of seeing and being seen—doubtless had to dominate their lives (Particularly since these women must live their lives beneath burkhas [sic], garments that restrict their movement and void their individuality by covering them from head to toe but for a gauze-like vent for the eyes.) This idea dominates *Osama* as well, with a twist [. . .]. *Osama* does have to do with disguise or masquerade, however: of a young girl as a boy.[32]

The film's focus on the figure of a young girl who passes as a boy actually serves to marginalize the very terms of visibility/invisibility, and particularly the gendered nature of the binary, in the Western media.

Further, the young girl's passing itself is meant not to mark a woman's passage into visibility, nor her punishment by domestic sexual slavery for transgressing the laws of sexual difference, but rather the distortions of ideological forces on human subjects. When the grandmother reflects on the young girl's transformation into a boy, she stresses its functionality, as in the narration cited above beginning with the assertion that "Men and women are equal." The figure of Osama thus does not conform to the constraining figurations of gender in the Greimasian square outlined above, but instead articulates a form of revolutionary humanism in the face of the Taliban's structure of sexual difference.[33] The protagonist's passage between femininity and masculinity is meant to articulate the divisions within Afghan society, and the toll of civil war, religious fundamentalism and patriarchal ideologies on society as a whole. The young girl's imprisonment as a sexual slave to her new husband at the end of the film reflects the mirroring of public and private, as well as the reproduction of patriarchal ideologies in the family (with the complicity of the court system, the division of labor, the tenuous forms of civil society and the politics of war).

Passing the Rainbow

Schäfer and Brandenburger's film similarly begins with a black screen and the sound of voices: "Are you recording?" "Yes." "Is the tape rolling?" "Yes, that's the microphone." "We've covered the lens so that no images will be recorded." On the audio soundtrack, the women choose the names they will use in the film and explain that they do not want to be identified, since their members working in Kabul would be harassed. When the image appears, the women debate whether or not to wear a veil; one woman explains that the film will be shown exclusively in German cinemas and not Afghan ones, and thus that she need not veil herself. This framing mechanism opens on to the subject of the film: the political, social and economic effects of representation; the structure of nascent media industries in Afghanistan; and the transnational circuits of visuality in which many of the women interviewed in the film participate.

The film's subjects are frequently actors in other films—*Osama*, *At Five in the Afternoon* (2003), domestic action films such as *The Law* (2004) and educational videos funded by American NGOs. They reflect on conditions of life both under the Taliban and in the contemporary moment, as well as media culture itself and the effect of representation on rendering the truth of social life. As such, *Passing the Rainbow* reveals the intersecting transnational, national and local modes of cultural production, and mediates between them by exposing their conditions of production and reflecting with the actors involved on the staging of contemporary Afghan life.

The opening scene of the film (after the framing narrative has indicated the complexity of processes of mediation) records the opening scene of Barmak's *Osama*, thus beginning also with the visible field of bottom-up camera work and icons of invisibility. Here though, the immediacy is even further interrupted through the recording of the film set, the director and assistants, separate takes and preparations for filming. Although Barmak arrests the grounded perspective that initiates the viewer's entry into Afghanistan under the Taliban, Schäfer and Brandenburger refuse immediacy of any kind, focusing instead on the acts of mediation that produce privileged points of view. Prior to the footage from the film set, the camera approaches Kabul in a moving vehicle, as the filmmakers interview Marina Golbahari, the actress who plays Osama in the film. She recounts that she was chosen because Barmak visited her orphanage and asked if anyone in their family had been martyred; since her sister had recently died, Golbahari burst into tears. She notes, "They saw that my story reflected real life, the life that the film *Osama* is also about. So they thought that I could play this role."

Throughout *Passing the Rainbow*, the film *Osama* is taken as an object of analysis, one that had effects on the actors who played in the film, on viewers in Afghanistan and on the narrativization of the truth of life under the Taliban. The film includes interviews with the women who play the demonstrators, who note that the scene of the demonstration represents "exactly how it happened in real life." Also included is a scene in a girls' classroom, where a young girl recounts the film's narrative. The teacher (who is not only a teacher at the school but also the actor who plays the main character in *At Five in the Afternoon*) asks the girls whether, were the story of *Osama* true, they would like to be boys; the young girl responds in the negative: "Because we are girls and we have a right to live [...]. Why should we become boys?"

The most striking commentary on the film *Osama* occurs in the interviews with Hamida Refah and Zobaida Sahar, who play Osama's mother and grandmother, respectively. Sahar notes, "Everything shown in the film *Osama* is true." When the interviewer asks whether they liked the ending of the film, however, Sahar says, "The ending is sad." She continues,

In our opinion, it would have been nice...My role as the Mother should have been to save my daughter. My role was too small. When the old man was taking the girl away, the Mother should have been able to meet him on the way. Then she would have gotten into an argument with him. I would have allied myself with my daughter to defeat the old man. That would have made the film more successful.

Sahar's rewriting of *Osama*'s ending demonstrates that Schäfer and Brandenburger's goal is not to verify the accuracy of the film so much as to engage the social context in which the film circulates, its conditions of production and the impact of Afghanistan's nascent media industry itself. Central to such a project is an engagement with processes of self-narration among the women involved in the film (and in various media projects in Afghanistan), and thus a reflection on the possibilities that dramatization and performance might open up for the representation of women's experience during the Taliban regime and after.

The allegory of "passing under the rainbow" in *Osama* is thus taken as a central metaphor for *Passing the Rainbow*, since the conditions of acting, performing and passing open onto the social conditions of representation in Afghanistan, entailing the orchestration of visibility by various parties. The film contrasts the young girl who refuses the offer to be transformed into a boy with a day laborer, Maleka, who has passed as a boy since the age of six in order to work to support her family. It also contrasts interviews with theatrical reenactments ("stagings") of short family dramas that expose the gendered dynamics of the family and society. Through one figure that is included in multiple scenes in the film—a woman who is rendered as a black-and-white videographic figure—these contrasts are framed explicitly as part of the film's work of representation or mythical figuration. Passing under the rainbow thus involves not only disguising as a boy but also the multiple transformations available to different figures in and through representation. Filming itself becomes a means of "passing under the rainbow," of fictionalizing, dramatizing, visualizing and documenting.

The framing of mediation itself as an act of passing under the rainbow is closely tied to the situatedness of media objects in the expanded field of visual culture. As noted above, the conditions of reception of *Passing the Rainbow* itself are foregrounded from the outset of the film. The interviews surrounding the film *Osama* are also meant to elucidate how the film functions in the emerging sphere of national cinema, as a cultural product that speaks not only *of* but also *to* contemporary Afghan society.

Passing the Rainbow reflects on several other historical and contemporary examples of Afghan media production. For example, in one scene, two women (one of whom is the videographic figure of a woman) watch the 1974 film, *Rabia of Balkh*, based on the real tenth-century poet and princess, Rabia-e Balkhi, who fell in love with a slave, Bakhtash, and was murdered by her brother Hares out of envy and lust for power. Her death provoked a slave uprising led by Bakhtash, which liberated the province from the tyranny of Hares. The film was one of the country's first feature film, and became a sensation when it was released in 1974. Under the Soviet occupation, the film was condemned, and was further threatened as part of the Taliban's quest to destroy Afghanistan's film archives in 1996. A recent review of *Rabia of Balkh* in the British newspaper *The Independent* noted:

> [...] by 1996 it exemplified everything the Taliban feared and detested: a lavish historical epic with an enchanting queenly figure at its centre who could be seen, most dangerously, as the embodiment of the sexually liberated, political emboldened woman. Fuelling the Taliban's ire, the role was played by the sultry Afghan actress Seema, clad in sumptuous, tightly tailored costumes, who was cast opposite Abdullah Shadaan, also the director of the film.[34]

The film *Rabia of Balkh* thus plays an important role in the history of Afghan cinema, but also in the figuration of a proto-feminist political agency, one that in many respects resembles the ethical call for justice in Sophocles's *Antigone*.[35] The embedding of the film within the frame of *Passing the Rainbow* articulates a history of feminine protagonists whose private acts (in this case Rabia's love for Bakhtash; in *Osama*, the young girl's defiance of the Taliban's ban on women in public activities) have critical ethico-political effects on the law.

Passing the Rainbow not only examines instances of Afghan's national cinema, however, but also the position of these films within the expanded media landscape. For instance, the film includes several scenes from low-budget, domestic action films produced by Film Saba Ltd. The director of these films, Saba Sahar, is also an actor who frequently uses martial arts to combat crimes, such as kidnapping and sexual harassment. In an interview, she explains, "Sadly I must say that the Afghans have forgotten their own art and have developed a great taste for foreign films, such as Indian and American films, which feature a lot of action." Another scene in *Passing the Rainbow* records the set of a public service announcements funded by the American NGO Peace Eye, entitled *Little Carpet Makers* (2004). The director explains that Peace Eye runs facilities to help prevent pregnancy, provide free clinics and doctors and supply pharmacies with free medicines. The educational film, on the subject of birth control, would be shown in border regions and villages for free through a mobile cinema apparatus.

All of these instances reverse the relation between top-down and bottom-up media outlined in the Greimasian schema above. What appear to be grassroots media—low-budget educational video—or local television productions—Sahar's *The Law* among others—are built on imported popular cultures (Hollywood or Bollywood) or directly funded by transnational NGOs. Conversely, national cinema (with its highly orchestrated and aesthetic rendering of everyday life) provides a space for dramatizing social life under the Taliban and under repressive regimes more broadly.

In this light, the interview with RAWA in *Passing the Rainbow* is of particular interest. The documentary crew asks the representative from RAWA whether they work with other women's organizations that make films, citing the example of the Self-Employed Women's Association (SEWA) in India, an organization that makes films on the experiences of women who want to divorce and who were beaten or raped. The interviewer asks, "Are you in contact with such or similar projects in other countries?" The RAWA representative responds as follows:

> We have no direct organizational contacts with them in the sense that they can force their views on us and we have to conform to them. Unquestionably a person's thoughts and mentality depend on his or her social environment. In less developed countries, of which Afghanistan is one, women have been told for years that they should only perform certain activities. In Europe, women already engage in all these activities. I'll give you a little example. It doesn't apply to everyone, but some people here think like this. Above

all, those men who have a backward and misogynistic mentality. They say: "Women can neither do agricultural work nor work as an engineer!" But that is simply not true! What a European woman can do, an Afghan woman can do, as well. There are no mental or anatomical differences between us. A European woman, for example, has very different expectations and ideas. Maybe her notion of equality is different. A European woman who works in a factory demands the same wages as a man. But the Afghan woman doesn't even think about such demands. And why not? Because in Afghanistan there aren't even the factories in which women could work. Even if some women in Afghanistan do not yet have the self-confidence, for some the main issue is finding work!

Whereas the question invites the possibilities of exchanges and collaborations among feminist media activists in different locations—the possibility Mohanty raises of a "feminism without borders"—the response defends against a possible co-optation of RAWA by outside influence.[36] Given the mobilization of RAWA and its videographic projects in the expanded field of wartime visual culture, it seems logical that RAWA would defend its work against the accusation that it be a mouthpiece for other interests, including transnational feminist politics.

More than this, though, the RAWA representative's reflection on feminist consciousness in Afghanistan works to overturn the U.S. rhetoric on the "plight of Muslim women." In his 2002 State of the Union address, George W. Bush said, "The last time we met in this chamber the mothers and daughters of Afghanistan were captives in their own homes, forbidden from working or going to school. Today women are free, and are part of Afghanistan's new government."[37] The RAWA representative stresses that the very term *equality* (particularly as defined within Western feminism) cannot be a basis for feminist politics in Afghanistan where unemployment, poverty and lack of access to basic necessities cross gender lines. RAWA's focus on providing education and basic medicine thus reframes the terms of feminist politics in the Afghan context, and does so in such a manner as to subvert the join of visibility and equality in U.S. discourses on Afghanistan in the post-9/11 era. That the representative responds in this manner to a question on media collaborations with activists in other parts of the world indicates the stakes of locating media production, first within the context of the transnational field of visual culture and second within the material conditions of existence in a given location.

The representational strategies of *Passing the Rainbow* not only trace the location of specific media in culture and their effects on self-representation, but also seek to find other channels of representation, channels that rupture the ideological closure of the field of visual culture.

Two key strategies emerge in this regard: a reframing of the terms of invisibility and a valorization of theatricality in representing social life and contradictions in women's experiences. With regard to the former, *Passing the Rainbow* includes an interview with a day laborer, Maleka Mohammad, who has passed as a boy since the age of six. The interview unfolds over three separate scenes—the set of the film *Osama*, a square in Kabul where day laborers wait for work and the view of the city filmed through the film crew's vehicle. Unlike the character Osama, Maleka joins observations on the material necessities of her crossing (she notes that her mother was young and, when her father died, she had no alternative but to go out and work) with reflections on her own gender identity. In the first interview, for example, one of the translators remarks that her voice is very low, and in the final interview (which is the last scene in the film), the questions center on her gender identity:

Q: Wouldn't you like to walk through the rainbow and thereby actually become a boy?
Maleka: Sure, why not?
Q: You don't want to be a girl?
Maleka: Why not?
Q: Do you like to dress like a woman from time to time?
Maleka: No, I don't like women's things. Just kohl eyeliner. When women paint themselves with lipstick, it puts me off.
Another voice: You'll be amazed at how well she rides a bicycle. The same goes for motorcycles and cars, by God! They wanted to offer her a role in a film, but she would have had to wear a burka. She said, "I'll only go there in men's clothes." Even when I threatened to kill her, she refused to wear women's clothing.
Q: In the film *Osama*, the girl is in constant fear of getting found out. Is this fear justified?
Maleka: If my heart is pure, I have nothing to fear. When men stand before me, they're all like women in my eyes.

In many respects, this interview provides the most unmediated testimony in the film, a reflection on the young day laborer's experiences and identity, and the complex negotiation of passing at the social and subjective levels. That Maleka remains invisible throughout the film not only serves to protect her identity, but also highlights the political necessity of invisibility outside the iconic/iconoclastic binary outlined above. Invisibility is coded not by the language of the "shadowy enemy," nor by the rhetorical trope of the veil, but as a strategy of survival in a public space where gendered divisions continue to inform the material conditions of existence.

The second key strategy—the valorization of theatricality—in turn reverses the assumptions about visibility and rights in the iconic/iconoclastic binary. Rather than make visible through women's testimonies of life under the Taliban, *Passing the Rainbow* instead chooses to interview actors regarding their impressions of fictional film narratives. Moreover, the film records a series of "stagings," dramatizations of fictional scenes in which many of the women who participate in *Passing the Rainbow* act out elements from everyday life, fantasies, educational messages and so on. In one scene, a woman plays a brother who cannot find work, but forbids his sister from earning money through acting. The dramatization provides the sister with the occasion to discuss democracy and rights under the Karzai regime. Another dramatizes a female Afghani president who redresses a wrong for a family. Another enacts a report by the television anchor woman (the "staging" includes a woman with a chair on her head to simulate the television screen) informing the public on the importance of voting.

Schäfer and Brandenburger believe that these theatrical stagings provide sites for the "counter-production of representation, for new definitions and reinterpretations of gender roles and power relations."[38] These stagings seek to represent the emancipatory but unrealized wishes of participants, their accounting for but also subversion of social norms. The production of fictional visual narratives forms part of Schäfer and Brandenburger's social intervention through the film, opening the possibility that participants change roles, articulate freedoms and rights, dramatize conflicts from daily life and make visible the contradictions between constructed images and real living conditions. Thus, interrupting both the documentary footage of media production in the film and the interviews with actors about Afghan media culture, the stagings in fact refract the social conditions of life in Afghanistan. They represent not only the reality of daily life but also allegories, aspirations and conflicts in order to reflect critically on Afghan society and to shed light on the construction of representation.

Prismatic Media: Beyond Visibility, Invisibility

Judith Butler has stressed that while gaining representation is framed conventionally as increasing the likelihood that the subject will be humanized, the processes of humanization and dehumanization—how certain forms of representation contribute to the dehumanization of subjects—are in fact much more complex, where violence can happen in and through representation in multiple ways. There is the possibility of violence in both visibility and invisibility, and this is especially true in media representations in times of political conflict and war. Butler states,

The demand for a truer image, for more images, for images that convey the full horror and reality of the suffering has its place and importance. The erasure of that suffering through the prohibition of images and representations more generally circumscribes the sphere of appearance, what we can see and what we can know. But it would be a mistake to think that we only need to find the right and true images, and that a certain reality will then be conveyed. The reality is not conveyed by what is represented within the image, but through the challenge to representation that reality delivers.[39]

Although early feminist media often stressed the importance of producing positive images of women, this led both to boundary debates about what (formal, stylistic, or thematic) markers pointed to a specifically feminine or feminist aesthetic. They also contained the troubling presumption that the framing of gender might be overcome, that work might more directly translate the aims of feminist political activism.

Refraction and diffraction (as critical and creative methodologies) serve to flesh out a politics within feminist media studies and feminist cultural production that highlights how images might produce subjective and social contradictions as they engage individuals in articulating meanings. Analyses of media need therefore to consider who is made visible, how and for whom, and what work might be achieved by documentary and artistic projects. In the contemporary moment, the promise of access and democratization in grassroots media has renewed the demand for analyses that critically appraise the new channels, patterns and forms of alternative media, artwork and documentary, and assess the social relations mediated by new technologies. Analyses must examine more carefully the channels of media communication, structures of visibility, genres of expression, modes of spectatorship and social relations of production and display. What is brought into view by new media? Who is figured and for whom? How are the restrictive frameworks of mainstream representations challenged? What new forms of relationality and connectedness are produced? Which channels of identification and/or desire are allowed to flow or are dammed up? On the ground, yes, but whose ground? And on what grounds?

Epilogue: The Political Exigency of the Oblique

In 1992, the artist Mona Hatoum created the installation *Light Sentence* at the Chapter Arts Centre in Cardiff. The work consisted of a tall arrangement of wire-mesh lockers surrounding a single light bulb, which moved slowly up and down, suspended from a simple wire; the installation resembled a large cage or prison cell. Hatoum noted that the light projected the locker grid onto the walls of the exhibition space, creating the impression that the entire room was a cage in which one was enmeshed or entrapped: "because the light bulb [was] moving very, very slowly, there's a feeling of displacement, disorientation that's created by the simple movement of the light, which shifts the ground under your feet and gives you an uneasy feeling when you enter the space, that something is not quite right."[1] This work provides not only a poetic entanglement of the key themes that emerge in this book—imaging and mediation, refraction as a political and aesthetic strategy, eccentric subjectivity, political displacement and transnational circulation—but also a remarkable parable for the feminist scholar interested in signifying practices in the global present: as she focuses on the object illuminated before her, she risks obscuring the refracted light encircling her, effecting the projected cage in which artwork, gallery, maker and viewer are enclosed. In focusing on the projections in the institutional space, she may turn her back on the object itself. To see the two cages requires an eccentric and prismatic vision, attentive to the diffraction and refraction of light, as well as to active processes of mediation and semiosis.

The concept of *imaging* has provided a method for thinking the active signifying practices that constitute objects, subjects and social reality, and the processes of refraction and diffraction that bring them both to light. Imaging practices position cultural producers, those represented and spectators and inscribe them in ideological formations, which are grounded in binary structures (sexual and racial difference, for instance), and marked by differential and overlapping spatial scales. Prismatic vision has provided a methodology for seeing the active processes of mediation, for engaging questions of multiplicity, difference, disjuncture and deflection. Such strategies are particularly important in the period covered in this book—the late twentieth and early twenty-first centuries—marked not by the seamlessness of globalization, but by a forceful and disjunctive refiguring of the world order.

The historical period in which this book begins its study is one where the world is considerably refashioned politically, economically and culturally: the 1989 crumbling of the Berlin Wall, the dissolution of the Soviet Union, the end of the political system of Apartheid in South Africa, the confrontations of Tiananmen Square, the founding of the European Union and the beginnings of the Oslo Peace Process were met with the optimistic assertion that alternatives to capitalism had failed and that we had reached the "end of history" and the triumph of capitalism, and particularly the expansive force of globalization under capitalism. The case studies presented in this book have focused on the important political and cultural events in the waning decades of the twentieth century, as well as the refiguring of the world under the terms of economic crisis and war in the early twenty-first century.

While these case studies may initially appear discrete—crossing the United States, Europe, West Asia, Central Asia and South Asia—the chapters rather seek to articulate the complex nodes of a global system considerably redefined by modes of ethnic nationalism, the aggressive force of globalization and its capitalization of increasing aspects of daily life, and the increased militarization under the conditions of permanent war. They also identify specifically the sites of appeals to transnational feminism across local contexts, frequently in deep (and sometimes exploitative or oppressive) relations with other localities, and with the disjunctive dimensions of the global system itself. Sexual violence and exploitation, alienation and disenfranchisement, invisibility and oppression are topics that demand a "feminism without borders"—a feminism that pays attention to the historical and cultural specificity of ideological closures and political struggles, with an aim to transcend them through a complex and emancipatory coalitional politics.

Refraction and diffraction have been used throughout this study as metaphors for an engaged and poetic media practice, and have worked to supplement critical engagements with reflection and reflexivity. Emerging out of early optics, both refraction and diffraction point to interference patterns—to the diversion of light as it passes through media of varying density, and to the breaking apart of a beam of light at the edge of an opaque body. Refraction has proven a particularly compelling concept in examining media in the globalized present, as the passage of media through cultural contexts, across spatial scales or into different institutional and public spaces has involved deflection, translation and transformation.

Indeed, the Oxford English Dictionary includes an obsolete figurative definition for refraction involving mediation, alteration or distortion—usually of something pure or absolute—arising from the medium of expression, personal perspective, social context and suchlike.

Strategies of refraction and diffraction have involved different processes and targets in the case studies presented. In the first chapter, prismatic visions served not only to pry open totalizing representations of ethnicity and gender in the context of genocide and armed conflict, but also to resist the resolution of these two axes in post-conflict politics (by international peace organizations, on the one hand, and by transnational feminist organizations, on the other). Refraction thus interceded in the conflicts between ethnic nationalism and gendered discourse in the aftermath of the dissolution of the former Soviet Union. In the second chapter, prismatic strategies served to foreground the frictions between the expansive and limitless force of capitalist globalization in the context of India's emergence as a new economic and cultural force on the world stage, the structures of international good governance and pre-capitalist social formations. It thus served to highlight the tension between geopolitical scales in the emerging world system. The third chapter focused on prismatic mediations of territorial disputes and continued colonizing forces in Israel-Palestine, and thus highlighted the friction of border-crossing even as they articulated the emancipatory imaginaries of statehood and belonging. Finally, the fourth chapter examined how prismatic strategies charted the movement of media through ideological structures, particularly insofar as those structures were constituted by absolutist binaries. In this context, the binary visibility/invisibility in the war in Afghanistan placed cultural producers in an impossible location, one in which diffraction assisted in processes of signification that did not repeat or reaffirm the binary structure of media culture.

Through its progression, writing this book has also encountered the difficult work of prismatic mediation as a scholarly practice—in the interdisciplinary methods mobilized in individual chapters; in the scale-shifts between the subjective, social and semiotic dimensions of imaging; and across disparate geographical locations and different political struggles. Such prismatic thinking always risks skirting the very boundary between an emancipatory and an ever-expanding "feminism without borders," between complex coalitions and a proliferating scholarship that spreads, like the limitless force of global capitalism. The scale of the global risks always repeating the logic of globalization, of converting local specificity into exchange value and of deterritorializing in the name of universalizing drives whose forces are frequently renewed in the persistent modernizing imperatives of the contemporary world.

The focus on refraction and diffraction—within cultural practices and in their movements through transnational circuits—sought to resist the conversion of historical and cultural specificity and value into the coin of globalization. Prismatic visions have sought to ally experimental media with the critical and creative technologies for generating resistance and coalitional politics in a globalized present. In doing so, they affirm the importance of media experimentation to politics and ethics in the contemporary moment. The poetic, Spivak teaches us, disturbs the surface of language, its clearly indicated connections, by working "in the silence between and around words."[2] Without the rhetoricity and poetic experimentation of artworks, films and documentaries, media risk constructing local scenes for transnational audiences through neo-colonialist forms of visibility and authority. This is especially true given what Spivak calls the "traffic in accessibility," which in the context of this study entails the translation into dominant and recognizable media genres. While such legibility renders media accessible to the greatest number of people globally, it also risks "subsum[ing] a democratic ideal into the law of the strongest."[3]

Spivak's "task of the feminist translator" requires the translator to surrender to the text, to ask the text to show the limits of its language. This surrender stands against a politics that presupposes that women have a natural or "narrative-historical" solidarity. Traditional ethics are caught, on the one hand, by not wanting to assume a kinship with the other, and on the other hand, by not being able to have a full conception of the other as other or alterity. These ethics always involve some degree of turning the other into an instance of the same. The surrender of translation, however, is not a traditional ethical standpoint. Spivak's call for the radical surrender to the rhetoricity of the other lies in the disruption of figuration in social practice. Figuration becomes a method for "rusing with rhetoric."[4] Such (prismatic) engagements do not assume the authenticity, the logical systematicity or the transparency of other subjects, struggles and cultural contexts. Such rusing implicates feminist scholarship in oppositional reading and writing practices, acknowledging mediation down the chains of response and responsibility in the global system.

While the displacement of one's point of understanding and conceptual articulation is a fruitful arena for resisting the hegemonic sites of the articulation of race/gender/sexuality, displacement is also the site where social subjects are articulated across languages and cultural representations, or as de Lauretis notes, "en-gendered in the experiencing of race and class, as well as sexual relations, not unified but rather multiple, and not so much divided as contradicted."[5] Thus, rather than simply a record of authentic and unified experience, prismatic media might shed light on "the meanings attached to gender, race, class and age at various historical moments," and thus *theorize* rather than re-present experience.[6] Such strategies expose the speculative root of *theoria*, and are central to articulating such a relational feminism because of the manner in which they engage in complex accounts of gender, ethnicity and sexuality in and across the transnational circuits of media's increasing circulation. Undertaking such a project is not without its frictions and obstacles; however, one is reminded that prisms only refract light by presenting it with an obstacle. The resulting patterns give shape to the very substance of the visible world.

Notes

Prelims

1. Roland Barthes, "Death of the Author," in *Image—Music—Text* (New York: Hill & Wang, 1977), 148.

Introduction

1. Jacques Derrida, "Videor," in *Resolutions: Contemporary Video Practices*, ed. Michael Renov and Erika Suderburg (Minneapolis: University of Minnesota Press, 1996), 73.
2. Trinh Minh-ha, *Woman Native Other* (Bloomington: Indiana University Press, 1989), 23.
3. Martha Rosler, "Video: Shedding the Utopian Moment," in *Illuminating Video: An Essential Guide to Video Art*, ed. Doug Hall and Sally Jo Fifer (New York: Aperture, in association with the Bay Area Video Coalition, 1990), 31.
4. Beryl Korot, Phyllis Gershuny and Michael Shamberg, "Introduction," *Radical Software* 1, no. 1 (1970): 1.
5. It also specifically situated alternative media in the U.S. in the context of socialist and anti-imperial struggles, particularly in light of Mao Tse-Tung's articulation of revolution in *On Guerrilla Warfare* (1937). It is important to note also that questions of alternative media were raised in the global South, especially in the context of the New World Information and Communications Order proposed by the Movement of Non-Aligned Countries in Algiers in 1973. See Rafael Roncagliolo, "The Growth of the Audio-Visual Imagescape in Latin America," in *Video the Changing World*, ed. Nancy Thede and Alain Ambrosi (Montreal: Black Rose Books, 1991), 22–30.
6. Deirdre Boyle, *Subject to Change: Guerrilla Television Revisited* (New York: Oxford University Press, 1997), xv.
7. Lisa Nakamura raises the point that the appropriation of images of Native Americans as the archetype of the "cybernetic nomad" in counter-cultural movements focused on independence from mass culture was particularly problematic given, first, the exclusion of Native Americans from most counter-cultural movements, and second, the exploitation of Native labor on

Reservations to work in new electronics factories. Nakamura discussed her current research on race, labor and indigeneity at the workshop "The Politics of Visuality: Innovative Feminist Approaches to Race/Gender/Sexualities in Visual Culture and Social Media," held at Rutgers University, January 20, 2012. I am grateful for her presentation for bringing to my attention the contradictions between the use of Native Americans in Shamberg's manifesto.

8. This is true of activist video in the United States made by groups such as People's Video Theater and projects such as The Disarmament Video Survey. It served also as a model for community video by, among other groups, Video SEWA (which trained members coming from the informal sectors in video production) and the Canadian National Film Board's "Challenge for Change" activist documentary program, which ran from 1967 to 1980.

9. The term "Third Cinema" was first proposed by Argentinian filmmakers Fernando Solanas and Octavio Getino in 1969. Third Cinema opposed Hollywood's emphasis on "emotional manipulation", as well as its heavy debt to commercial industries. Instead, it was charged with promoting a critical understanding of social dynamics. Although no specific aesthetic forms were prescribed, filmmakers who identified with the genre of Third Cinema sought to make films which brought about socialist consciousness and change. See especially Michael Chanan's *Twenty-Five Years of the New Latin American Cinema* (London: BFI, 1983) for the original manifestos by Solanas and Getino, Julio García Espinosa, and Glauber Rocha.

10. Alain Ambrosi, "Alternative Communication and Development Alternatives," in *Video the Changing World*, ed. Nancy Thede and Alain Ambrosi (Montreal: Black Rose Books, 1991), 4–14. Although community video and indigenous self-representation are not the topic of this study, there are excellent studies in this field. See Faye Ginsburg, Lila Abu-Lughod and Brian Larkin, eds., *Media Worlds: Anthropology on New Terrain* (Berkeley: University of California Press, 2002); and Pamela Wilson and Michelle Stewart, eds., *Global Indigenous Media: Cultures, Poetics, and Politics* (Durham: Duke University Press, 2008); among others.

11. Jim Pines and Paul Willemen, eds., *Questions of Third Cinema* (London: BFI Publications, 1989), 12–13.

12. The term "imperfect cinema" derives from the Cuban filmmaker Julio García Espinosa, who calls for an end to the division between art and life and between intellectuals and "the people." See "For an Imperfect Cinema," in *Twenty-Five Years of New Latin American Cinema*, ed. Michael Chanan (London: British Film Institute, 1983), 28–33.

13. Nevertheless, Laura U. Marks's careful investigation of video art in the Arab world, and Beirut specifically, voices a word of caution also about the accessibility of video in certain cultural contexts. Her research finds that most Arab independent media is, in her terms, "intercultural," that is, tied to global and diasporic exchanges. Laura U. Marks, "What is That *and* between Arab Women and Video? The Case of Beirut," *Camera Obscura* 18, no. 2 (2003): 41–70.

14. Luis Camnitzer, Jane Farver and Rachel Weiss, *Global Conceptualism: Points of Origin, 1950s-1980s* (New York: Queens Museum of Art, 1999), viii.

15. László Beke, "Conceptual Tendencies in Eastern European Art," in Camnitzer, Farber and Weiss, 41–51.

16. Mari Carmen Ramírez, "Tactics for Thriving on Adversity: Conceptualism in Latin America, 1960–1980," in Camnitzer, Farber and Weiss, 66.

17. As such, video presages the debates surrounding and paradoxes inherent in the contemporary landscape of video art, activist and hacktivist media and experimental documentary.

18. Rosler, 43.

19. An important exception among others is Michael Renov and Erika Suderburg's edited volume *Resolutions: Contemporary Video Practices* (Minneapolis: University of Minnesota Press, 1996).

20. Michael Rush argues that 1997— the year when Sony released the first digital recorder in the U.S.—marks the definitive moment of media convergence for the field of video art. With this technology, cultural producers began using a combination of video, digital video, film, DVDs and computer-based imaging in their art projects. Michael Rush, *New Media in Late 20th Century Art* (London: Thames & Hudson, 1999).

21. Lucy Lippard makes a distinction between activist and political art, noting that political art is socially concerned, its artistic process is frequently bound to genre traditions and conventional modes of display. Activist art, on the other hand, is socially engaged and fights for cultural democracy. Lucy Lippard, "Trojan Horses: Activist Art and Power," in *Art After Modernism: Rethinking Representation*, ed. Brian Wallis (New York: The New Museum of Contemporary Art, 1984). While many of the works included in this study may be considered "political art" rather than "activist art" by this definition, attention to the circuits of transmission, the context of display, and the conditions of viewership considerably blur the boundaries between these two forms. Thus, while Milica Tomić's *Belgrade Remembers* engages in a public provocation on repression and resistance in the city of Belgrade— and in this regard might more clearly be identified as an activist artistic practice—Tomić's debt to the languages of feminist body and performance art complicate the work's singularly activist identification (Tomić's work is discussed in Chapter 1 of this study). Conversely, while Emily Jacir's *Memorial to the 418 Village That Were Destroyed, Depopulated and Occupied by Israel in 1948* was located in a traditional museum setting, the Queens Museum, the fact that this museum had served as a temporary home of the United Nations in the 1940s, at the moment when the UN General Assembly passed the resolution to partition Palestine, clearly adds an activist dimension to the work (Jacir's work is discussed in Chapter 3 of this book). These examples demonstrate that, while works themselves trespass disciplinary boundaries, historical scholarship frequently works to reify the division through conventions such as artists' monographs and exhibition catalogues, by dealing with activist and community video along sociological or political axes, or through issue-based collections.

22. I am thinking here explicitly of Okwui Enwezor's curatorial model at *Documenta XI*, which took place in a series of "platforms" and international symposia whose topics (Democracy Unrealized, Experiments with Truth: Transitional Justice and the Processes of Truth and Reconciliation, Créolité and Creolization, Under Siege: Four African Cities—Freetown, Johannesburg, Kinshasa, Lagos) sought to stretch the terms of the avant-garde and the emerging global public sphere. In doing so, it included film, video, digital installations and works that were conventionally located in the field of documentary or activist media. Another example of the kinds of curatorial interventions across these genres involves the artistic and curatorial work of the RAQS Media Collective.

23. T. J. Demos, "The Art of Darkness: On Steve McQueen," *October* 114 (Autumn 2005): 62–63.

24. Salah M. Hassan and Olu Oguibe, " 'Authentic/Ex-Centric' at the Venice Biennale: African Conceptualism in Global Contexts," *African Arts* 34, no.4 (Winter 2001): 65.

25. For an excellent and detailed consideration of scale-making and global-ization, see Anna Tsing, *Friction: An Ethnography of Global Connection* (Princeton: Princeton University Press, 2005).

26. In the British and North American context principally, artists' exploration of the medium of video emerged in relation to a newly emerging field of feminist film theory, and particularly Laura Mulvey's "Visual Pleasure and Narrative Cinema." Lynda Benglis, Dara Birnbaum, Coco Fusco, Lynn Hershman, Joan Jonas, Howardena Pindell, Adrian Piper and Martha Rosler (among many others) each addressed the structures of the gaze and the politics of representation with short video works. Further, artists associated with the Feminist Art Program at Fresno State College frequently used video to document per-formances, and thus associated video with the feminist political project of consciousness-raising.

27. Teresa de Lauretis, *Alice Doesn't: Feminism, Semiotics, Cinema* (Bloomington: Indiana University Press, 1984), 39.

28. Ibid., 48.

29. Although McLuhan certainly emphasized the contraction of the globe effected by electronic media, he by no means meant to suggest that village life would necessarily produce harmony or homogeneity. Nevertheless, his focus on the extension of perception and consciousness runs contrary to my focus, *per* de Lauretis, on both the binding force of imaging processes, their inscription of social and subjective processes in ideology, and the irruptive and eccentric positions open to different female subjects in the social, which construct a different measure of desire and frame of reference.

30. De Lauretis, *Alice Doesn't*, 39.

31. Ibid.

32. Teresa de Lauretis, "Eccentric Subjects," in *Figures of Resistance: Essays in Feminist Theory* (Urbana: University of Illinois Press, 2007), 152.

33. Rosalind Krauss, "The Aesthetics of Narcissism," *October* 1 (Spring 1976): 56.

34. Ibid., 56–57.
35. Ibid., 57.
36. De Lauretis, "Eccentric Subjects," 152.
37. Teresa de Lauretis, *Technologies of Gender: Essays on Theory, Film and Fiction* (Bloomington: Indiana University Press, 1987), 2.
38. De Lauretis, "Eccentric Subjects," 175.
39. Ibid., 151.
40. Ibid.
41. In this regard, de Lauretis's "eccentric subject" might be likened with the process of *décalage* articulated by Brent Hayes Edwards. In examining failed modes of black transnationalism, he emphasizes the subtle but indelible effects left behind, where "unevenness or differentiation marks a constitutive *décalage* in the very weave of culture." *Décalage* involves the restoration of a prior unevenness or diversity, a gap in time or space. See Brent Hayes Edwards, *The Practice of Diaspora: Literature, Translation, and the Rise of Black Internationalism* (Cambridge: Harvard University Press, 2003), 13. Kara Keeling takes up Edwards's notion of *décalage* to posit a form of oppositional consciousness characterized as "I = Another," a subject position which I will take up as central to the operation of prismatic media. See Kara Keeling, "I = Another: Digital Identity Politics," in *Strange Affinities: The Gender and Sexual Politics of Comparative Racialization*, ed. Grace Kyungwon Hong and Roderick A. Ferguson (Durham: Duke University Press, 2011), 53–75.
42. De Lauretis, "Eccentric Subjects," 175
43. De Lauretis, *Technologies of Gender*, 18.
44. Mary Ann Doane, "Indexicality: Trace and Sign," *differences* 18, no. 1 (2007): 4.
45. Tom Gunning, "Moving Away from the Index," *differences* 18, no. 1 (2007): 33.
46. A focus on Peircian semiotics emphasizes this point by distinguishing between the icon, which involves a relation of resemblance between the representamen and the object it comes to represent, and the index, which includes the "general hailing and deixic functions of language and gesture." See Gunning, 30.
47. Brian Winston characterizes direct cinema or *cinéma vérité* as including: minimal contact between filmmakers and their subjects; conformity between the documentary and the actual order of events filmed; long takes and jump cuts; low or no commentary or voice-over imposing a frame between subjects and audience; and no use of interviews. See Brian Winston, "Documentary: I Think We Are in Trouble," in *New Challenges for Documentary*, ed. Alan Rosenthal (Berkeley: University of California Press, 1988), 23.
48. Trinh Minh-ha, *When the Moon Waxes Red: Representation, Gender and Cultural Politics* (New York: Routledge, 1991), 33.
49. Bill Nichols, "The Voice of Documentary," in *New Challenges for Documentary*, 50.
50. Ibid., 50.

51. Ibid., 51.
52. Trinh, 42.
53. Homi Bhabha, "Signs Taken for Wonders," in *The Location of Culture* (New York: Routledge, 1994), 110.
54. Trinh, 46.
55. This is certainly an ideological necessity, the basis for human rights claims generally. Nevertheless, as Spivak's argument makes clear, "the enablement must be used even as the violation is re-negotiated." Gayatri Chakravorty Spivak, "Righting Wrongs" in *Human Rights, Human Wrongs*, ed. Nicholas Owens (Oxford: Oxford University Press, 2002), 169.
56. Roland Barthes, *Mythologies* (New York: Hill and Wang, 1972), 117.
57. James Clifford, "Post/Neo Colonial Situations: Notes on Historical Realism Today," in *Literatura e Viagens Pós-coloniais*, ed. Helena Carvalhão Buescu and Manuela Ribeiro Sanches (Lisbon: Centro de Estudos Comparatistas, 2002), 12.
58. Ibid., 16–17.
59. Ibid., 10.
60. Ibid., 16–17.
61. Ibid., 17.
62. In this regard, Caren Kaplan notes, with respect to the commercialization of romantic "safari" travel images, that literal and figurative representations of travel "[enable and reproduce] a dangerous 'global-sisterhood' model that asserts similarities based on essentialized categories." See Caren Kaplan, "A World Without Boundaries: The Body Shop's Trans/National Geographics," in *With Other Eyes: Looking at Race and Gender in Visual Culture*, ed. Lisa Bloom (Minneapolis: University of Minnesota Press, 1999), 141.
63. Trinh, 47.
64. Ibid., 48.
65. Ibid.
66. Fredric Jameson, *Postmodernism, or, The Cultural Logic of Late Capitalism* (Durham: Duke University Press, 1991), 72.
67. Ibid., 75. This is not to say that many of the video works examined in this study do not employ narrative forms that are literary or filmic; indeed, it is to note that—insofar as video works organize narrative time—they borrow from the expressive capacities of other genres as a formal residue. When narratives cycle into looping mechanisms, real time, and collage, they articulate a form of mediation Jameson calls "video."
68. Jameson, 86.
69. Chandra Talpade Mohanty, *Feminism without Borders: Decolonizing Theory, Practicing Solidarity* (Durham: Duke University Press, 2003), 107–9.
70. Donna Haraway, *Modest_Witness@Second_Millenium.FemaleMan©_Meets_ OncoMouse™: Feminism and Technoscience* (New York: Routledge, 1997), 16–17.
71. Ibid., 16.

72. While Karen Barad takes up Haraway's notion of diffraction at length, her commitment to what she calls "nonrepresentational methodological approaches" or "material practices of intra-acting within and as part of the world" is specifically at odds with my articulation of an aesthetic strategy for representing complex and empancipatory feminist coalitional politics. See Karen Barad, *Meeting the Universe Halfway: Quantum Physics and the Entanglement of Matter and Meaning* (Durham: Duke University Press, 2007), 88–90.

73. Chela Sandoval, *Methodology of the Oppressed* (Minneapolis: University of Minnesota Press, 2000), 44–61.

74. Theodor Adorno and Max Horkheimer, "The Culture Industry: Enlightenment as Mass Deception," in *Dialectic of Enlightenment* (New York: Continuum, 1993), 411.

75. De Lauretis, *Alice Doesn't*, 38–39. In this regard, the conceptual and aesthetic strategy of refraction or diffraction allies certain media with the feminist articulation of standpoint theory, and especially with its focus on multiplicity and complexity, on the incorporation of multiple and competing views as a strategy for knowledge and cultural production. Mary Hawkesworth asserts that feminist standpoint analysis "acknowledges that claims about the world are theoretically mediated and value-laden—constructed in relation to a range of partial perspectives and determinate interests." See Mary Hawkesworth, *Feminist Inquiry: From Political Conviction to Methodological Innovation* (New Brunswick: Rutgers University Press, 2006), 178.

76. I thank Laura Christian for bringing this example to my attention in our conversations around reflexivity.

77. Gayatri Chakravorty Spivak, *Death of a Discipline* (New York: Columbia University Press, 2003), 13.

78. De Lauretis, "Eccentric Subjects," 152.

79. Teresa de Lauretis, "Aesthetics and Feminist Theory: Rethinking Women's Cinema," in *Female Spectators: Looking at Film and Television*, ed. E. Deirdre Pribam (London: Verso, 1988), 181.

80. This is not to say that standpoint theory resolves the question of "standpoint"—nor that refraction necessarily redirects media contents in politically fruitful directions. Wendy Brown, in problematizing standpoint theory and the category of experience, argues, "When the notion of a unified and coherent subject is abandoned, we [. . .] cease to be able to speak of woman or for women in an unproblematic way [. . .] dispensing with the unified subject does not mean ceasing to be able to speak about our experiences as women, only that our words cannot be legitimately deployed or construed as larger or longer than the moments of the lives they speak from." See Wendy Brown, *States of Injury: Power and Freedom in Late Modernity* (Princeton: Princeton University Press, 1995), 40–41. Similarly, Hawkesworth asks, "If the experiences of situated knowers are identified as the grounds for the construction of competing standpoints, how can feminists avoid forms of subjectivism, which sustain both an unshakable conviction in the veracity of

one's own experience and relativist resignation concerning the impossibility of adjudicating incompatible, experience-based claims?" Hawkesworth, 202.

81. Mohanty, 111–12.

82. Caren Kaplan, "The Politics of Location as Transnational Feminist Critical Practice," in *Scattered Hegemonies: Postmodernity and Transnational Feminist Practices*, ed. Inderpal Grewal and Caren Kaplan (Minneapolis: University of Minnesota Press, 1994), 138.

83. Ibid., 139.

84. Ibid., 148.

85. Mohanty, 118.

86. In this regard, it is important to acknowledge also the manner in which this study participates in the "traffic in accessibility," emerging out of the North American academy, examining works available to Western audiences, frequently translated or subtitled in English or French. In taking up the question of transnational circuits, in opening up to the effect of cultural production and transmission for feminisms in a globalized present, this study seeks to articulate a commitment to a feminism without borders that attends to frictions, ruptures, uneven privileges and the very terms of transmission. De Lauretis reminds us that feminist theory is itself also a technology of gender, that "the construction of gender is also effected by its deconstruction." This assertion stresses the implication of the feminist scholar, her complicity with ideologies, and argues that the work of feminist theory begins by recognizing our location, articulating the "situatedness—political-historical and personal-political—of its own thought." De Lauretis, *Technologies of Gender*, 2.

87. James Clifford, *Routes: Travel and Translation in the Late Twentieth-Century* (Cambridge: Harvard University Press, 1997), 11.

88. Gayatri Chakravorty Spivak, *An Aesthetic Education in an Era of Globalization* (Cambridge: Harvard University Press, 2012), 1. It should be noted that this book was released shortly before the completion of the manuscript, and thus while the book's subject is captivating and utterly relevant to this study, I have been unable to fully consider the book's implications here.

89. Tsing, *Friction*, 1.

90. Ibid., 5.

91. Spivak, *An Aesthetic Education*, 12.

92. Mohanty, 124.

93. Norma Alarcón, Caren Kaplan and Minoo Moallem, *Between Woman and Nation: Nationalisms, Transnational Feminisms and the State* (Durham: Duke University Press, 1999), 1.

94. De Lauretis, *Alice Doesn't*, 39.

95. Gayatri Chakravorty Spivak, *Death of a Discipline* (New York: Columbia University Press, 2003), 34. In a much earlier text, Spivak fleshes out this imaginative mode: "[. . .] if we must think a relationship between the subject of onto/epistemology [. . .] and the object of onto/axiology (that disenfranchised woman, not even graduated into that subject, whose historicity or

subjectship we cannot imagine beyond the regulation 'women's union' or 'personal pain' human interest anecdote) the hope behind the political desire will be that the possibility for the name [subaltern] will be finally erased [. . .] In search of irreducibles, after the chastening experience of coming close to the person who provides that imagined name, I want to be able not to lament when the material possibility for the name will have disappeared." Like the seduction of the name "subaltern" in Spivak's text, the seduction of visibility is foregrounded by the tensions between revelation and refraction that shape the works included in this study. Gayatri Chakravorty Spivak, "Feminism and Deconstruction, Again: Negotiations," in *Outside in the Teaching Machine* (New York: Routledge, 1993), 140.

96. I thank Prof. Gina Dent for drawing my attention to this unusual formulation and what it might mean, during an independent reading group organized around Gayatri Spivak's work held at the University of California, Santa Cruz in Winter 2004.

97. Spivak, *An Aesthetic Education*, 3.

98. Ibid., 4.

99. With regard to the "lure of the local," Miwon Kwon has critiqued Lucy Lippard for presenting a holistic vision of place, tied to a sense of rooted identity. Instead of a retrieval and resuscitation of a sense of place (and the presumption that what was lost can be found again), Kwon argues for the possibility of engaging at once the desires for both "right" and "wrong" places, and the social conventions, ideological regimes and habits of familiarity which set distinctions between propriety and impropriety. See Miwon Kwon, "The Wrong Place," *Art Journal* 59, no. 1 (Spring, 2000): 33–43.

100. Spivak, *An Aesthetic Education*, 28.

101. See Clifford, *Routes.*

Chapter 1

1. http://milicatomic.wordpress.com/works/one-day-instead-of-one-nighta-burst-of-machine-gun-fire-will-flash-if-light-cannot-come-otherwise/.

2. Although I examine both video installations and experimental documentaries in this chapter, my argument throughout will strive to show the common conditions of cultural production and similar strategies employed by both artists and documentarians in addressing the postwar representational landscape in Serbia, Bosnia, Croatia and internationally.

3. Cited in Expert Report of Renaud de la Brosse, "Political Propaganda and the Plan to Create "A State for All Serbs": Consequences of Using Media for Ultra-Nationalist Ends," compiled at the request of the Office of the Prosecutor of the International Criminal Tribunal for the Former Yugoslavia, 40, accessed April 27, 2006, http://hague.bard.edu/icty_info.html.

4. The Brosse Report cites five examples from different authors, all published in the major newspaper *Politika* from November 1998 to May 1990.

5. Anne McClintock, "No Longer in a Future Heaven: Nationalism, Race and Gender," in *Imperial Leather: Race, Gender and Sexuality in the Colonial Context* (New York: Routledge, 1995), 353.

6. Ibid., 353.

7. Nira Yuval-Davis and Floya Anthias, *Women-Nation-State* (London: Macmillan, 1989), 7. Cited in McClintock, 355.

8. This is certainly the case with many of the texts included in the anthology *Mass Rape: The War Against Women in Bosnia-Herzegovina*, ed. Alexandra Stiglmayer (Lincoln: University of Nebraska Press, 1994), and particularly Catherine MacKinnon's article, cited below in the chapter.

9. Beverly Allen, *Rape Warfare: The Hidden Genocide in Bosnia-Herzegovina and Croatia* (Minneapolis: University of Minnesota Press, 1996), 87.

10. The malleability of ethnic categories is the subject of a work of art by Mary Kelly entitled *The Ballad of Kastroit Rexhepi* (2002). Here, Kelly was struck by a *Los Angeles Times* article in 1999 that described the situation of a young boy who had been left for dead as his Albanian parents escaped a sustained Serbian attack. When he was found alive on the battleground, he was given a Serbian name (Zoran) and left behind at a hospital. When the Serbs retreated, the young boy was renamed with an Albanian name (Lirim). While the news story had the tenor of a human-interest story, Kelly was marked by how it compressed large-scale historical events into the young boy's body. She created a wall text consisting of three stanzas, formed on collected drier lint, which she collected while drying thousands of pounds of black and white cotton clothing. The stanzas read, "Unnatural spring: metal seedpods germinating bloody flora anticipating the 'expulsions.' Still, there is no escape from the facile affirmation of the media: 'Summer, 1999 happy ending in the Times.'" In using drier lint, Kelly sought to make connections between the detritus of everyday life and the "waste of war." See Ernest Larsen, "About a Boy," *Art in America* (December 2002): 98–101. I would like to thank Jennifer González for bringing this work to my attention.

11. Vesna Kesić, "Muslim Women, Croatian Women, Serbian Women, Albanian Women . . . ," in *Balkan as Metaphor: Between Globalization and Fragmentation*, ed. Dušan I. Bjelić and Obrad Savić (Cambridge: The MIT Press, 2002), 311.

12. This view was most famously propounded by Catherine MacKinnon, who wrote an article published in *Ms. Magazine* in 1993, entitled "Turning Rape into Pornography: Postmodern Genocide." The article was reproduced in *Mass Rape: The War Against Women in Bosnia-Herzegovina*, ed. Alexandra Stiglmayer (Lincoln: University of Nebraska Press, 1994), 73–81.

13. Kesić, 317.

14. Catherine MacKinnon, "Turning Rape into Pornography: Postmodern Genocide." *Ms. Magazine* (July/August 1993): 24–30.

15. The *Ms. Magazine* article also followed on the heals of the 1992 Canadian Supreme Court ruling (the "Butler Decision"), which incorporated elements of Dworkin and MacKinnon's ordinances into existing Canadian obscenity laws. This ruling was controversial especially because the first case prosecuted under

the decision involved a story of consensual lesbian SM that appeared in a queer magazine entitled *Bad Attitude*.

16. Roland Barthes, "Myth Today," in *Mythologies* (New York: Hill& Wang, 1972), 111.
17. Ibid., 113–117.
18. Ibid., 119.
19. See, for example, the interview with Milica Pesić, director of the European Center for War, Peace, and the News Media, on National Public Radio's program *All Things Considered*. April 12, 1999.
20. Brosse, 5–6.
21. Cited in Roy Gutman, *A Witness to Genocide* (New York: Macmillan Publishing Company, 1993), x.
22. The Brosse Report also noted that the SRNA, the Bosnian Serb television station, reported that Muslims fed Serbian women and children to hungry lions at the Sarajevo zoo: see Brosse, 77. Newspapers in Serbia also published reader's letters reporting that Albanians were raping hundreds of Serbian women in Kosovo: see Brosse, 50.
23. Teresa de Lauretis, "The Violence of Rhetoric: Considerations on Representation and Gender," in *Technologies of Gender: Essays on Theory, Film and Fiction* (Basingstoke: Macmillan Publishers, 1989), 4.
24. Ibid., 5.
25. Ibid., 6–7.
26. Ibid., 1–2.
27. Lynda E. Boose, "Crossing the River Drina: Bosnian Rape Camps, Turkish Impalement, and Serb Cultural Memory," *Signs* 28, no. 1, Gender and Cultural Memory (Autumn 2002): 71–96.
28. Ibid., 75–6.
29. Kosovar Albanians (who are Muslim) are descendants of the Illyrians (who arrived in the Balkans around 8 B.C.E.) have been the target of a discreditation campaign by Serbian scientific, academic and political groups, who sought to revise and cast doubt on the primordiality of this group in the region: see Boose, 76.
30. Boose, 78.
31. Ibid., 79.
32. Ibid., 85.
33. Such a construction begs the question why Serbians do not act against Bosnian and Croatian men rather than against women. One might surmise that such acts would constitute, in the view of those committing these crimes, a threat to Serbian masculinity, the fear of being viewed as sodomites. Thus, it would seem that homophobia is partially responsible for the shifting gender (from Turkish men to Croatian women, for example) in "ethnic cleansing" campaigns, and thus the campaigns reconstitute a heteronormative gender binary through the sexual violence of rape and forced pregnancy.
34. The mobilization of a technology of gender in the politics of ethnic nationalism is also true of the institutions of high culture. Tom Holert noted that,

when the director of the Museum of Contemporary Art Belgrade (MOCAB) was fired in 1993, the venue was transformed into a site for the articulation of Serbian nationalist culture. Holert mentions specifically MOCAB's new director, Radislav Trkulja, who "promulgated an invented history of Serbian art based largely on mythico-erotic painting that aimed to legitimize an official politics based on violence (and, implicitly, sex) in the name of ethnic superiority." See Tom Holert, "The New Normal," *ArtForum* XLIV, no. 6 (February 2006): 83–84.

35. De Lauretis makes clear the important ties between violence and rhetoric, reversing the phrase "the rhetoric of violence" to understand how rhetoric itself might also be the site of violence. Her understanding is central to the point I am making here about the representation of women in ethnic nationalism in the former Yugoslavia. See Teresa de Lauretis, "The Violence of Rhetoric."

36. Strikingly, the question of mixed-race identity became repressed from the mythical narratives of forced pregnancies.

37. De Lauretis, 2.

38. Ibid., 10–11.

39. Marcia Vetrocq, "The 1997 Venice Biennale: A Space Odyssey," *Art in America* (September 1997): 76.

40. Ibid., 75. See also documentation of the Venice Biennale 1997 by the New School International Art Tour, accessed January 12, 2006, http://www.online. newschool.edu/iat97/FPP/abram.html.

41. Vetrocq, 76.

42. Ibid.

43. Zoe Kosmidou, "Transitory Objects: A Conversation with Marina Abramović," *Sculpture* 20, no. 9 (November 2001): 31.

44. Maureen Turim, "Marina Abramović's Performance: Stresses on the Body and Psyche in Installation Art," *Camera Obscura 54* 18, no. 3 (2003): 106.

45. Kosmidou, 28.

46. Barthes, 128. The mythical function of these images might also be read through Barthes's distinction between denotation and connotation in "The Rhetoric of the Image." In this re-reading, the three ways of reading myth might be articulated as follows: in the first case, one might focus on the denotative sign and mobilize it so as to connote another meaning (as the myth-maker does). In the second, one might separate out the original connotative message of the sign from its new connotative message (to return to the sign prior to its appropriation by myth and thus de-mythologize the sign). In the third, the connotative meaning is intimately tied to the sign itself, and one examines how this proximate relation is shaped historically and socially. While this later work is clearer on the question of connotative meanings, Barthes's attention to the filling and emptying of the mythic signifier is particularly relevant to the figuration of woman/nation that I am concerned with here, and particularly with the violent effects of such rhetorical moves. See Roland Barthes, "The Rhetoric of the Image," in *The Responsibility of Forms: Critical Essays on Music, Art and Representation* (Berkeley: University of California Press, 1991), 1–17.

47. Tomić also created a web-based artwork where the viewer is presented with a close-up of the same image of Tomić that appears in the video installation, except that the statements in various languages frame the image with a band of text. When the viewer clicks on the image, her statement appears in a particular language and the text is then replaced with a wound (such as a nose bleed, a gash in her chest or neck, or a trickle of blood from behind her ear). When the viewer clicks the wound, the image of Tomić fades behind the text, and a series of symbols appear: a baby pram, a pipe, a stick figure of a yogi, a finger sprouting leaves and two schematic female figures. Each of these figures covers a statement ("I am a mother," "I am a smoker," "I am a transcendental meditator," "I am a homosexual," "I am a vegetarian,"). The page then links to an article by Ernesto Laclau, entitled "Universalism, Particularism and the Question of Identity." The "Question of Identity" becomes a link that returns the viewer to the original image of Tomić, unwounded. The declarative statements in different iterations of the work often contradict each other, destabilizing the truthfulness of the statements with respect to Tomić herself. The viewer is also placed in the awkward position of inflicting the wounds on Tomić as she navigates through the artwork. See *The Reality Check: I Am Milica Tomić*, accessed May 31, 2006, http://realitycheck.c3.hu/milica/index.html.

48. Emily Jacir's work is discussed at greater depth in Chapter 2; Lida Abdul's work is discussed in Chapter 4.

49. Maura Reilly, "Art Essay: Curating Transnational Feminisms," *Feminist Studies* 36, no. 1 (Spring 2010), 156.

50. Barthes, "Myth Today," 128.

51. Rita Manchanda makes this argument with regard to the naturalization of the relation between women and peace in South Asian conflicts. See Rita Manchanda, "Where are the Women in South Asian Conflicts?" in *Women, War and Peace in South Asia: Beyond Victimhood to Agency* (New Delhi: Sage Publications, 2001), 16–17.

52. A later video work by Marina Abramović, entitled *The Hero* (2001), sought specifically to memorialize her late father as a Yugoslavian national hero. In it, Abramović sat on a white horse and held up a long staff topped with the Yugoslavian flag. Posed like a chivalric painting, Abramović sang the former Yugoslavian national anthem. The performance ended when she could no longer hold up the flag with her outstretched arm. In this work also, the figure of the father and of the "fatherland" are thoroughly entangled, and Abramović seems to be at once memorializing her father's loss, and the loss of her country. The piece was exhibited, among other places, at the Cetinje Biennale V in 2004 under the theme "Balkans in the Balkan."

53. Of course, the video itself loops continuously in the site of the installation. The viewer is then given a sense not of the doubling of the testimony, but rather of the repeated circulation of the traumatic narrative.

54. We might recall in this regard the force of the Serbian myth of Turkish impalement. Given the construction of gender through violence, the hole in the father's chest can certainly be read as an emasculation of the father, similar

to the actual practice (reportedly widespread) of actual castration of prisoners in detention camps.

55. A clear example of this is Catherine MacKinnon's, "Rape, Genocide and Women's Human Rights," in *Mass Rape: The War Against Women in Bosnia-Herzegovina*, ed. Alexandra Stiglmayer (Lincoln: University of Nebraska Press, 1994),183–197. In this article, MacKinnon argues that the politics of "ethnic cleansing" by Serbian forces is simply a manifestation of the "rape, forced motherhood, prostitution, pornography, and sexual murder, on the basis of sex and ethnicity together, that is inflicted on women every day in every country in the world." She further argues that the explosion of pornography in post-Socialist Yugoslavia led to the forms of sexualized violence committed against women during the genocide in the 1990s. Throughout her argument, she relies on a totalizing and singular category, "woman," that violently excludes how women are constituted through difference in specific historical and social contexts, and by particular semiotic and socio-cultural apparatuses.

56. Jennifer A. González, "Autotopographies," in *Prosthetic Territories: Politics and Hypertechnologies*, ed. Gabriel Brahm Jr. and Mark Driscoll (Boulder: Westview Press, 1995), 136. González notes that this reflects also the distinction, in Marcel Proust, between intellectual and involuntary memory (*mémoire involontaire*).

57. For example, the use of actors to represent those in captivity disrupts the relay of testimony, and thus the figure of the witness. This is most pointedly revealed by the fact that Steve Buscemi, Jo Andres's partner, appears in the video as one of the people in hiding in the theater basement. This recognizable actor reinforces the artifice of the video, not in the service of the psychic life of objects, but at an excessive remove from the actual conditions and social relations of Sarajevo under siege.

58. Mandy Jacobson is originally from South Africa, where she was a community worker, specializing in gender issues and urban development, and an activist, producing community videos for various progressive organizations. Karmen Jelincić was born in Croatia and raised in the United States. She has been active with Bosnian refugees in New York and Croatia, and has worked for the Lawyers Committee for Human Rights specifically in relation to the work of the International War Crimes Tribunal for the former Yugoslavia.

59. The documentary emerged at a time when feminist human rights activists were pushing for wartime rape to be tried as a rape crime. Also at this time, other documentarists were using testimonial video documents in human rights work; for example, Ellen Bruno's *Satya* (1993), based on the experiences of Tibetan Buddhist nuns who were imprisoned and tortured for their protests against the Chinese occupation of Tibet. *Calling the Ghosts* was screened around the United States, and Cigelj and Sivac were present for discussions following the viewing. HBO organized a meeting between Cigelj and Sivac and the Council on Foreign Relations in New York, with the Undersecretary of State for Human Rights John Shattuck, the Chair of the Committee to Protect Journalists Kati Marton, and the executor of the Dayton

Accord Richard Holbrooke. The documentary was also screened at film festivals in Toronto, Sarajevo and Minsk. See http://www.centerforsocialmedia. org/ documents/callingtheghosts.pdf.

60. Martha Minow, *Between Vengeance and Forgiveness: Facing History after Genocide and Mass Violence* (Boston: Beacon Press, 1998), 5.

61. Katarzyna Marciniak, "Pedagogy of Anxiety," *Signs* 35, no. 4 (Summer 2010), 871.

62. From *Calling the Ghosts*, cited in Marciniak, 871.

63. Their campaign was ultimately successful, and in June 1996, the International Criminal Tribunal for the former Yugoslavia in The Hague indicted eight Serbian men for sexual assault as a war crime.

64. In "Aesthetics and Feminist Theory," Teresa de Lauretis notes how Chantal Akerman's *Jeanne Dielman* (1975) constructs a picture of female experience that "addresses the spectator as female." De Lauretis argues that "narrative suspense is not built on the expectation of a 'significant event' [. . .] but is produced by the tiny slips in Jeanne's routine, the small forgettings, the hesitations between real-time gestures as common and 'insignificant' as peeling potatoes, washing dishes or making coffee—and then not drinking it." Abramović's and Andres's attention to cooking, cleaning, gathering water, and so on also recall this specifically female experience of war. See Teresa de Lauretis, "Aesthetics and Feminist Theory: Rethinking Women's Cinema," in *Female Spectators: Looking at Film and Television*, ed. E. Deirdre Pribram (London: Verso, 1988), 178–9.

65. Marlise Simons, "Milošević Died of Heart Attack, Autopsy Shows," *New York Times*. International Section. March 13, 2006, http://www.nytimes.com/2006/ 03/13/international/europe/13milosevic.html.

66. Giorgio Agamben, *Remnants of Auschwitz: The Witness and the Archive* (New York: Zone Books, 2002), 20.

Chapter 2

1. Elahe Massumi, *A Kiss Is not a Kiss*, 2000.

2. Ross Kauffman and Zana Briski, *Born into Brothels*, 2004.

3. Elahe Massumi, *The Hijras*, 2000.

4. The central instrument, the *Convention on the Rights of the Child* (1989), mandates countries to protect children from trafficking and any forms of sexual exploitation and abuse, and to prevent the abduction, sale or trafficking of children. Since 2000, however, a series of protocols have been passed to address the exploitation of children, including the *Optional Protocol to the Convention on the Rights of the Child on the Sale of Children, Child Prostitution and Child Pornography* (2000), the *Protocol to Prevent, Suppress and Punish Trafficking in Persons, Especially Women and Children* (2000) and the *Internal Labour Organization Convention 182 Concerning the Prohibition and Immediate Action for the Elimination of the Worst forms of Child Labour* (1999). See UN General Assembly, "Preamble," *Optional Protocol to the Convention on the Rights*

of the Child on the Sale of Children, Child Prostitution and Child Pornography (May 2000), accessed May 13, 2012, http://www.unhcr.org/refworld/docid/3ae6b38bc.html.

5. See, for example, the emphasis on indigenous self-representation in Faye Ginsburg, Rene Vautier, Jean Rouch, Wapikoni Mobile, Vincent Carelli, the Medvedkin Group (Chris Marker), among others.

6. Hal Foster, *The Return of the Real* (Cambridge: MIT Press, 1996).

7. Ibid., 174.

8. Patricia Thomson, "Transforming Young Lives in Calcutta," *American Cinematographer* 86, no. 2 (February 2005): 91.

9. Kauffman and Briski.

10. *Kids with Cameras* is an NGO that was founded by Briski in 2002 as a result of the photography workshops she organized in Kolkata's red-light district. The foundation seeks to raise money for children by selling photographs, as well as through exhibitions and film festivals. Funds are used to teach children photography "to empower them, building confidence, self-esteem and hope." Workshops have been conducted in Kolkata, Haiti, Jerusalem and Cairo. See "Mission," Kids with Cameras, accessed May 13, 2012, http://kids-with-cameras.org/mission/. Sarah Brouillette stresses that "Key to the film, the charity and each piece of attendant media is this linking of the production and circulation of art to a comprehensive global aid program that helps secure disadvantaged children's right to education." Sarah Brouillette, "Human Rights Markets and *Born into Brothels*," *Third Text* 25, no. 2 (March 2011), 172.

11. The film's ending is nevertheless lukewarm. While Avijit chooses to enter the Future Hope School, inspired by his trip to Amsterdam, the film ends by recapping the situation of the other children: Suchitra, who is being pushed by her aunt to "join the line," is unable to leave the brothel. Two of the three girls who were placed in boarding school return to the brothel. One boy refuses to go to the school altogether.

12. Renée Green, "Slippages," in *Radiotemporaire* (Grenoble: Magasin, 2002), 12.

13. Jennifer A. González, *Subject to Display: Reframing Race in Contemporary Installation Art* (Cambridge: MIT Press, 2008), 12.

14. See Coco Fusco, "Ethnicity, Politics, and Poetics: Latinos and Media Art," in *Illuminating Video*, ed. Doug Hall and Sally Jo Fifer (New York: Aperture, in association with the Bay Area Video Coalition, 1990), 304–316.

15. Rob Wilson and Wimal Dissanayake, eds., *Global/Local* (Durham: Duke University Press, 1996), cited in Green.

16. Serena Nanda, *Neither Man Nor Woman* (Belmont: Wadsworth Publishing, 1999). Nanda explains that hijras join particular households through a mentor who both introduces them to the community and collects a portion of their earnings throughout their lives.

17. Elahe Massumi, conversation with author, New York, June 20, 2004.

18. Walter Benjamin, "The Author as Producer," *New Left Review* I, no. 62 (July/August 1970): 2.

19. Trinh T. Minh-ha, "Outside In Inside Out," in *Questions of Third Cinema*, ed. Jim Pines and Paul Willemen (London: BFI Publishing, 1989), 137.

20. Benjamin, 8.

21. Gayatri Spivak, "Woman in Difference," in *Outside in the Teaching Machine* (New York: Routledge, 1993), 78.

22. Ibid., 82.

23. I am thinking specifically of Joan Jonas's *Vertical Roll* (1972), discussed in the Introduction.

24. Spivak, 82.

25. Bill Nichols, "Axiographics: Ethical Space in Documentary Film," in *Representing Reality* (Bloomington: Indiana University Press, 1991), 76.

26. Laura Mulvey, "Visual Pleasure in Narrative Cinema" (1975), in *Feminism and Film*, ed. E. Ann Kaplan (Oxford: Oxford University Press, 2000), 34–47.

27. Ibid., 40.

28. Nichols, 83.

29. Laura U. Marks, *Touch: Sensuous Theory and Multisensory Media* (Minneapolis: University of Minnesota Press, 2002), 3–4.

30. Ibid., 4.

31. Ibid., xii.

32. Ibid., 13.

33. Ibid.

34. Linda Williams notes that pornography is a "moving" medium, regardless of whether it provokes pleasure (for its audience) or outrage (for its detractors). In fact, Williams traces how this moving quality has stood at the basis of pro-censorship definitions of pornography (Does it provoke outrage? It must then be pornography). See Linda Williams, *Hard Core: Power, Pleasure and the 'Frenzy of the Visible'* (Berkeley: University of California Press, 1989).

35. Marks, 12.

36. I showed *A Kiss Is not a Kiss* to students in my Histories of Video in the U.S. class in the summer of 2004. They were extremely discomforted by the images, even as I performed a formal analysis of the movement between cinematic and digital modes of viewing. This reaction emphasized for me how uncomfortable the viewer is made to feel in watching Massumi's work.

37. Alicia Murría, "Elahe Massumi: Fiction and Veracity," in *Narraciones: Elahe Massumi* (Madrid: Fundación Telefónica, 2004), 116–117.

38. James T. Clifford, *Routes: Travel and Translation in the Twentieth-Century* (Cambridge: Harvard University Press, 1997), 34.

39. Ibid., 38.

40. Jean-Léon Gerôme was a French painter and sculptor, a student of Paul Delaroche, who traveled extensively in Turkey, Egypt and North Africa. He is best known for his Oriental scenes, including "The Guard of the Harem," "The Great Moorish Bath" and "The Dance of the Almeh," all of which include central nude female figures in bathhouses, public markets or harems. The texture of Massumi's mise-en-scène closely resembles—indeed appears to cite—these Orientalist paintings, evoking the history of colonial and imperial representations of colonized bodies.

41. Among these were the Sundance Film Festival, Seattle International Film Festival, Full Frame Documentary Film Festival, Cleveland International Film

Festival, Bermuda International Film Festival and U.S. Academy Award for Best Documentary Feature, all in 2004.

42. Pooja Rangan, "Immaterial Child Labor: Media Advocacy, Autoethnography and the Case of *Born into Brothels,*" *Camera Obscura* 75, 25, no. 3 (2011), 144. Rangan also draws the reader's attention to the letter of protest by Swapna Gayen, the secretary of the Durbar Mahila Samanwaya Committee, an activist organization working on health and labor issues among sex works in the Sonagachi neighborhood, which critiqued Kauffman and Briski first for not sharing the film with their ethics committee and second for their portrayal of sex workers as unconcerned for the future of their children.

43. The final scene is strikingly similar to the end of Mahasweta Devi's short story "Douloti," where a sex worker, her body riddled with disease, dies over a map of India drawn by the school children in the district. For Spivak, Douloti's death (she is "all over India" in the story's final words) signals a critique of nationalism based on the super-exploitation of a gendered subaltern subject. Not only this, though, her name, Douloti, can also mean "traffic in wealth." Hence, both the body of woman (no longer producing value but instead disease) and the social conditions of her exploitation are both figured by the image of the woman dying over the postcolonial national map. See Spivak, "Woman In Difference," 95.

Chapter 3

1. Indeed, these questions articulate precisely Edward Said's "predicament" (in James Clifford's terms), that he envisioned and was invested in a non-absolutist Palestinian "state." I thank James Clifford for raising this important point with me.

2. Edward Said, "Reflections on Exile," in *Reflections on Exile and Other Essays* (Cambridge MA: Harvard University Press, 2000), 176.

3. Smadar Lavie and Ted Swedenburg, *Displacement, Diaspora, and Geographies of Identity* (Durham: Duke University Press, 1996), 12.

4. This crisis in rights-based structures is very clear in the shifting conceptualization of the "refugee problem." In April 2006, the UN Human Rights Commission's Refugee Agency published a report entitled *The State of the World's Refugees 2006.* In its introduction, the Report pointed out that "States have serious concerns about 'uncontrolled' migration in today's era of globalization." In the post-WWII era, displaced populations in Europe and elsewhere were managed through a three-pronged approach: repatriation, local integration and third-country resettlement. The two key actors in implementing this approach were national governments and international (UN-based) agencies. The 2006 UNHCR Report, by contrast, voices a concern with the large-scale "mixed migration" caused by the forces of globalization, and the difficulty in sorting out political refugees, migrant workers (economic refugees) and emigrants more broadly. It has thus sought to shift the scale of its response to include NGOs, experts on refugee issues and multi-lateral bodies. See

UNHCR, "The State of the World's Refugees 2006: Human Displacement in the New Millenium," accessed August 15, 2006, http://www.unhcr.org/cgi-bin/texis/vtx/template?page= publ&src=static/sowr2006/toceng.htm

5. The condensation of messages in these objects is evident in the multiple names for the wall being constructed in Israel on the border (and into the territory) of the West Bank. It has been referred to as a "security barrier," a "protection wall" and an "Apartheid wall."

6. The term "borderlands" deploys (with a difference) Gloria Anzaldúa's terminology in *Borderlands = La Frontera: The New Mestiza* (San Francisco: Spinsters/Aunt Lute, 1987).

7. See Kathryn Kanjo, *La Frontera/The Border: Art About the Mexico/United States Experience* (San Diego: Centro Cultural La Raza and the Museum of Contemporary Art of San Diego, 1993), and Guillermo Gomez-Peña, *The New World Border: Prophecies, Poems & Loqueras for the End of the Century* (San Francisco: City Lights, 1996), among others.

8. See Smadar Lavie, "Blowup in the Borderzones" in *Displacement, Diaspora, and Geographies of Identity*, ed. Smadar Lavie and Ted Swedenburg (Durham: Duke University Press, 1996), 69.

9. Smadar Lavie and Ted Swedenburg, eds., *Displacement, Diaspora, and Geographies of Identity* (Durham: Duke University Press, 1996), 16.

10. Alarcón, Kaplan and Moallem, 6–7.

11. Lavie and Swedenburg, 20–22.

12. Chandra Talpade Mohanty, *Feminism Without Borders: Decolonizing Theory, Practicing Solidarity* (Durham: Duke University Press, 2003), 2.

13. In this regard, Radhakrishnan Rajagopalan draws out the gendered implications of Partha Chatterjee's analysis of the join between the binaries inner/outer and home/world. Chatterjee argues, "The world is the external, the domain of the material; the home represents our inner spiritual self, our true identity. The world is a treacherous terrain of the pursuit of material interests, where practical considerations reign supreme. It is also typically the domain of the male. The home is its essence and must remain unaffected by the profane activities of the material world—and woman is its representation." Radhakrishnan Rajagopalan, "Nationalism, Gender, and the Narrative of Identity" in *Diasporic Mediations: Between Home and Location* (Minneapolis: University of Minnesota Press, 1996), 192.

14. Irit Rogoff, *Terra Infirma: Geography's Visual Culture* (London: Routledge, 2000), 88.

15. Jaleh Mansoor, "A Spectral Universality: Mona Hatoum's Biopolitics of Abstraction." *October* 133 (Summer 2010), 56.

16. Mona Hatoum, interview with Michael Archer in *Mona Hatoum*, ed. Michael Archer, Guy Brett and Catherine de Zegher (London: Phaidon, 1997), 26–29.

17. Hatoum, interview with Archer, 26.

18. It was also installed at the Third SITE Santa Fe Biennial in 1999 and the exhibit "Around the World in Eighty Days" at the South London Gallery in 2006, among others. It is in the permanent collection of the L.A. Museum of

Contemporary Art. It is important that the piece, which figures a precarious world system, has itself moved and been reconstructed in so many locations. To move the work, of course, is to reconstruct it; thus, its very routes through the global system involve processes of destruction and construction in order to figure its precariousness.

19. See for example an *ArtForum* review noting that Hatoum's map "seemed to invite visitors to 'explore' the world by literally taking a stand in it, at the very perceptible risk of dispersing the whole thing—and possibly breaking a few bones in the process." See Miriam Rosen, "Orbis Terrarum," *ArtForum* 39, no. 4 (December 2000): 155. An *Artnet* review also noted that "visitors to the show repeatedly found themselves literally stumbling into the piece, sending bits of the world skittering across the concrete, in what is a convincing metaphor for the various human depredations of Mother Earth." See Walter Robinson, "Theater Santa Fe," *Artnet Magazine*, July 9, 1999, http://www.artnet.com/magazine_pre2000/reviews/robinson/robinson7-9-99.asp. A blog post noted specifically the displacements I refer to above. See "Mona Hatoum's Map Around the World in 80 Days," *Rodcorp*, July 20, 2006, accessed August 20, 2006, http://rodcorp.typepad.com/rodcorp/2006/07/mona_hatoums_ma.html.

20. Urs Steiner and Samuel Herzog, "The Idea is What Matters! Interview with Mona Hatoum," *Neue Zürcher Zeitung*, November 20, 2004, reproduced on *Quantara*, accessed August 18, 2006, http://www.qantara.de/webcom/show_article.php/_c-310/_nr-144/i.html

21. James Clifford, *Routes: Travel and Translation in the Late Twentieth-Century* (Cambridge MA: Harvard University Press, 1997), 2.

22. Museum of Contemporary Art (MOCA) Los Angeles, "Press Release: Mona Hatoum, accessed August 20, 2006, http://www.moca.org/museum/exhibitioninfo_printable.php?useGallery=1&id=333

23. Jean Laplanche and Jean-Bertrand Pontalis, "Fantasy and the Origins of Sexuality," in *Formations of Fantasy*, ed. Victor Burgin (London: Routledge, 1989), 27.

24. Inderpal Grewal and Caren Kaplan, "Introduction: Transnational Feminist Practices and Questions of Postmodernity," in *Scattered Hegemonies: Postmodernity and Transnational Feminist Practices*, ed. Inderpal Grewal and Caren Kaplan (Minneapolis: University of Minnesota Press, 1994), 1–36.

25. I have unfortunately been unable to re-view the piece *Border* for this chapter, although its deconstruction of the Israeli/Lebanese border as a site of affect and phobia by those security guards who patrol the "good fence" surely contributes to the kinds of resistance to abstraction I am discussing here.

26. The "good fence" is the name given to the 80-mile stretch of border that separates Israel and Lebanon. From Israel's foundation to the 1970s, the border between Israel and Lebanon was relatively peaceful. With the start of the Lebanese civil war in the mid-1970s, Israel sought to "neutralize" the border region from attacks by PLO guerrillas or Syrian military units. The fence that had been created to keep out Palestinian guerrillas also included gates through

which Israeli forces could conduct raids on PLO bases in Southern Lebanon. As part of its Good Fence Policy, then Israeli Defence Minister Shimon Peres in turn opened those gates to Lebanese seeking food or medical assistance in Israel. The Good Fence Policy also stipulated that Israel would launch heavy retaliatory raids across the Lebanese border should the opening of the gates encourage guerrillas to enter the area of Southern Lebanon. In 1978, Israel launched the Litani Operation, and in 1982 the Operation Peace for Galilee to create a "buffer zone" in Southern Lebanon and to attack and destroy the PLO. Rovner's site-specific installation was created four years before Israel's withdrawal from Southern Lebanon.

27. This piece recalls a project by Carmela Castrejón. When a 13-mile long steel fence was built on the Mexican-U.S. border in 1991, Castrejón hung a row of blood-stained garments along the fence. Coinciding with the year of the Gulf War, Castrejón sought to represent "the dead in the Middle East, as well as those over here, victims of another type of slow war, silent and without any truce." This reflected not only on the coincidence of borders, but also the fact that the fence was being built with leftover materials from the Gulf War. See María Eraña, "From a Border of Canyons and Sand," in *La Frontera/The Border: Art About the Mexico/United States Experience*, ed. Kathryn Kanjo (San Diego: Centro Cultural La Raza and the Museum of Contemporary Art of San Diego, 1993).

28. Rogoff, 7.

29. Ibid., 113.

30. Menick notes that she could only distribute the pamphlet if it were specifically requested, and that it needed to include a label reading "I reprinted this brochure from the 1964 World's Fair as my artwork—Emily Jacir." See John Menick, "Undiminished Returns: The Work of Emily Jacir 1998–2002," in *Emily Jacir Belongings: Arbeiten/Works 1998–2003*, ed. Martin Sturm (Linz: O.K. Center for Contemporary Art Upper Austria/O.K. Books, 2004), 39.

31. Between the proposal of the project and its final installation, Jacir was challenged by the time-consuming labor involved in embroidering the 418 names into the fabric of the refugee tent. She sent emails to friends and listservs asking for help with the project. John Menick argues that, as a result of this, the project took on new social dimensions: "On some nights, over a dozen people would participate in order to sew the letters. A few of these who showed up wanted to find the villages where their families came from; several people learned of the expulsion for the first time. Palestinians, Israelis, Americans, Egyptians, Syrians, Yemenis, Spaniards and others sewed, told stories, joked and gossiped." The piece was installed unfinished at PS1's Clocktower Gallery, emphasizing the importance of the process of production over the final installation. The installation included a day-by-day roster of sewing participants along with texts they had written about their experiences in the studio. See Menick, 24.

32. It is important to emphasize also that Jacir does not work with literal maps. Because of her focus on lived experience, the relation between the body

traveling through space and the objects that frame conditions of belonging/ unbelonging, she refuses transcendental viewpoints. In this sense, Jacir is on to the trick Hatoum identifies in *Present Tense*, that the abstract ceding of pockets of territory will mean cementing Palestinian space as a space of violence, fragmentation and isolation. Her dedication to understanding national space through the lived experience of specific bodies thus both articulates the experience of fragmentation and loss of Palestinians, and refuses solutions that instantiate that very fragmentation.

33. Rovner's installation was presented by Deitch Projects in collaboration with the Chase Manhattan Art Program. It is caught, therefore, as many contemporary site-specific art works are, in the position of both depending on and critiquing the conditions of its exhibition all at once—something I believe Rovner does successfully in this work.

34. Edward Leffingwell, "Michal Rovner at 410 Park Avenue," *Art in America* 88, no.11 (November 2000): 169.

35. Michal Rovner, "In conversation with Leon Golub," in *Michal Rovner: The Space Between*, ed. Sylvia Wolf (New York: Whitney Museum of Art; Göttingen: Steidl Verlag, 2002), 165.

36. Michael Rush, " 'There Will be Silence': The Video Art of Michal Rovner" in *Michal Rovner: The Space Between*, ed. Sylvia Wolf (New York: Whitney Museum of Art; Göttingen: Steidl Verlag, 2002), 196.

37. Rovner, In Conversation with Golub, 161.

38. Clifford, 9.

39. Emily Jacir, "Interview with Stella Rollig," in *Emily Jacir Belongings: Arbeiten/Works 1998–2003*, ed. Martin Sturm (Linz: O.K. Center for Contemporary Art Upper Austria/O.K. Books, 2004), 28.

40. Jacir, Interview with Rollig, 9.

41. Said, 177.

42. Teresa de Lauretis, *Alice Doesn't: Feminism, Semiotics, Cinema* (Bloomington: Indiana University Press, 1984), 38.

43. Clifford, 10.

44. Laplanche and Pontalis, 27.

45. Alarcón, Kaplan and Moallem, 14.

46. Henri Lefebvre, *The Production of Space*, trans. Donald Nicholson-Smith (Malden: Blackwell Publishing, 1991), 71.

47. Lefebvre, 73.

48. Jacir, Interview with Rollig, 18.

49. This is also true of Akram Zaatari's *This Day*, which carries the viewer along through his multiple modes of travel in the Syrian Desert, through Beirut and Amman. Often, Zaatari shoots through the front windshield of a moving car, the windshield framing the scene unfolding before him, and the rearview mirror capturing the driver's eyes. Zaatari also sometimes includes his own reflection, in the screen of the television set he uses to edit the video, as well as in the glass of a cable car he shoots from. In all these scenes, Zaatari, like Jacir, makes clear that the camera moving through space is also the body

moving through space, and that the body is both discursively apprehending space (as already existing) and actively producing spaces (the sites of social encounter).

50. See Smadar Lavie, "Blowup in the Borderzones" in *Displacement, Diaspora, and Geographies of Identity*, ed. Smadar Lavie and Ted Swedenburg (Durham: Duke University Press, 1996), 69.

51. In this regard, Emily Jacir's *Memorial to 418 Palestinian Villages which were Destroyed, Depopulated and Occupied by Israel in 1948* (2001) might more closely be allied with the historical project of Zaatari. Nevertheless, it would be a mistake to see Zaatari's project as purely historical and retrospective.

52. Given the violence that has erupted since 2003 in Beirut, and most recently in 2008, *This Day* might be seen as presaging the continued explosive tension within the landscape of Beirut.

53. Rogoff, 113.

54. Ibid.

55. Ibid.

56. In his introductory remarks to "From the History of an Infantile Neurosis (1918)," Freud argues that "The length of road over which an analysis must travel with the patient, and the quantity of material which must be mastered on the way, are of no importance in comparison with the resistance which is met with in the course of the work, and are only of importance at all in so far as they are necessarily proportional to the resistance. The situation is the same as when to-day an enemy army needs weeks and months to make its way across a stretch of country which in times of peace was traversed by an express train in a few hours and which only a short time before had been passed over by the defending army in a few days." Sigmund Freud, *Three Case Histories.* (New York: Touchstone, 1996), 167.

57. Hatoum, "Interview with John Tusa, BBC Radio 3," accessed August 4, 2006, http://www.bbc.co.uk/radio3/johntusainterview/hatoum_transcript. shtml.

58. Clifford, 3.

59. Jacir, Interview with Rollig, 18.

60. This impossible but necessary demand resembles Said's call for a secular and multi-ethnic state solution to the Israeli/Palestinian conflict.

61. Jacqueline Rose, *States of Fantasy* (Oxford: Clarendon Press, 1996), 5. Rose is committed to Freud's understanding of fantasy prior to Freud's abandonment of the seduction theory, however, and thus makes a quick move from fantasy to morality ("how subjects tie themselves ethically to each other and enter a socially viable world") through forms of transgenerational haunting, guilt for crimes not committed, and so on. This leaves to the side Freud's later development of fantasy which, in Laplanche and Pontalis's detailed elaboration, speaks more readily to the prismatic mediations that are at issue here.

62. De Lauretis, 56.

63. This is true not only of the social worlds that form the basis of this chapter, but also in the art world where the ink spilled on the art world's global character

at times blots out the complex social relations and longstanding histories of exchange, collaboration, influence, resistance and exploitation that constitute the domain of the cross-cultural.
64. Jacir, Interview with Rollig, 9.
65. Ibid.
66. Clifford, 3.
67. Theodor Adorno and Thomas Y. Levin, "On the Question 'What is German?' " *New German Critique*, no. 36 (Fall 1985): 121–131, cited in Rogoff, 6.
68. De Lauretis, 39.

Chapter 4

1. Anne McClintock, "Paranoid Empire: Specters from Guantanamo and Abu Ghraib," *Small Axe* 13, no. 1: 52.
2. Robert Stam, "Mobilizing Fictions: The Gulf War, the Media, and the Recruitment of the Spectator," *Public Culture* 4, no. 2 (Spring 1992): 102.
3. Finbarr Barry Flood, "Between Cult and Culture: Bamiyan, Islamic Iconoclasm, and the Museum," *Art Bulletin* LXXXIV, no. 4 (December 2002): 641.
4. Cornelia Brink, "Secular Icons: Looking at Photographs from Nazi Concentration Camps." *History and Memory* 12, no. 1 (2000): 141–44.
5. Lila Abu-Lughod, "Do Muslim Women Really Need Saving? Anthropological Reflections on Cultural Relativism and Its Others," *American Anthropologist* 104, no. 3 (September 2002): 784.
6. Ibid., 784.
7. Donna Haraway, *Modest_Witness@Second_Millenium.FemaleMan©_Meets_ OncoMouse™: Feminism and Technoscience* (New York: Routledge, 1997), 16.
8. The video is available on the CBC's website at http://www.cbc.ca/national/ blog/special_feature/fighting_ghosts/. It has also been posted on *YouTube* at http://www.youtube.com/watch?v= BE7ANG2HS-w.
9. McClintock, 55–57.
10. Ibid., 62.
11. Saskia Sassen, *Globalization and Its Discontents* (New York: The New Press, 1998), 177.
12. Fredric Jameson, *The Political Unconscious: Narrative as a Socially Symbolic Act* (Ithaca: Cornell University Press, 1981), 46.
13. Ibid., 47.
14. Teresa de Lauretis, "The Violence of Rhetoric: Considerations on Representation and Gender," in *Technologies of Gender: Essays on Theory, Film and Fiction* (Basingstoke: Macmillan Publishers, 1989), 5.
15. Most notably, it represented Afghanistan at the Venice Biennale in 2005 and was included in the *Global Feminisms* exhibit at the Brooklyn Museum in 2007.
16. Andreas Huyssen, "Nostalgia for Ruins," *Grey Room* 23 (Spring 2006): 6–21.

17. Mariam Rawi, "Betrayal," *Reproductive Health Matters* 12, no. 23 (May 2004): 118.
18. It is worth noting also that, following 9/11, the U.S. military appropriated some of the RAWA images for use in flyers dropped by U.S. warplanes over Afghanistan.
19. The names of these, taken together, highlight the rhetorical force of bringing into visibility: Undercover Social Worker, Post Office Undercover, Undercover Debt Collector, Undercover Mosque, Undercover Mother, Undercover in the Secret State, Undercover with New Labour, Iran Undercover.
20. Gareth McLean, "TV Review: To hell and back," *The Guardian (London)*, Features Pages (June 27, 2001): 22.
21. See, for example, Janelle Brown, "How a Taliban enemy fights beneath the veil: An underground resistance group of Afghani women risks torture and execution to alert the world to the regime's atrocities," *The Ottawa Citizen*, October 6, 2001 (Saturday Final Edition), News, B4.
22. This impression is further confirmed by the fact that one of Shah's visits (to what she calls "the most subversive place of all") is to a secret beauty parlor. For Shah, this is the location where women are able to maintain their dignity, providing resistance to the regime of the Taliban and its curtailment of women's freedoms.
23. Malek Alloula, *The Colonial Harem*, trans. Myrna Godzich and Wlad Godzich, intro. Barbara Harlow (Minneapolis: University of Minnesota Press, 1986).
24. Flood, 641.
25. Hamid Naficy, *An Accented Cinema: Exilic and Diasporic Filmmaking* (Princeton: Princeton University Press, 2001), 10.
26. Bert Cardullo, "An Afghan Is a Woman," *The Hudson Review* 58, no. 2 (Summer 2005): 302.
27. Ibid., 305.
28. André Bazin, "An Aesthetic of Reality: Neorealism," in *What Is Cinema?* (Berkeley: University of California Press, 2005), 24–25.
29. It is important to note that the foreign filmmaker emerges only diegetically at the end of the film, put on trial on the same day as Osama, convicted and led away to be executed by a firing squad.
30. Gilles Deleuze, *Cinema 1: The Movement-Image*, trans. Hugh Tomlinson and Barbara Habberjam (Minneapolis: University of Minnesota Press, 2003), 33.
31. Ibid., 37.
32. Cardullo, 304.
33. This point is elucidated further by contrasting *Osama* with Samira Makhmalbaf's *At Five in the Afternoon*, also produced in 2003, whose central character, Nogreh, must negotiate the complex shifting structures of female identity in the post-Taliban era, both the sites of possible liberation and the persistent forms of traditionalism that bind contemporary Afghanistan.
34. Arifa Akbar, "Jewel of Afghan Cinema Saved from the Taliban," *The Independent*. May 9, 2009, accessed April 22, 2012, http://www.independent.co.uk/news/world/middle-east/jewel-of-afghan-cinema-saved-from-the-taliban-

1681824.html. The article mentions also that the film was rescued, alongside up to six thousand others, by the archivists at the National Film Archive, who concealed the film reels behind a hastily constructed false wall prior to the Taliban's campaign against the archives. Siddiq Barmak is quoted in the article as saying, "It was created in the first private studios in Afghanistan and it was about a historical, classical subject that every Afghan learnt at school. I remember seeing the posters and wanting to go and see it in a movie theatre. It had the most famous names of the day but it also faced a lot of problems in its making, with four directors working on it and no government funding."

35. Although it is beyond the scope of this chapter, Antigone has been raised in contemporary critical thought as a figure for ethico-political (and specifically feminist) acts. Antigone must either obey the laws of the state or follow her sense of justice, bury her brother Polyneices's body and publicly declare her act of defiance. This defiance transgresses not only state edicts but also the circumscribed role of women as non-citizens, as well as proper kinship relations (she desires, after all, to lie down in the ground with her brother). In revealing her act to Creon, she asserts the ethical choice she makes, and invites the punishment the edict requires. Creon thus banishes her to a cave (a permutation of the sentence of death by stoning).

36. There are multiple instances of this response throughout the film, either in order to acknowledge the right of a director or official to make decisions, or to resist the implication that one is a mouthpiece for a specific group or interest. The repetition of this response itself indicates the nature of free speech in the political climate of Afghanistan.

37. George W. Bush, "The State of the Union: Present Bush's State of the Union Address to Congress and the Nation," *New York Times*, January 30, 2002, Section A, 22.

38. Sandra Schäfer, *Stagings. Kabul, Film & Production of Representation* (Berlin: b_books, 2009).

39. Judith Butler, *Precarious Life the Powers of Mourning and Violence* (London: Verso, 2004), 146.

Epilogue: The Political Exigency of the Oblique

1. "Mona Hatoum," Interviewed by Gray Watson, *Audio Arts Magazine* 13, no. 4 (1993).

2. Gayatri Chakravorty Spivak, "The Politics of Translation" in *Outside in the Teaching Machine* (New York: Routledge, 1994), 181.

3. Ibid., 182.

4. Ibid., 187.

5. Teresa De Lauretis, *Technologies of Gender: Essays on Theory, Film and Fiction* (Basingstoke: Macmillan, 1989), 2.

6. Chandra Talpade Mohanty, *Feminism Without Borders: Decolonizing Theory, Practicing Solidarity* (Durham: Duke University Press, 2003), 118.

Bibliography

Abu-Lughod, Lila. "Do Muslim Women Really Need Saving? Anthropological Reflections on Cultural Relativism and Its Others." *American Anthropologist* 104, no. 3 (September 2002): 783–790.

Adorno, Theodor, Walter Benjamin, Ernst Bloch, Bertold Brecht, and Georg Lukács. *Aesthetics and Politics*. London: Verso, 1980.

Agamben, Giorgio. *Remnants of Auschwitz: The Witness and the Archive*. New York: Zone Books, 2000.

Agosín, Marjorie. *Women, Gender, and Human Rights: A Global Perspective*. New Brunswick: Rutgers University Press, 2001.

Alarcón, Norma, Caren Kaplan, and Minoo Moallem. *Between Woman and Nation: Nationalisms, Transnational Feminisms and the State*. Durham: Duke University Press, 1999.

Alexander, M. Jacqui, and Chandra Talpade Mohanty, eds. *Feminist Genealogies, Colonial Legacies, Democratic Futures*. New York: Routledge, 1997.

Allen, Beverly. *Rape Warfare: The Hidden Genocide in Bosnia-Herzegovina and Croatia*. Minneapolis: University of Minnesota Press, 1996.

Alloula, Malek. *The Colonial Harem*. Translated by Myrna Godzich and Wlad Godzich. Minneapolis: University of Minnesota Press, 1986.

Alshaibi, Sama. "Memory Work in the Palestinian Diaspora." *Frontiers: A Journal of Women Studies* 27, no. 2 (2006): 30–53.

Althusser, Louis. *Lenin and Philosophy, and Other Essays*. London: New Left Books, 1971.

An-Na'im, Abdullahi Ahmed, ed. *Human Rights in Cross-Cultural Perspectives*. Philadelphia: University of Pennsylvania Press, 1992.

Anderson, Benedict. *Imagined Communities: Reflections on the Origin and Spread of Nationalism*. London: Verso, 1983.

Anzaldúa, Gloria. *Borderlands = La Frontera: The New Mestiza*. San Francisco: Spinsters/Aunt Lute, 1987.

Appadurai, Arjun. *Modernity at Large: Cultural Dimensions of Globalization*. Minneapolis: University of Minnesota Press, 1996.

Baer, Ulrich. *Spectral Evidence: The Photography of Trauma*. Cambridge: The MIT Press, 2002.

Balibar, Etienne. "Paradoxes of Universality." In *Anatomy of Racism*, edited by David Theo Goldberg, 283–294. Minneapolis: University of Minnesota Press, 1990.

Barker, Francis, Peter Hulme, and Margaret Iversen, eds. *Colonial Discourse/ Postcolonial Theory*. Manchester: Manchester University Press, 1994.

Barlow, Melinda. "Feminism 101: The New York Women's Video Festival, 1972– 1980." *Camera Obscura* 18, no. 3 (2003): 3–39.

Barrett, Michèle. *Women's Oppression Today*. London: Verso, 1988.

Barrett, Michèle, and A. Phillips, eds. *Destabilizing Theory: Contemporary Feminist Debates*. Cambridge: Polity Press, 1992.

Barthes, Roland. *Camera Lucida: Reflections on Photography*. New York: Hill and Wang, 1980.

———. *Image-Music-Text*. London: Fontana, 1977.

———. "L'effet De Réel." In *Le Bruissement De La Langue*, 153–174. Paris: Editions du Seuil, 1993.

———. *Mythologies*. New York: Hill and Wang, 1972.

———. *The Responsibility of Forms: Critical Essays on Music, Art, and Representation*. Berkeley: University of California Press, 1991.

Bazin, André. "An Aesthetic of Reality: Neorealism." In *What is Cinema? Volume 2*. Translated by Hugh Gray, 16–40. Berkeley: University of California Press, 2005.

Bender, Gretchen, and Timothy Druckrey, eds. *Culture on the Brink: Ideologies of Technology*. Seattle: Bay Press, 1994.

Benjamin, Walter. "The Author as Producer." *New Left Review* I, no. 62 (July/August 1970): 1–9.

———. "The Task of the Translator: An Introduction to the Translation of Baudelaire's Tableaux Parisiens." Translated by Harry Zohn. In *The Translation Studies Reader*, edited by Lawrence Venuti, 75–82. London: Routledge, 2000.

Berger, John. *Ways of Seeing*. London: Penguin, 1990.

Bhabha, Homi K. *The Location of Culture*. New York: Routledge, 1994.

Birringer, Johannes. "Video Art/Performance: A Border Theory." *Performing Art Journal* 13, no. 3 (September 1991): 54–84.

Bishop, Claire. *Participation (Documents of Contemporary Art)*. Cambridge: The MIT Press, 2006.

Bjelić, Dušan I., and Obrad Savić. *Balkan as Metaphor: Between Globalization and Fragmentation*. Cambridge: The MIT Press, 2002.

Bloom, Lisa, ed. *With Other Eyes: Looking at Race and Gender in Visual Culture*. Minneapolis: University of Minnesota Press, 1999.

Bock, Gisela, and Susan James. *Beyond Equality and Difference: Citizenship, Feminist Politics and Female Subjectivity*. London: Routledge, 1992.

Boeri, Stefano. "Border Device(s)." *Parachute*, no. 120 (October-December 2005): 28–39.

Bolton, Richard, ed. *The Contest of Meaning: Critical Histories of Photography*. Cambridge: The MIT Press, 1989.

Boose, Lynda E. "Crossing the River Drina: Bosnian Rape Camps, Turkish Impalement, and Serb Cultural Memory." *Signs* 28, no. 1 (2002): 71–96.

Bourriaud, Nicolas. *Relational Aesthetics*. Translated by Simon Pleasance and Fronza Woods. Dijon: Les Presses du Réel, 2002.

Boyle, Deirdre. *Subject to Change: Guerrilla Television Revisited*. New York: Oxford University Press, 1997.

Brah, Avtar. *Cartographies of Diaspora: Contesting Identities*. London: Routledge, 1996.

Bright, Deborah. "Introduction: Pictures, Perverts and Politics." In *The Passionate Camera: Photography and Bodies of Desire*, edited by Deborah Bright, 1–22. London: Routledge, 1998.

Brink, Cornelia. "Secular Icons: Looking at Photographs from Nazi Concentration Camps." *History and Memory* 12, no. 1 (2000): 135–150.

Brown, Wendy. *Politics out of History*. Princeton: Princeton University Press, 2001.

———. *States of Injury: Power and Freedom in Late Modernity*. Princeton: Princeton University Press, 1995.

Brouillette, Sarah. "Human Rights Markets and *Born into Brothels*." *Third Text* 25, no. 2 (March 2011): 169–176.

Bunch, Charlotte. "Women's Rights as Human Rights: Towards a Revision of Human Rights." *Human Rights Quarterly* 12 (1990): 486–498.

Burgin, Victor. *In/Different Spaces: Place and Memory in Visual Culture*. Berkeley: University of California Press, 1996.

———. *Thinking Photography*. New Jersey: Humanities Press, 1982.

Burnett, Ron. "Video: The Politics of Culture and Community." In *Resolutions: Contemporary Video Practices*, edited by Michael Renov and Erika Suderburg, 283–303. Minneapolis: University of Minnesota Press, 1996.

Butler, Judith. *Antigone's Claim: Kinship between Life and Death*. New York: Columbia University Press, 2000.

———. *Bodies That Matter*. New York: Routledge, 1993.

———. *Excitable Speech: A Politics of the Performative*. New York: Routledge, 1997.

———. *Precarious Life: The Powers of Mourning and Violence*. London: Verso, 2004.

Butler, Judith, and Joan W. Scott, eds. *Feminists Theorize the Political*. New York: Routledge, 1992.

Camnitzer, Luis, Jane Farver, and Rachel Weiss. *Global Conceptualism: Points of Origin, 1950s-1980s*. New York: Queens Museum of Art, 1999.

Canclini, Néstor García. "Remaking Passports: Visual Thought in the Debate on Multiculturalism." In *The Visual Culture Reader*, edited by Nicholas Mirzoeff, 180–189. London: Routledge, 1998.

Cardullo, Bert. "An Afghan is a Woman." *The Hudson Review* 58, no. 2 (Summer 2005): 302–310.

Carr, Robert. "Crossing the First World/Third World Divides: Testimonial, Transnational Feminisms, and the Postmodern Condition." In *Scattered Hegemonies: Postmodernity and Transnational Feminist Practices*, edited by Inderpal Grewal and Caren Kaplan, 153–172. Minneapolis: University of Minnesota Press, 1994.

Chaney, David. "Cosmopolitan Art and Cultural Citizenship." *Theory, Culture & Society* 19, nos. 1–2 (2002): 157–174.

Charlesworth, Hilary. "Alienating Oscar? Feminist Analysis of International Law." In *Reconceiving Reality: Women and International Law*, edited by Dorinda G. Dallmeyer, 1–18. Washington: American Society of International Law, 1993.

———. "What Are 'Women's International Human Rights'?" In *Human Rights of Women: National and International Perspectives*, edited by Rebecca J. Cook, 58–85. Philadelphia: University of Pennsylvania Press, 1994.

Charlesworth, Hilary, Christine Chinkin, and Shelley Wright. "Feminist Approaches to International Law." *American Journal of International Law* 85 (1991): 613–645.

Cheah, Pheng, and Bruce Robbins, eds. *Cosmopolitics: Thinking and Feeling Beyond the Nation*. Minneapolis: University of Minnesota Press, 1998.

Chow, Rey. *Ethics after Idealism: Theory-Culture-Ethnicity-Reading*. Bloomington: Indiana University Press, 1998.

———. *Primitive Passions: Visuality, Sexuality, Ethnography, and Contemporary Chinese Cinema*. New York: Columbia University Press, 1995.

Clifford, James T. "Post/Neo Colonial Situations: Notes on Historical Realism Today." In *Literatura E Viagens Pós-Coloniais*, edited by Helena Carvalhào Buescu and Manuela Ribeiro Sanches. Lisbon: Ediçòes Colibri, 2002.

———. *The Predicament of Culture: Twentieth-Century Ethnography, Literature and Art*. Cambridge: Harvard University Press, 1988.

———. *Routes: Travel and Translation in the Late Twentieth Century*. Cambridge: Harvard University Press, 1997.

Clover, Carol J. "Law and the Order of Popular Culture." In *Law in the Domains of Culture*, edited by Austin Sarat and Thomas R. Kearns, 97–119. Ann Arbor: University of Michigan Press, 1998.

Cook, Rebecca J., ed. *Human Rights of Women: National and International Perspectives*. Philadelphia: University of Pennsylvania Press, 1994.

Cooke, Miriam. *Women Claim Islam: Creating Islamic Feminism through Literature*. New York: Routledge, 2001.

Coomaraswamy, Radhika. "Reinventing International Law: Women's Rights as Human Rights in the International Community." *Harvard Law School Human Rights Program*. Accessed March 15, 2006. http://www.law.harvard.edu/programs/hrp/publications/radhika.html.

Coombes, Annie E. "Museums and Formation of National and Cultural Identities." *Oxford Art Journal* 11, no. 2 (1988): 58–68.

———. "The Recalcitrant Object: Cultural Contact and the Question of Hybridity." In *Colonial Discourse/Postcolonial Theory*, edited by Francis Barker, Peter Hulme and Margaret Iversen. Manchester: Manchester University Press, 1994.

Cornell, Drucilla. *At the Heart of Freedom: Feminism, Sex and Equality*. Princeton: Princeton University Press, 1998.

Cornell, Drucilla, Michael Rosenfeld, and David Gray Carlson, eds. *Deconstruction and the Possibility of Justice*. New York: Routledge, 1992.

Coutts-Smith, Kenneth. "Cultural Colonialism." *Third Text* 16, no. 1 (2002): 1–14.

Crary, Jonathan. *Suspensions of Perception: Attention, Spectacle and Modern Culture*. Cambridge: The MIT Press, 1999.

———. *Techniques of the Observer: On Vision and Modernity in the Nineteenth Century*. Cambridge: The MIT Press, 1990.

Cubitt, Sean. *Videography: Video Media as Art and Culture*. London: MacMillan Education Ltd, 1993.

Culler, Jonathan. *On Deconstruction; Theory and Criticism after Structuralism*. Ithaca: Cornell University Press, 1982.

Dallmeyer, Dorinda G., ed. *Reconceiving Reality: Women and International Law*. Washington: The American Society of International Law, 1993.

Davis, Emily S. "The Intimacies of Globalization: Bodies and Borders On-Screen." *Camera Obscura* 21, no. 2 (2006): 33–73.

Debord, Guy. *The Society of the Spectacle*. New York: Zone Books, 1967.

DeCerteau, Michel. *The Practice of Everyday Life*. Berkeley: University of California Press, 1984.

De Lauretis, Teresa. "Aesthetics and Feminist Theory: Rethinking Women's Cinema." In *Female Spectators: Looking at Film and Television*, edited by E. Deirdre Pribram, 174–195. London: Verso, 1988.

———. *Alice Doesn't: Feminism, Semiotics, Cinema*. Bloomington: Indiana University Press, 1984.

———. "Eccentric Subjects." In *Figures of Resistance: Essays in Feminist Theory*, 151–182. Urbana: University of Illinois Press, 2007.

———. "Popular Culture, Public and Private Fantasies: Femininity and Fetishism in David Cronenberg's *M. Butterfly*." *Signs: Journal of Women in Culture and Society* 24, no. 2 (Winter 1999): 303–334.

———. *Technologies of Gender: Essays on Theory, Film and Fiction*. Basingstoke: Macmillan, 1989.

———. *The Practice of Love: Lesbian Sexuality and Perverse Desire*. Bloomington: Indiana University Press, 1994.

Deleuze, Gilles. *Cinema 1: The Movement-Image*. Translated by Hugh Tomlinson and Barbara Habberjam. Minneapolis: University of Minnesota Press, 1986.

———. *Difference and Repetition*. Translated by Paul Patton. New York: Columbia University Press, 1994.

Deleuze, Gilles, and Félix Guattari. *A Thousand Plateaus: Capitalism and Schizophrenia*. Translated by Brian Massumi. Minneapolis: University of Minnesota Press, 1987.

Demos, T. J. "Desire in Diaspora: Emily Jacir." *Art Journal* 62, no. 4 (2003): 68–78.

———. "The Art of Darkness: On Steve McQueen." *October* 114 (Autumn 2005): 61–89.

Derrida, Jacques. "Force of Law: The 'Mystical Foundation of Authority.'" In *Deconstruction and the Possibility of Justice*, edited by Drucilla Cornell, Michael Rosenfeld and David Gray Carlson, 1–67. New York: Routledge, 1992.

———. "Videor." In *Resolutions: Contemporary Video Practices*, edited by Michael Renov and Erika Suderburg, 73–77. Minneapolis: University of Minnesota Press, 1996.

Deutsche, Rosalyn. "Not-Forgetting: Mary Kelly's *Love Songs*." *Grey Room* 24 (Summer 2006): 26–37.

Dirlik, Arif. "The Postcolonial Aura: Third World Criticism in the Age of Global Capitalism." In *Dangerous Liaisons: Gender, Nation, and Postcolonial*

Perspectives, edited by Anne McClintock, Aamir Mufti and Ella Shohat, 501–528. Minneapolis: University of Minnesota Press, 1997.

Djurić, Dubravka, and Misko Suvaković, eds. *Impossible Histories: Historic Avant-Gardes, Neo-Avant-Gardes, and Post-Avant-Gardes in Yugoslavia, 1918–1991*. Cambridge: The MIT Press, 2003.

Doane, Mary Ann. "Indexicality: Trace and Sign." *differences* 18, no. 1 (2007): 1–6.

Downey, Anthony. "The Spectacular Difference of Documenta XI." *Third Text* 17, no. 1 (2003): 85–92.

Edwards, Brent Hayes. *The Practice of Diaspora: Literature, Translation, and the Rise of Black Internationalism*. Cambridge: Harvard University Press, 2003.

El Guindi, Fadwa. *Veil: Modesty, Privacy and Resistance*. Oxford: Berg, 1999.

Engle, Karen. "Female Subjects of Public International Law: Human Rights and the Exotic Other Female." *New England Law Review* 26 (1992): 1509–1526.

Enwezor, Okwui. *Snap Judgments: New Positions in Contemporary African Photography*. Göttingen: Steidl, 2006.

Enwezor, Okwui, and Octavio Zaya. *In/Sight: African Photographers, 1940 to Present*. New York: Guggenheim Museum, 1996.

Eraña, María. "From a Border of Canyons and Sand." In *La Frontera/the Border: Art About the Mexico/United States Experience*, edited by Kathryn Kanjo. San Diego: Centro Cultural La Raza and the Museum of Contemporary Art of San Diego, 1993.

Espinosa, Julio García. "For an Imperfect Cinema." In *Twenty-Five Years of New Latin American Cinema*, edited by Michael Chanan, 28–33. London: British Film Institute, 1983.

Evans, David T. *Sexual Citizenship: The Material Construction of Sexualities*. London: Routledge, 1993.

Fanon, Frantz. *Black Skin, White Masks*. New York: Grove Press, 1967.

———. *The Wretched of the Earth*. New York: Grove Press, 1968.

Featherstone, Mike, ed. *Global Culture: Nationalism, Globalization and Modernity*. London: Sage Publications, 1990.

Feldman, Allen. "Memory Theaters, Virtual Witnessing, and the Trauma-Aesthetic." *Biography* 27, no. 1 (2004): 163–202.

Felman, Shoshana, and Dori Laub. *Testimony: Crises of Witnessing in Literature, Psychoanalysis, and History*. New York: Routledge, 1992.

Flood, Finbarr Barry. "Between Cult and Culture: Bamiyan, Islamic Iconoclasm, and the Museum." *Art Bulletin* 84, no. 4 (December 2002): 641–659.

Foster, Hal. *The Return of the Real: The Avant-Garde at the End of the Century*. Cambridge: The MIT Press, 1996.

Foster, Kevin. "New Faces, Old Fears: Migrants, Asylum Seekers and British Identity." *Third Text* 20, no. 6 (2006): 683–691.

Foucault, Michel. *Discipline & Punish: The Birth of the Prison*. Translated by Alan Sheridan. New York: Random House, 1977.

———. "Of Other Spaces." *Diacritics* 16 (Spring 1986): 22–27.

Freud, Sigmund. *Group Psychology and the Analysis of the Ego*. edited and translated by James Strachey. New York: W.W. Norton & Co, 1959.

————. "On Narcissism: An Introduction," and "Thoughts for the Times on War and Death." In *Standard Edition of the Complete Psychological Works of Sigmund Freud*, Volume 14, edited and translated by James Strachey, 73–102, 273–303. London: Vintage: Hogarth Press and the Institute of Psycho-Analysis, 1914.

Fusco, Coco. *English Is Broken Here*. New York: New Press, 1995.

————. "Ethnicity, Politics and Poetics: Latinos and Media Art." In *Illuminating Video*, edited by Doug Hall and Sally Jo Fifer, 304–316. New York: Aperture, in association with the Bay Area Video Coalition, 1990.

Gaines, Jane M. "Political Mimesis." In *Collecting Visible Evidence*, edited by Jane M. Gaines and Michael Renov, 84–102. Minneapolis: University of Minnesota Press, 1999.

Gaines, Jane M., and Michael Renov, eds. *Collecting Visible Evidence*. Minneapolis: University of Minnesota Press, 1999.

Gilroy, Paul. *The Black Atlantic: Modernity and Double Consciousness*. Cambridge: Harvard University Press, 1993.

Ginsburg, Faye, Lila Abu-Lughod and Brian Larkin, eds. *Media Worlds: Anthropology on New Terrain*. Berkeley: University of California Press, 2002.

Gomez-Peña, Guillermo. *The New World Border: Prophecies, Poems & Loqueras for the End of the Century*. San Francisco: City Lights, 1996.

González, Jennifer A. "Autotopographies." In *Prosthetic Territories: Politics and Hypertechnologies*, edited by Gabriel Brahm Jr and Mark Driscoll, 133–149. Boulder: Westview Press, 1995.

————. *Subject to Display: Reframing Race in Contemporary Installation Art*. Cambridge: The MIT Press, 2008.

Graham-Brown, Sarah. *Images of Women: The Portrayal of Women in Photography of the Middle East 1860–1950*. London: Quartet Books, 1988.

Green, Renée. "Slippages." In *Radio Temporaire*, edited by Zeigam Azizov, Sylvie Desroches, Dean Inkster, Adrian Laubscher, Alejandra Riera, Caecilia Tripp, Grenoble: Ecole du Magasin, 2002.

Grewal, Inderpal. "Global Identities: Theorizing Transnational Studies of Sexuality." *GLQ* 7, no. 4 (2001): 663–679.

————. *Transnational America: Feminisms, Diasporas, Neoliberalisms*. Durham: Duke University Press, 2005.

Grewal, Inderpal, and Caren Kaplan. *Scattered Hegemonies: Postmodernity and Transnational Feminist Practices*. Minneapolis: University of Minnesota Press, 1994.

Grossberg, Lawrence. *Bringing It All Back Home*. Durham: Duke University Press, 1997.

Grosz, Elizabeth. *Space, Time and Perversion: Essays on the Politics of Bodies*. New York: Routledge, 1995.

Grusin, Richard, and Jay David Bolter, eds. *Remediation: Understanding New Media*. Cambridge: The MIT Press, 1999.

Gunning, Isabelle R. "Arrogant Perception, World-Travelling and Multicultural Feminism: The Case of Female Genital Surgeries." *Columbia Human Rights Law* 23 (1991): 189–247.

Gunning, Tom. "Moving Away from the Index: Cinema and the Impression of Reality." *differences* 18, no. 1 (2007): 29–52.

Gutman, Roy. *A Witness to Genocide.* New York: Macmillan Publishing Company, 1993.

Hadria, Michèle Cohen. "Nothing New under the Western Sun: Or the Rise of the Arab Experimental Documentary." *Third Text* 19, no. 1 (2005): 33–43.

Hall, Doug, and Sally Jo Fifer, eds. *Illuminating Video: An Essential Guide to Video Art.* New York: Aperture, in association with the Bay Area Video Coalition, 1990.

Hall, Stuart. "Minimal Selves." In *Black British Cultural Studies*, edited by Houston A. Baker Jr., Manthia Diawara and Ruth H. Lindeborg, 114–119. Chicago: University of Chicago Press, 1996.

———. "New Ethnicities." In *Stuart Hall: Critical Dialogues in Cultural Studies*, edited by David Morley and Kuan-Hsing Chen, 442–451. London: Routledge, 1996.

———. "The Local and the Global: Globalization and Ethnicity." In *Culture, Globalization and the World System*, edited by Anthony D. King, 19–40. Minneapolis: University of Minnesota Press, 1991.

Halleck, DeeDee. *Hand-held Visions: The Impossible Possibilities of Community Media.* New York: Fordham University Press, 2002.

Hanley, JoAnn, and Ann-Sargent Wooster, eds. *The First Generation: Women and Video, 1970–75.* New York: Independent Curators International, 1994.

Haraway, Donna J. "Ecce Homo, Ain't (Ar'n't) I a Woman, and Inappropriate/d Others: The Human in a Post-Humanist Landscape." In *Feminists Theorize the Political*, edited by Judith Butler and Joan W. Scott, 86–100. New York: Routledge, 1992.

———. *Modest_Witness@Second_Millenium.Femaleman_Meets_Oncomouse: Feminism and Technoscience.* New York: Routledge, 1997.

———. *Simians, Cyborgs, and Women: The Reinvention of Nature.* London: Routledge, 1991.

———. "The Persistence of Vision." In *The Visual Culture Reader*, edited by Nicholas Mirzoeff, 677–684. London: Routledge, 1998.

Harvey, David. *Spaces of Capital: Towards a Critical Geography.* New York: Routledge, 2001.

Hassan, Ihab. "Realism, Truth, and Trust in Postmodern Perspective." *Third Text* 17, no. 1 (2003): 1–13.

Hassan, Salah M., and Olu Oguibe. " 'Authentic/Ex-Centric' at the Venice Biennale: African Conceptualism in Global Contexts." *African Arts* 34, no. 4 (Winter 2001): 64–75.

Hatoum, Mona, Michael Archer, Guy Brett, and M. Catherine de Zegher *Mona Hatoum.* London: Phaidon Press, 1997.

Hawkes, Martine. "Transmitting Genocide: Genocide and Art." *M/C Journal* 9, no. 1 (March 2006). Accessed June 9, 2012. http://journal.media-culture.org.au/0603/09-hawkes.php.

Hesford, Wendy S. "Documenting Violations: Rhetorical Witnessing and the Spectacle of Distant Suffering." *Biography* 27, no. 1 (Winter 2004): 104–144.

Hibbitts, Bernard J. "Making Sense of Metaphors: Visuality, Aurality, and the Reconfiguration of American Legal Discourse." *Cardozo Law Review* 16, no. 2 (1994): 229–236.

Hillis, Ken. *Digital Sensations*. Minneapolis: University of Minnesota Press, 1999.

Hilsdon, Anne-Marie, Martha McIntyre, Vera Mackie, and Maila Stivens, eds. *Human Rights and Gender Politics: Asia-Pacific Perspectives*. London: Routledge, 2000.

Huyssen, Andreas. "Nostalgia for Ruins." *Grey Room* 23 (Spring 2006): 6–21.

Innis, Robert E., ed. *Semiotics: An Introductory Anthology*. Bloomington: Indiana University Press, 1985.

Jameson, Fredric. *Postmodernism, or, The Cultural Logic of Late Capitalism*. Durham: Duke University Press, 1991.

———. *The Political Unconscious: Narrative as a Socially Symbolic Act*. Ithaca: Cornell University Press, 1981.

Jansen, Sue Curry, Jefferson Pooley and Lora Taub-Pervizpour, eds. *Media and Social Justice*. New York: Palgrave MacMillan, 2011.

Jayawardena, Kumari. *Feminism and Nationalism in the Third World*. London: Zed Books, 1986.

Jones, Amelia. *Body Art: Performing the Subject*. Minneapolis: University of Minnesota Press, 1998.

———. *Self/Image*. New York: Routledge, 2006.

Juhasz, Alexandra. "No Woman Is an Object: Realizing the Feminist Collaborative Video." *Camera Obscura* 18, no. 3 (2003): 71–97.

———. "The Future Was Then: Reinvesting in Feminist Media Practice and Politics." *Camera Obscura* 21, no. 1 (2006): 53–57.

———, ed. *Women of Vision: Histories in Feminist Film and Video*. Minneapolis: University of Minnesota Press, 2001.

Kanjo, Kathryn, ed. *La Frontera/the Border: Art About the Mexico/United States Experience*. San Diego: Centro Cultural La Raza and the Museum of Contemporary Art of San Diego, 1993.

Kaplan, Caren. "A World without Boundaries: The Body Shop's Trans/National Geographics." In *With Other Eyes: Looking at Race and Gender in Visual Culture*, edited by Lisa Bloom. Minneapolis: University of Minnesota Press, 1999.

Kaplan, Janet A. "Flirtations with Evidence: The Factual and the Spurious Consort in the Works of the Atlas Group/Walid Raad." *Art in America* 92 (October 2004): 134–138.

Keeling, Kara. "I = Another: Digital Identity Politics." In *Strange Affinities: The Gender and Sexual Politics of Comparative Racialization*, edited by Grace Kyungwon Hong and Roderick A. Ferguson, 53–75. Durham: Duke University Press, 2011.

Kesić, Vesna. "Muslim Women, Croatian Women, Serbian Women, Albanian Women…" In *Balkan as Metaphor: Between Globalization and Fragmentation*, edited by Dušan I. Bjelić and Obrad Savić, 311–321. Cambridge: The MIT Press, 2002.

Kester, Grant. *Art, Activism and Oppositionality: Essays from Afterimage*. Durham: Duke University Press, 1998.

———. *Conversation Pieces: Community and Communication in Modern Art*. Berkeley: University of California Press, 2004.

King, Anthony D., ed. *Culture, Globalization and the World System*. Minneapolis: University of Minnesota Press, 1991.

Korot, Beryl, Phyllis Gershuny, and Michael Shamberg. "Presentation." *Radical Software* 1, no. 1 (1970).

Kosmidou, Zoe. "A Conversation with Marina Abramović." *Sculpture* (November 2001): 27–31.

Krauss, Rosalind. "Video: The Aesthetics of Narcissism." *October* 1 (Spring 1976): 50–64.

Kristeva, Julia. *The Powers of Horror: An Essay on Abjection*. Translated by Leon S. Roudiez. New York: Columbia University Press, 1982.

Kwon, Miwon. *One Place after Another: Site-Specific Art and Locational Identity*. Cambridge: The MIT Press, 2002.

———. "The Wrong Place." *Art Journal* 59, no. 1 (Spring 2000): 33–43.

Lacan, Jacques. *The Seminar of Jacques Lacan, Book VII: The Ethics of Psychoanalysis, 1959-60*. Translated by Dennis Porter. Edited by Jacques-Alain Miller. New York: Norton, 1992.

Laplanche, Jean. *Essays on Otherness*. London: Routledge, 1999.

Laplanche, Jean, and Jean-Bertrand Pontalis. "Fantasy and the Origins of Sexuality." In *Formations of Fantasy*, edited by Victor Burgin, James Donald, and Cora Kaplan, 5–34. London: Methuen & Co. Ltd, 1986.

Lavie, Smadar. "Blowups in the Borderzones: Third World Israeli Authors' Gropings for Home." In *Displacement, Diaspora, and Geographies of Identity*, edited by Smadar Lavie and Ted Swedenburg, 55–96. Durham: Duke University Press, 1996.

Lavie, Smadar, and Ted Swedenburg, eds. *Displacement, Diaspora, and Geographies of Identity*. Durham: Duke University Press, 1996.

Lefebvre, Henri. *The Production of Space*. Translated by Donald Nicholson-Smith. Malden: Blackwell Publishing, 1991.

Levi Strauss, David, Ben Okri, and Alfredo Jaar. *Let There Be Light: The Rwanda Project 1994-1998*. Barcelona: Actar, 1998.

Limqueco, Peter, and Peter Weiss, eds. *Prevent the Crime of Silence: Reports from the Sessions of the International War Crimes Tribunal*. London: Bertrand Russell Peace Foundation Ltd, 1971.

Lippard, Lucy. "Escape Attempts." In *Six Years: The Dematerialization of the Art Object from 1966-1972*, edited by Lucy Lippard, vii–xxii. New York: Praeger, 1973.

———. *Mixed Blessings: New Art in a Multicultural America*. New York: Pantheon Books, 1990.

———. *The Lure of the Local: Senses of Place in a Multicentered Society*. New York: New Press, 1997.

———. *The Pink Glass Swan: Selected Essays on Feminist Art*. New York: New Press, 1995.

————. "Trojan Horses: Activist Art and Power" In *Art After Modernism: Rethinking Representation*, edited by Brian Wallis, 341–358. New York: The New Museum of Contemporary Art, in association with David R. Godine, Publisher, Inc., Boston, 1984.

Litowitz, Douglas E. *Postmodern Philosophy and Law*. Lawrence: University Press of Kansas, 1997.

Louria-Hayon, Adi. "Existence and the Other: Borders of Identity in Light of the Israeli/Palestinian Conflict." *Afterimage* 34, nos. 1–2 (July-October 2006): 22–27.

Lowe, Lisa. *Critical Terrains: French and British Orientalisms*. Ithaca: Cornell University Press, 1991.

MacDonald, Sharon, ed. *The Politics of Display: Museums, Science, Culture*. London: Routledge, 1998.

MacDonald, Sharon, and G. Fyfe, eds. *Theorizing Museums: Representing Identity and Diversity in a Changing World*. Oxford: Blackwell Publishers, 1996.

Maddock, Peter. "The Imagini Mundi of Gulammohammed Sheikh: An Exercise in the Dedifferentiation of the Global and Local Ecumene." *Third Text* 20, no. 5 (2006): 539–553.

Manchanda, Rita. *Women, War and Peace in South Asia: Beyond Victimhood to Agency*. New Delhi: Sage Publications, 2001.

Mansoor, Jaleh. "A Spectral Universality: Mona Hatoum's Biopolitics of Abstraction." *October* 133 (Summer 2010): 49–74.

Marciniak, Katarzyna. "Cinematic Exile: Performing the Foreign Body on Screen in Roman Polanski's *The Tenant*." *Camera Obscura* 15, no. 1 (2000): 1–43.

————. "Pedagogy of Anxiety." *Signs: Journal of Women in Culture and Society* 35, no. 4 (Summer 2010): 869–892.

Marks, Laura U. *Touch: Sensuous Theory and Multisensory Media*. Minneapolis: University of Minnesota Press, 2002.

————. "What Is That *and* between Arab Women and Video? The Case of Beirut." *Camera Obscura* 18, no. 3 (2003): 40–69.

Maxwell, Anne. *Colonial Photography and Exhibitions: Representations of the 'Native' and the Making of European Identities*. London: Leicester University Press, 1999.

McClintock, Anne. *Imperial Leather: Race, Gender and Sexuality in the Colonial Contest*. New York: Routledge, 1995.

————. "No Longer in a Future Heaven: Gender, Race and Nationalism." In *Dangerous Liaisons: Gender, Nation and Postcolonial Perspectives*, edited by Anne McClintock, Aamir Mufti and Ella Shohat, 89–112. Minneapolis: University of Minnesota Press, 1997.

————. "Paranoid Empire: Specters from Guantanamo and Abu Ghraib." *Small Axe* 13, no. 1 (2009): 50–74.

McClintock, Anne, Aamir Mufti, and Ella Shohat, eds. *Dangerous Liaisons: Gender, Nation and Postcolonial Perspectives*. Minneapolis: University of Minnesota Press, 1997.

McCormick, Richard W. "Rape and War, Gender and Nation, Victims and Victimizers: Helke Sander's *Befreier Und Befreite*." *Camera Obscura* 16, no. 1 (2001): 99–141.

McQuire, Scott. *Visions of Modernity: Representation Memory, Time and Space in the Age of the Camera*. London: Sage Publications, 1998.

Mercer, Kobena. *Welcome to the Jungle: New Positions in Black Cultural Studies*. New York: Routledge, 1994.

Mernissi, Fatima. *Dreams of Trespass: Tales of a Harem Girlhood*. Reading: Addison-Wesley Publishing Company, 1994.

———. *The Veil and the Male Elite*. Reading: Addison-Wesley Publishing Company, 1991.

———. *Women's Rebellion and Islamic Memory*. London: Zed Books, 1996.

Mieli, Paola. *Actualité De L'hystérie*. Paris: Erès, 2002.

Minow, Martha. *Between Vengeance and Forgiveness: Facing History after Genocide and Mass Violence*. Boston: Beacon Press, 1998.

Mirzoeff, Nicholas, ed. *The Visual Culture Reader*. London: Routledge, 1998.

Mitchell, W. J. T. *The Reconfigured Eye*. Cambridge: The MIT Press, 1994.

Mohanty, Chandra Talpade. *Feminism Without Borders: Decolonizing Theory, Practicing Solidarity*. Durham: Duke University Press, 2003.

———. "Women Workers and Capitalist Scripts: Ideologies of Domination, Common Interests, and the Politics of Solidarity." In *Feminist Genealogies, Colonial Legacies, Democratic Futures*, edited by M. Jacqui Alexander and Chandra Talpade Mohanty, 3–29. New York: Routledge, 1997.

Moore, Lindsey. "Women in a Widening Frame: (Cross-)Cultural Projection, Spectatorship, and Iranian Cinema." *Camera Obscura* 20, no. 2 (2005): 1–33.

Morley, David, and Kuan-Hsing Chen, eds. *Stuart Hall: Critical Dialogues in Cultural Studies*. London: Routledge, 1996.

Mouffe, Chantal. "Feminism, Citizenship, and Radical Democratic Politics." In *Feminists Theorize the Political*, edited by Judith Butler and Joan W. Scott, 369–384. New York: Routledge, 1992.

———. *The Return of the Political*. London: Verso, 1993.

Mulvey, Laura. "Visual Pleasure and Narrative Cinema." *Screen* 16, no. 3 (1975): 6–18.

Murría, Alicia. "Elahe Massumi: Fiction and Veracity." In *Narraciones: Elahe Massumi*. Madrid: Fundación Telefónica, 2004.

Naficy, Hamid. *An Accented Cinema: Exilic and Diasporic Filmmaking*. Princeton: Princeton University Press, 2001.

Nanda, Serena. *Neither Man nor Woman: The Hijras of India*. Belmont: Wadsworth Publishing Co, 1999.

Nava, Mica. "Cosmopolitan Modernity: Everday Imaginaries and the Register of Difference." *Theory, Culture & Society* 19, nos. 1–2 (2002): 81–99.

Nayar, Jayan. "A People's Tribunal against the Crime of Silence? The Politics of Judgement and an Agenda for People's Law." *Law, Social Justice and Global Development* 2, no. 2 (2001). Accessed June, 9 2012, http://www2.warwick.ac.uk/fac/soc/law/elj/lgd/2001_2/nayar..

Neumaier, Diane, ed. *Reframings: New American Feminist Photographies*. Philadelphia: Temple University Press, 1995.

Newton, Julianne H. *The Burden of Visual Truth: The Role of Photojournalism in Mediating Reality*. Mahwah: Lawrence Erlbaum Associates, 2001.

Nichols, Bill. *Representing Reality*. Bloomington: Indiana University Press, 1991.

——. "The Voice of Documentary." In *New Challenges for Documentary*, edited by Alan Rosenthal, 48–63. Berkeley: University of California Press, 1988.

Oguibe, Olu. *The Culture Game*. Minneapolis: University of Minnesota Press, 2004.

Otto, Diane. "NGOs in the UN System: The Emerging Role of International Civil Society." *Human Rights Quarterly* 18 (1996): 107.

Owens, Nicholas ed. *Human Rights, Human Wrongs*. Oxford: Oxford University Press, 2002.

Papastergiadis, Nikos. "Hybridity and Ambivalence: Places and Flows in Contemporary Art and Culture." *Theory, Culture & Society* 22, no. 4 (2005): 39–64.

Parsberg, Cecilia. "Networking on the Wall." *Eurozine*. May 30, 2006, accessed June 9, 2012, http://www.eurozine.com/articles/2006-05-30-parsberg-en.html.

Phelan, Peggy. "Marina Abramović: Witnessing Shadows." *Theatre Journal* 56, no. 4 (2004): 569–577.

Phillips, Anne ed. *Feminism and Politics*. Oxford: Oxford University Press, 1998.

Pines, Jim and Paul Willemen, eds. *Questions of Third Cinema*. London: BFI Publications, 1989.

Pratt, Mary Louise. *Imperial Eyes*. London: Routledge, 1992.

Raad, Walid. "Missing Lebanese Wars." *Public Culture* 11, no. 2 (1999): i–xiv.

Rabaté, Jean-Michel. *Writing the Image after Roland Barthes*. Philadelphia: University of Pennsylvania Press, 1997.

Rajagopalan, Radhakrishnan. *Diasporic Mediations: Between Home and Location*. Minneapolis: University of Minnesota Press, 1996.

Rabinowitz, Paula. *They Must Be Represented*. London: Verso, 1994.

Rai, Shirin M., and Geraldine Lievesley. *Women and the State: International Perspectives*. London: Taylor & Francis, 1996.

Raj, Rita, Charlotte Bunch, and Elmira Nazombe, eds. *Women at the Intersection: Indivisible Rights, Identities and Oppressions*. New Brunswick: Rutgers University Press, 2002.

Ralph, Jan, ed. *Visions: Fifty Years of the United Nations*. New York: Hearst Books, 1992.

Rand, Erica. "The Passionate Activist and the Political Camera." In *The Passionate Camera: Photography and Bodies of Desire*, edited by Deborah Bright, 366–384. London: Routledge, 1998.

Randall, Vicky, and Georgina Waylen, eds. *Gender, Politics and the State*. London: Routledge, 1998.

Rangan, Pooja. "Immaterial Child Labor: Media Advocacy, Autoethnography and the Case of *Born into Brothels*." *Camera Obscura* 25, no. 3 (2011): 143–177.

Rawi, Mariam. "Betrayal." *Reproductive Health Matters* 12, no. 23 (May 2004): 116–119.

Reilly, Niamh. *Without Reservation: The Beijing Tribunal on Accountability for Women's Human Rights*. New Brunswick: Rutgers University Press, 1996.

Renov, Michael ed. *Theorizing Documentary*. New York: Routledge, 1993.

————. *The Subject of Documentary*. Minneapolis: University of Minnesota Press, 2004.

————. "Toward a Poetics of Documentary." In *Theorizing Documentary*, edited by Michael Renov, 12–36. New York: Routledge, 1993.

Renov, Michael, and Erika Suderburg, eds. *Resolutions: Contemporary Video Practices*. Minneapolis: University of Minnesota Press, 1996.

Riley, Denise. *Am I That Name? Feminism and the Category 'Women' in History*. Minneapolis: University of Minnesota Press, 1988.

Rogoff, Irit. *Terra Infirma: Geography's Visual Culture*. London: Routledge, 2000.

Rony, Fatimah Tobing. *The Third Eye: Race, Cinema, and Ethnographic Spectacle*. Durham: Duke University Press, 1996.

Rose, Jacqueline. *States of Fantasy*. Oxford: Clarendon Press, 1996.

Rose, Nikolas. "The Politics of Life Itself." *Theory, Culture & Society* 18, no. 6 (2001): 1–30.

Rosenthal, Alan ed. *New Challenges for Documentary*. Berkeley: University of California Press, 1988.

Rosler, Martha. "Video: Shedding the Utopian Moment." In *Illuminating Video: An Essential Guide to Video Art*, edited by Doug Hall and Sally Jo Fifer, 31–50. New York: Aperture, in association with the Bay Area Video Coalition, 1990.

Rotas, Alex. "Is 'Refugee Art' Possible?" *Third Text* 18 no. 1 (2004): 51–60.

Rubin, Gayle. "The Traffic in Women: Notes on the 'Political Economy' of Sex." In *Toward an Anthropology of Women*, edited by Rayna R. Reiter, 157–210. New York: Monthly Review Press, 1976.

Rush, Michael. *New Media in Late 20th-Century Art*. London: Thames & Hudson, 1999.

————. *Video Art*. London: Thames & Hudson, 2003.

Said, Edward W. *Orientalism*. London: Penguin Books, 1995.

————. "Reflections on Exile." In *Reflections on Exile and Other Essays*, edited by Edward W. Said, 173–186. Cambridge: Harvard University Press, 2000.

Salloum, Joyce. "In/Tangible Cartographies: New Arab Video." *Third Text* 19, no. 1 (2005): 27–31.

Samantrai, Ranu. "Cosmopolitan Cartographies: Art in a Divided World." *Meridians: Feminism, Race, Transnationalism* 4, no. 2 (2004): 168–194.

San Juan Jr., E. *Beyond Postcolonial Theory*. New York: St. Martin's Press, 1998.

Sandoval, Chela. *Methodology of the Oppressed*. Minneapolis: University of Minnesota Press, 2000.

Sarat, Austin, and Thomas R. Kearns, eds. *Law in the Domains of Culture*. Ann Arbor: University of Michigan Press, 1998.

Sassen, Saskia. "Digital Networks and the State: Some Governance Questions." *Theory, Culture & Society* 17, no. 4 (2000): 19–33.

————. "Europe's Migrations: The Numbers and the Passions Are Not New." *Third Text* 20, no. 6 (2006): 635–645.

————. "Excavating Power: In Search of Frontier Zones and New Actors." *Theory, Culture & Society* 17, no. 1 (2000): 163–170.

————. *Globalization and Its Discontents: Essays on the New Mobility of People and Money*. New York: New Press, 1998.

Schiller, Herbert I. "Media, Technology and the Market: The Interacting Dynamic." In *Culture on the Brink: Ideologies of Technology*, edited by Gretchen Bender and Timothy Druckrey, 31–46. Seattle: Bay Press, 1994.

Scott, Joan W. "Experience." In *Feminists Theorize the Political*, edited by Judith Butler and Joan W. Scott, 22–40. New York: Routledge, 1992.

Sekula, Alan. *Photography against the Grain: Essays and Photo Works, 1973–1983*. Halifax: Press of the Nova Scotia College of Art and Design, 1984.

Sharpe, Jenny. "A Conversation with Gayatri Chakravorty Spivak: Politics and the Imagination." *Signs: Journal of Women in Culture and Society* 28, no. 2 (2002): 609–624.

Shohat, Ella, ed. *Talking Visions: Multicultural Feminism in a Transnational Age*. Cambridge: The MIT Press, 1998.

Shohat, Ella, and Robert Stam. "Narrativizing Visual Culture: Towards a Polycentric Aesthetics." In *The Visual Culture Reader*, edited by Nicholas Mirzoeff, 27–49. London: Routledge, 1998.

Silverman, Kaja. *The Threshold of the Visible World*. New York: Routledge, 1996.

Sklair, Leslie. *Globalization: Capitalism and Its Alternatives*. Oxford: Oxford University Press, 2002.

Sobchack, Vivian. "'Presentifying' Film and Media Feminism." *Camera Obscura* 21, no. 1 (2006): 65–69.

Solomon-Godeau, Abigail. *Photography at the Dock: Essays on Photographic History, Institutions and Practices*. Minneapolis: University of Minnesota Press, 1994.

————. "Representing Women: The Politics of Self-Representation." In *Reframings: New American Feminist Photographies*, edited by Diane Neumaier, 296–310. Philadelphia: Temple University Press, 1995.

Sontag, Susan. *On Photography*. New York: Anchor Books, 1977.

————. *Regarding the Pain of Others*. New York: Farrar, Straus and Giroux, 2003.

Spivak, Gayatri Chakravorty. *A Critique of Postcolonial Reason: Toward a History of the Vanishing Present*. London: Harvard University Press, 1999.

————. *An Aesthetic Education in the Era of Globalization*. Cambridge: Harvard University Press, 2012.

————. *Death of a Discipline*. The Wellek Library Lectures in Critical Theory. New York: Columbia University Press, 2003.

————. "Can the Subaltern Speak?" In *Colonial Discourse and Post-Colonial Theory: A Reader*, edited by Patrick Williams and Laura Chrisman, 66–111. New York: Columbia University Press, 1994.

————, ed. *Imaginary Maps*. New York: Routledge, 1995.

————. *Outside in the Teaching Machine*. New York: Routledge, 1993.

————. "Resident Alien." In *Relocating Postcolonialism*, edited by David Theo Goldberg and Ato Quayson, 46–65. Oxford: Blackwell Publishers, 2002.

————. "Righting Wrongs." In *Human Rights, Human Wrongs*, edited by Nicholas Owens, 188–227. Oxford: Oxford University Press, 2002.

Squires, Carol ed. *The Critical Image: Essays on Contemporary Photography.* Seattle: Bay Press, 1990.

Stam, Robert. "Mobilizing Fictions: The Gulf War, the Media, and the Recruitment of the Spectator." *Public Culture* 4, no. 2: 101–126.

Stiglmayer, Alexandra ed. *Mass Rape: The War against Women in Bosnia-Herzegovina.* Lincoln: University of Nebraska Press, 1994.

Stivens, Maila. "Introduction: Gender Politics and the Re-Imagining of Human Rights in the Asia-Pacific." In *Human Rights and Gender Politics: Asia-Pacific Perspectives,* edited by Anne-Marie Hilsdon, Martha Macintyre, Vera Mackie and Maila Stivens, 1–36. London: Routledge, 2000.

Stupples, Peter. "Visual Culture, Synthetic Memory and the Construction of National Identity." *Third Text* 17, no. 2 (2003): 127–139.

Sturken, Marita. "The Politics of Video Memory: Electronic Erasures and Inscriptions." In *Resolutions: Contemporary Video Practices,* edited by Michael Renov and Erika Suderburg, 1–12. Minneapolis: University of Minnesota Press, 1996.

Tagg, John. *The Burden of Representation: Essays on Photographies and Histories.* Minneapolis: University of Minnesota Press, 1993.

Thede, Nancy and Alain Ambrosi, eds. *Video the Changing World.* Montreal: Black Rose Books, 1991.

Thomas, Julia. *Reading Images.* Houndsmills: Palgrave Publishers Ltd, 2000.

Trinh, T Minh-ha. "Outside In Inside Out." In *Questions in Third Cinema,* edited by Jim Pines and Paul Willemen, 133–149. London: DFI Publishing, 1989.

———. *When the Moon Waxes Red: Representation, Gender and Cultural Politics.* New York: Routledge, 1991.

———. *Woman Native Other.* Bloomington: Indiana University Press, 1989.

Tsing, Anna. *Friction: An Ethnography of Global Connection.* Princeton: Princeton University Press, 2005.

Turim, Maureen. "The Image of Art in Video." In *Resolutions: Contemporary Video Practices,* edited by Michael Renov and Erika Suderburg, 36–40. Minneapolis: University of Minnesota Press, 1996.

———. "Marina Abramović's Performance: Stresses on the Body and Psyche in Installation Art." *Camera Obscura* 18, no. 3 (2003): 99–117.

Venuti, Lawrence. "Translation, Community, Utopia." In *The Translation Studies Reader,* edited by Lawrence Venuti, 468–488. London: Routledge, 2000.

Vetrocq, Marcia E. "The 1997 Venice Biennale: A Space Odyssey." *Art in America* (September 1997): 66–77.

Wayne, Mike. *Theorising Video Practice.* London: Lawrence & Wishart Ltd, 1997.

Williams, Linda. *Hard Core: Power, Pleasure and the Frenzy of the Visible.* Berkeley: University of California Press, 1989.

Williams, Raymond. *Television: Technology and Cultural Form.* New York: Routledge, 2003.

Wilson, Pamela, and Michelle Stewart, eds. *Global Indigenous Media: Cultures, Poetics, and Politics.* Durham: Duke University Press, 2008.

Wilson, Rob and Wimal Dissanayake, eds. *Global/Local.* Durham: Duke University Press, 1996.

Wing, Adrien Katherine. *Global Critical Race Feminism*. New York: New York University Press, 2000.

Winston, Brian. "Documentary: I Think We Are in Trouble." In *New Challenges for Documentary*, edited by Alan Rosenthal, 21–33. Berkeley: University of California Press, 1988.

Wolf, Sylvia, ed. *Michal Rovner: The Space Between*. New York; Göttingen: Whitney Museum of Art; Steidl Verlag, 2002.

Woodiwiss, Anthony. "Human Rights and the Challenge of Cosmopolitanism." *Theory, Culture & Society* 19, nos. 1–2 (2002): 139–155.

Wooster, Ann-Sargent. "The Way We Were." In *The First Generation: Women and Video, 1970-75*, edited by JoAnn Hanley and Ann-Sargent Wooster. New York: Independent Curators International, 1994.

Young, James Edward. *At Memory's Edge: After-Images of the Holocaust in Contemporary Art and Architecture*. New Haven: Yale University Press, 2000.

Yuval-Davis, Nira. *Gender & Nation*. London: Sage Publications, 1997.

Yuval-Davis, Nira, and Floya Anthias,. *Women-Nation-State*. London: Macmillan, 1989.

Yuval-Davis, Nira, and Pnina Werbner, eds. *Women, Citizenship and Difference*. London: Zed Books, 1999.

Zimmerman, Patricia R. *States of Emergency: Documentaries, Wars, Democracies*. Minneapolis: University of Minnesota Press, 2000.

Žižek, Slavoj. "Melancholy and the Act." *Critical Inquiry* 26, no. 4 (Summer 2000): 657–681.

Index

Printed in the United States of America